The Anatomy of
THE ISRAELI ARMY

Gunther E. Rothenberg

The Anatomy of
THE ISRAELI ARMY

The Israel Defence Force, 1948–78

Hippocrene Books, Inc.
New York, N.Y.

First published 1979
Copyright Gunther Rothenberg 1979
All Rights Reserved

Hippocrene Books, Inc.
171 Madison Avenue
New York, N.Y. 10016

ISBN 0 88254 491 8
Library of Congress Catalog Card Number 79-88523
Printed in Great Britain

Dedicated to the memory of Heinz (Chaim) Politzer, a Jewish soldier from Palestine, killed in action in the Western Desert, 19 July 1942.

Contents

List of Illustrations

List of Maps

Acknowledgments

The author and publishers wish to thank the following for their kind permission to reproduce copyright illustrations: Camera Press Ltd (5, 6, 18, 19, 20, 23, 26, 29); Israel Information (3, 18); Keystone Press Agency Ltd (1, 2, 4, 7, 8, 9, 10, 12, 13, 14, 15, 16, 17, 21, 22, 24, 25, 27, 28, 30, 31, 32); Radio Times Hulton Picture Library (11).

Preface

At the opening of the Geneva Peace Conference in December 1973, Secretary of State Henry Kissinger observed that, except for uneasy cease-fires and armistices, the Arab–Israeli conflict constituted one continued war that 'has already lasted 25 years'. And six years later, though for the first time two of the parties to the conflict have signed a peace agreement and are continuing to openly negotiate face to face, Israel still is isolated and besieged, relying for survival on her Army, the Israel Defence Forces, IDF or ZAHAL.

To understand this situation in true perspective, it is necessary to recall the small beginnings, the ups and downs, apparent weaknesses and unsuspected strength that have characterized the history of the Israeli Army during the last three decades. Though organized in chronological form, this book is not a history of the wars and campaigns which historians have dissected and about which journalists have written colourful accounts. The central theme of this book is how within a single generation a small people – 650,000 in 1948 – lacking arms and training for modern war, managed to build an army that in four wars defeated much larger and better equipped enemies. To achieve this, the new Israeli Army, unlike others emerging in the post-World War II era, did not accept ready-made military doctrines, though it borrowed or modified ideas regarding unconventional warfare advocated principally by certain British officers – Wingate, Liddell Hart, and Fuller. But overall, political and economic constraints compelled the Israelis to develop their own military structures, tactics, and strategies. On occasion these were very advanced and effective, sometimes they were merely different, and on occasion they were faulty.

Changing security needs and developments in weaponry have led to a continual debate over the relative importance of various branches and arms within the Army, and the success or failure of a particular concept have brought repeated fundamental revisions in the Army's thinking and force structure. In addition, changes were determined by the attitudes of larger powers, providing or, more often, withholding items of major equipment. In turn, this forced the IDF to develop or modify its own weaponry, to work out substitute strategies and tactics, and to develop a substantial and advanced arms industry. These developments will be discussed and brief analyses of the various wars and other actions are offered in this context.

Finally, and perhaps even more than other armies, the IDF remains a citizen army, reflecting the society which created it and which it serves. Not only the political structure of a democratic and highly diverse nation, but also the social and ethnic complexities of a people still struggling to achieve a common cultural denominator, are reflected in the Israeli Army. Moreover, though there is a considerable element of continuity in the higher ranks of the officer corps, with veteran commanders who have served in the pre-state under-ground forces only now moving off the stage for good, the practice of early retirement for senior officers, who on mobilization are recalled to active duty but otherwise often assume prominent political and social roles, has created yet another, sometimes problematical link, between the Army and society.

At the same time, despite the pre-eminent role of the armed forces in the life of a nation which over three decades has fought four major wars and countless minor actions and where the continuing hostility of her neighbours and the Communist World has placed a staggering burden on her people and economy, Israel, in contrast with most other nations that became independent after World War II, has not turned into a military dictatorship, but has remained a lively, contentious, and often exasperating parliamentary de-mocracy. Perhaps the most important lesson which Western defence specialists can draw from the history of the IDF is that even a very small democratic state can successfully withstand enemies superior in numbers and materiel. Against the current of contemporary despair, anxiety, and adulation of leftist authoritarian regimes, supposed to have inherent military advantages over democracies, Israel furnishes proof to the contrary.

Despite the plethora of books, pamphlets, and articles on the IDF, little is known about its internal structure and organization, development, doctrine, and problems of arms procurement. The aim of this volume is to provide this needed background. Of course, in writing on recent events, especially where national security is at stake, very little official documentation is available and much has to be deduced from circumstantial evidence. Even some of the events of 1948 are still shrouded in secrecy and, if anything, access to Israeli archives has become more restrictive than it has been in the past. And the author, though he has served as a soldier both before and during Israel's War of Independence, can claim no special connections, interviews, or access to confidential information. But then perhaps such claims, often the result of a hasty guided tour of the battlefields and some briefings by military spokesmen may provide a false picture. In fact, as Colonel Dunkelman, a Canadian officer who commanded an Israeli brigade in 1948, recently complained, many accounts of campaigns and operations 'display an astounding degree of inaccuracy'. This, he believed, stemmed in part from incorrect information furnished to writers by the various commanders whose personal prestige was at stake. This, of course, is true of soldiers everywhere and not unique to the IDF. For the IDF, however, difficulties are compounded by the fact that throughout its existence its composition has been fluid and its forces have so often been expanded, reorganized, or formed into temporary groupings that an accurate order of battle has never been established and there exist wide discrepancies in figures.

Finally, this volume should be regarded primarily as an attempt to provide an analysis of a singular military establishment and not as a justification or a condemnation of any of the participants. Still, I confess that this is not a value-free book. In dealing with an issue as emotional and current as the Arab–Israeli conflict the author has in any case little chance of escaping being charged with bias. I accept this, though I hope that I have dealt fairly with both sides. At the same time, I would like to make it clear that while I have talked with numerous former and serving officers and men of the IDF, opinions, judgements, and other details are mine and are totally and completely unofficial. Moreover, in writing this book I have not received assistance or funding from any source, beyond the constant encouragement and support provided by my wife Ruth. All errors of commission and omission are mine, and mine alone.

A Note on Ranks

During the underground period the Jewish defence organizations employed functional rank designations only, i.e. platoon commander, company commander, chief of the Palmach and so on. When the Army was formed, Ben Gurion and Yadin insisted on the introduction of standard ranks on the British pattern. The highest rank was the *aluf*, the equivalent of a brigadier-general, in charge of a front or a major branch. After the War of Independence the chief of staff held the rank of *rav aluf*, then equivalent to major-general while the *aluf mishne* rank, equal to colonel, was introduced for brigade commanders. To provide an appropriate rank for divisional task force commanders, the *tat aluf* was interposed between the colonel and the brigadier rank, the *aluf* became a major-general, while the rank of *rav aluf*, now equivalent to lieutenant-general, remained reserved for the chief of staff. Naval and Air Force ranks were and remain identical with those of the ground forces.

I

The Foundations: 1907–47

'With one hand they engaged in the work while the other held the spear.'

Nehemiah 4: 11

On 14 May 1948, eight hours before the British mandate expired at midnight, David Ben Gurion, the acting head of the Provisional National Administration and its director of security affairs, proclaimed the 'establishment of a Jewish state in Palestine to be called the State of Israel'. Even as he spoke before a packed audience representing the various organizations of the *Yishuv*, the Jewish population in Palestine, the new state was fighting for its very existence. Since December 1947 Arab irregulars and pararegulars had been locked in bitter combat with Jewish defence units and throughout that day reports, both hopeful and grave, flowed into Ben Gurion's military headquarters. There were advances, but there also were setbacks. The most ominous news was that after ten days of desperate resistance the last position in the Etzion bloc, a group of Jewish settlements on the southern approaches to Jerusalem, had fallen before the armoured cars of Transjordan's Arab Legion and that the regular armies of four other Arab states – Egypt, Iraq, Lebanon, and Syria – stood poised for invasion on the frontiers of Palestine.

There was rejoicing that night, but there was also apprehension. The question was whether the 650,000 Jews of Israel could meet the test of open war against a full-scale assault by regular forces. Although the development of armed forces had preceded the establishment of the state, these forces were still weak and lacked both offensive and defensive capabilities. The Jewish forces did not even have a name; the decree officially establishing the Israel Defence Force (ZAHAL or IDF) was not published until 26 May. But that, of course, was a mere formality. Organization, doctrine, and command structures were already in place, though armament was poor and training in most cases inadequate. The Jewish chief operations officer, Yigael Yadin, believed that the

13

chances of holding back the invasions were at best 'delicately balanced', while Arab, British and American military experts estimated that the Arab armies would reach Haifa and Tel Aviv within ten days.

The repulse and eventual defeat of these armies was due in large measure to the soldiers of Israel, who displayed courage, resourcefulness, and initiative, coupled with a high standard of combat leadership at all levels. And these qualities have remained characteristic of the Israeli Army, repeatedly defying calculations based on men, materiel, and firepower alone. To understand how these qualities were developed it is necessary to look back at the evolution of the modern Jewish settlement in Palestine because there was an inseparable connection between the political, social, and economic aspects of the Jewish community and the development of military strength.

The Historical and Political Setting

After the Roman legions destroyed the Second Jewish Commonwealth in AD 70, a Jewish remnant remained in Palestine and survived the Arab conquest, the Crusades, and the Mamelukes. Moreover, scattered throughout the diaspora, Jews everywhere retained strong religious ties with their ancient land. The return to Zion, *aliyah* in Hebrew, remained a constant dream and there was no century in which some did not attempt to realize it. The advent of Turkish rule provided more tolerable conditions and from the sixteenth century on pious Jews by the thousands lived in the holy cities of Jerusalem, Safed, Hebron, and Tiberias. This population, Ashkenazim, that is Jews from almost all of Europe, as well as Sephardim, originally the community expelled from Spain, but by extension also including Jews from Yemen, Morocco, Iraq, and Turkey, had no political ambitions. They had come to pray and die in the 'Land of Israel', and sustained themselves by charity, petty trade, and crafts. In the 1870s a small number, helped by Jewish benefactors from abroad, had moved out of their crowded quarters in the cities and established a few agricultural settlements.

Modern political Zionism, the Jewish national liberation movement, appeared in the latter decades of the nineteenth century when racial antisemitism shattered earlier hopes for equality and tolerance in Europe.[1] The Zionists held that the Jewish problem could be resolved only by the foundation of a national home where a persecuted people could find sanctuary and self-determination. Many prominent Zionists, including Theodor Herzl, the movement's official founder, believed that this could be achieved through negotiations with the Sultan, the Kaiser, or the British Foreign Office. Others, however, argued that the Jewish national home required a regeneration of the Jewish people. Jews could not become a healthy normal people unless they abandoned intellectual and middle-class pursuits for physical labour on the land. The first of this group of settlers, pioneers – or *chalutzim* as they called themselves – arrived in the 1880s but had little success. Jewish self-labour did not appeal to the established *Yishuv*, urban or rural, and the new settlements created by this group foundered on primitive conditions and the ever-present malaria. Baron Edmond de Rothschild, a generous benefactor, came to their aid, but his patronage deprived the settlers of independence, turning their communities into philanthropic institutions. By the turn of the century the survivors of this first *aliyah* had largely abandoned the concept of Jewish labour. They hired Arab workers and entrusted their security to Arab watchmen. Around the turn of the century it appeared that the *Yishuv* would become an oriental ghetto and its farmers colonial planters living off cheap native labour.

The turning point came in 1904 with the arrival of the second wave of immigration. Composed mostly of young people influenced by the revolutionary movement in Russia, these newcomers had abandoned the strict religious observance of their forefathers; they were true believers combining an almost mystic faith in the regenerative powers of physical labour with a wide spectrum of socialist creeds, nationalist ideas, and Tolstoyan idealism. They were given to continuous factional disputes as to how to build a society based on equality and social justice. Unable to find work in the established villages, which preferred Arab labourers, they set up agricultural co-operatives to contract for work and to prepare themselves for their own settlement on the land. These groups provided the seminal beginnings for novel forms of communal settlements: the kibbutz, and the co-operative smallholders' village, moshav, as well as the eventual Labour Federation, the Histadrut, which Ben Gurion, one of the members, would call a 'community of state builders'. Another co-operative, *ha-Shomer*, the Watchman, contracted the guarding of Jewish villages against the endemic banditry prevalent in the country.

This combination of socialist pioneering with the concept of Jewish self-defence was the lasting contribution of the second *aliyah*. Despite considerable attrition among these pioneers caused by disease, poverty, and disillusionment, those who survived and remained in the country became the leaders of the Zionist Labour movement and prominent among the eventual founders of the state. To be sure, later waves of immigrants, often refugees driven by necessity rather than idealisms, did not share all these concepts, but Labour Zionism set much of the tone for the modern *Yishuv* and also shaped its military establishment.

All this, of course, was still far in the future. For the moment the Labour Zionists were merely a struggling group of workers, living hand to mouth, in Palestine, their aspirations not only opposed by the authorities, but also not shared by the majority of the *Yishuv* or by Jewry abroad. In the decade after 1904, however, Professor Chaim Weizmann, an eminent Russian-born British scientist, succeeded in uniting the diverse approaches within the Zionist movement. Without discarding diplomacy, he simultaneously supported the step-by-step approach of the Labour Zionists and, within its limited means, the organization began to acquire land in Palestine.

Land acquisitions, mainly in areas shunned by the Arabs, set the future pattern of Jewish settlement. Because of the disturbed history of Palestine, most villages had been established in the hills. Being not easily accessible, they were therefore more secure. The coastal plain, the Jezreel and the Jordan Valleies, by contrast, had been abandoned and neglected. Here land was available and thus the pattern of Jewish settlement in the plains – often marshy and malarial – and Arab hill villages emerged.

Before much could be accomplished, the outbreak of World War I created entirely new political circumstances. The importance of Palestine and indeed the entire eastern Mediterranean basin, had been greatly enhanced by the development of the Suez Canal and the progressive enfeeblement of the Ottoman Empire. Great Britain, especially, was interested in securing ties with forces within that empire to strengthen its own position in the area and to this end had established relations with Hussein, the Sherif of Mecca, promising him the Arab portions of the Turkish Empire, with the exception of Palestine. Simultaneously, the British government approached Weizmann and other Jewish personalities to enlist their support. In November 1917, Britain issued the Balfour Declaration. 'His Majesty's Government', the document read, 'view with favour the establishment in Palestine of a national home for the Jewish people, and will use their best endeavours to facilitate the achievement of this object, it being clearly understood that nothing shall be done which may prejudice the civil and religious rights of the existing non-Jewish communities in Palestine.'

The Zionist leadership expected that relations with these communities, essentially Moslem and Christian Arabs, and Druze, would be harmonious. They were not unaware of the Arab aspirations, but they believed that material progress would reconcile even the most serious national conflicts. For that matter T.E. Lawrence, the Arabs' champion, predicted that the Zionist venture would prove both beneficial and welcome to the Arab world.

In 1919 the Emir Feisal, acting for his father Hussein, met with Zionist leaders. They signed an agreement which 'mindful of the racial kinships and bonds existing between the Arab and the Jewish people' pledged close co-operation in the development of the Arab state and of Palestine. At this time Palestine included Transjordan, while the Arab state referred to a greater Syrian kingdom. But the arrangement collapsed when the French took over

Syria and ejected Feisal. In consolation, the British named him King of Iraq and in 1922 cut away four-fifths of the area of Palestine and created a new Arab state, Transjordan, for Feisal's brother, the Emir Abdullah. This first partition of Palestine was a blow to the Zionists, but they accepted it. Moreover, Weizmann fervently hoped that the British would be awarded the mandate for Palestine and this was officially done in 1922 when the League of Nations Council unanimously ratified Britain as mandatory power, with the responsibility of 'securing the establishment of the Jewish home' and of 'facilitating Jewish immigration'.

Immigration was indeed the crucial issue. In 1917 the Jewish population, partly as a result of Turkish pressures, numbered only 60,000 as against 600,000 Arabs. Immediately after the war, in 1919–20, more than 10,000 Jews, the third *aliyah*, entered the country – mainly from Russia. The Arabs, fearing an eventual Jewish majority, lashed out in riots in the spring of 1920, and the British authorities responded by limiting Jewish immigration to 16,500 a year. Only 8,000 immigrants came in 1921, but in May 1921 another 'disturbance' – the Colonial Office could find no stronger word for it – brought more bloodshed. This time the authorities temporarily halted all immigration and reopened it with the proviso that it be limited by the 'economic capacity of Palestine to absorb new immigrants'. To further appease Arab resentments, Amin el Husseini, one of the chief instigators of the riots, was appointed Mufti of Jerusalem, religious leader of the Palestine Moslems.

All this did little to 'facilitate immigration'. During the next 15 years the Jews made important progress in fashioning their own self-contained society, culturally distinctive and economically viable, with political, social, and economic agencies of their own. They created a great number of political parties, including the General Federation of Jewish Labour, an elected council of delegates of the Jewish community, the *Vaad Leumi*, and a Hebrew education system including a university. These advances were assisted by the Jewish Agency, an international non-government body whose aims were to assist and encourage settlement in Palestine. Its executive and that of the Zionist Organization usually were identical. At the same time, however, Jewish numbers grew slowly. By 1925 the Jewish population in the country had increased to only 108,000, while the Arab population had risen to 800,000, both by natural increase and by immigration from neighbouring countries. In 1926 immigration fell off sharply and in the following year the exodus was greater than the influx. There was heavy unemployment in the Jewish urban areas and many kibbutzim were on the verge of collapse.

The apparent weakness of the Jewish position, coupled by a sharp cutback in the police force and the military garrison, down to only two battalions and one RAF squadron, encouraged Arab extremists, led by the Mufti of Jerusalem, to deliver what might become a death blow. Fanned by agitation that the Jews had sinister designs against the Moslem holy places in Jerusalem, in August 1929 there were attacks against Jews in that city, quickly spreading to the rest of the country. In several places, notably in Hebron and Safed, numerous Jews were brutally murdered. It was three days before army reinforcements arrived to restore order; meanwhile the administration refused to use Jewish police or issue arms to defenceless settlements.

These events, however, halted Jewish immigration only temporarily. The growing crisis in Europe, first in Poland and then in Germany, brought the mass immigration of the 1930s. Between 1933 and 1936 more than 160,000 Jews arrived in the country, while for a short period the Jewish birthrate temporarily approached that of the Moslems and surpassed that of the Palestinian Christians. If immigration continued at the rate of 62,000 a year, the number reached in 1935, the day was not far off when Jews would constitute the majority in the country. To contain this peril, the Arabs in 1935 demanded the creation of a Palestinian parliament, an end to Jewish land purchases, and a halt to immigration. When Whitehall refused, the Arabs raised the standard of revolt. An Arab Higher Committee was formed to call for a general strike, followed by attacks against Jewish transport, settlements, and individuals. From there the revolt escalated into an attack on British rule. In 1937 a Royal Commission of Inquiry, the Peel Commission, determined that the mandate was unworkable – that is, that it could not be implemented without the use of massive force, something that Whitehall was not prepared to do. The commission therefore recommended partition of Palestine into Jewish and Arab states, with a British enclave from Jaffa to Jerusalem. Faced by the need to provide an immediate refuge, the Jews reluctantly accepted partition; the Arabs rejected it outright. Turbulence continued while the government looked for an alternative solution.

The solution, it turned out, was adverse to the Jews. In February 1939, Jews and Arabs were summoned to a conference at St James's Palace in London. Concerned about its position in the Middle East, the government invited not only representatives from the two rival communities but also delegations from the Arab states. The conference failed. The Arabs refused to even meet with the Jews. By this time, with war on the horizon, the British government had decided, since Zionism disrupted relations with the Arab world, containing not only the sources of oil but also sitting astride the imperial communications line, to abandon the policy of supporting Zionist aspirations. Great Britain had no wish to jeopardize her relations with the Arabs and Jewish support in an Anglo-German war could be taken for granted. On 17 May 1939 the government published the White Paper. There would be only limited land purchase and immigration and after ten years Palestine would become an independent state with a Jewish minority. The Balfour Declaration was repudiated.

The new policy came under heavy attack in Parliament where Winston Churchill called it a 'plain breach of a solemn obligation'. There were angry speeches, demonstrations, and riots in Palestine, but basically the Jews were unable to retaliate with force. When war did come in September, Ben Gurion, now the leader of the dominant Labour Party, Mapai, declared that the *Yishuv* would fight the war as if there was no White Paper and the White Paper as if there was no war. Brave words, but in practice this stand, endorsed by all major parties, meant that the Jewish community in Palestine ranged itself behind the British war effort. The Arabs, having achieved political victory, halted their rebellion, though their extremists remained unsatisfied. For the most part the Arabs remained neutral during the war, showing a leaning towards the Axis when things appeared dark for the British Empire. Some persisted in open hostility. The Mufti, having earlier fled to Lebanon, spent the war years in Berlin, recruiting Moslems for Hitler's forces and encouraging the Germans in their programme for extermination of the Jews.

Although slow to realize that relations with the British were permanently changed, Zionism between 1939 and 1945 made major transformation of goals and methods. Before the war political sovereignty had not been a primary concern. Zionist leaders, including the ultra-nationalist chief of the revisionist movement, Zeev Jabotinsky, regarded England as the most civilized nation and gladly would have settled for a Hebrew commonwealth within the empire. But when, even as the dimensions of the Jewish catastrophy in Europe became clear, the local authorities in Palestine and the Colonial Office in London proved utterly without compassion for the agony of the Jews, when shiploads of 'illegal' refugees were sent back to certain death, and when offers to form a Jewish division to fight the common enemy were repeatedly rejected, admiration turned to bitterness. And with the systematic carnage of European Jewry before its eyes, Zionists and non-Zionist Jews alike adopted the creation of an independent Jewish state that would guarantee immigration and provide future security as their political goal.

During the first years of the war resistance to the White Paper was limited towards evading its restriction on land purchases and immigration. Moreover, especially during the critical period of 1941–2, the British military and the Jews were only too willing to co-operate in the defence of the Middle East. But as the war receded from the region, British policy became less flexible, while the *Yishuv* shifted slowly from co-operation to resistance. At first only the most extremist group, the so-called 'Stern group', attacked British installations and personnel. By 1944, however, fighting units of the revisionist movement also opened operations against the British, though for the next two years the Jewish

Agency and the Labour Party, both for tactical and ideological reasons, tried to repress these 'dissidents', as they were called. Hope still remained that a post-war Labour government in Britain would honour its many pro-Zionist pledges. When Labour came to power in July 1945, however, these expectations proved vain. Concerned over imperial interests, grimly holding on to a position which had lost almost all of its purpose with the decision to give up India, the Labour government reneged on its promises. The White Paper, Prime Minister Attlee stated, would guide policy and he even refused American requests to allow 100,000 survivors of the death camps to enter Palestine. Arab wishes, Attlee told President Truman, had to be considered lest the whole Middle East go up in flames. And with British troops committed in Greece, India, and in the occupation of Germany, the additional troops necessary to implement such immigration could not be found. Jewish refugees would have to be treated like all others and not allowed to jump 'to the head of the queue'.

At this point, late in 1945, Ben Gurion reluctantly decided to join forces with the 'dissidents'. He ordered the main Jewish defence organization, the Haganah, to sabotage military installations, support civil disobedience, and intensify its efforts to bring in immigrants in defiance of the White Paper. Ben Gurion wanted to demonstrate to the British that they could not control Palestine. But British Foreign Secretary Bevin was an obstinate man and Britain suddenly found the additional troops. Violence, however, could not be neatly contained and resistance, repression, and terror escalated, turning Palestine into 'John Bull's other Ireland'. The British fought what was fast becoming a full-scale Jewish insurrection with long curfews, arms searches, mass arrests, deportations, and executions. By 1946 over 90,000 British soldiers, sailors, airmen, and police were engaged in this effort. The spectacle of British troops herding Jews behind barbed wire and of British sailors chasing small refugee boats caused mounting domestic and international criticism. In the midst of a severe economic crisis, the price for maintaining a British presence in Palestine was becoming too steep. Early in 1947, Bevin told the House of Commons that the Palestine problem would be submitted to the United Nations. Perhaps the foreign secretary hoped that the UN would ask Britain to retain the mandate, but with modifications that would eliminate the obligation to a Jewish National Home.

In the spring of 1947 a United Nations Special Commission for Palestine (UNSCOP) was established. It found that the claims of the opposing communities, some 600,000 Jews and 1,200,000 Arabs, were irreconcilable. The commission voted unanimously to terminate the British mandate and by a majority vote it recommended partition: the creation of two separate states, Jewish and Arab, joined in an economic union. Jerusalem was to be excluded from both and administered by the UN. There followed intense diplomatic manoeuvring. Great Britain, the Arab states, the US State Department, and the oil interests all opposed partition; the Soviet Union strongly supported it. In the end President Truman overrode the State Department and instructed the American delegations to work for partition. On 29 November 1947, with a vote of 33 to 13, with 10 abstentions, the partition plan was passed by the General Assembly. Angered, Great Britain announced that it would provide no aid in its implementation, while the Arabs proceeded to resist partition by force of arms.

Throughout the summer of 1947 the Arab Higher Committee and the Arab states threatened war. 'The partition line proposed', Jamal Husseini, the committee's spokesman, told the UN on 24 November, 'shall be nothing but a line of fire and blood.' Now the Arabs made good their threat. The first shots were fired on 30 November. Road transport was fired upon; Jewish settlements and urban areas were attacked, and in some towns a mutual exodus of people living in mixed areas began. By the end of the first two weeks nearly 100 Jews had been killed. The long and bloody War of Independence had begun.

The First Steps towards a Jewish Self-Defence: 1907–29

Although some armed Jewish watchmen could be found in the Ottoman Palestine of the 1880s, the roots of the Army of Israel began in the days of the second *aliyah*.[2] In 1907 a group of young romantics formed a secret military society, Bar Giora. Never more than a dozen strong, in 1909 it merged with other like-minded men and women to establish the society of Jewish watchmen, the famed *ha-Shomer*. Part of the socialist labour movement, the group had a hard time selling its services to the independent Jewish farmers, though some of the early kibbutzim employed *shomrim* to augment their own manpower. But the socialist ideology of the *ha-Shomer*, with never more than a couple hundred members, repelled the independent farmers, while the highly individualist and elitist tone of the society created friction with the egalitarian-minded Jewish workers. During World War I it urged the Turkish authorities to form a Jewish militia, ostensibly to help and defend the country. But the Turks, rightfully wary of the deeper motives, denied the request, arrested some of the leaders, and expelled others, together with several thousand suspected Jewish activists. The incidental discovery of a Jewish espionage network, the Nili run by the Aaronson family, confirmed Turkish suspicions and there were more arrests, executions, and expulsions. *Ha-Shomer* survived the war, but in May 1920 dissolved itself.

A different course of Jewish military activity was proposed by the Russian Jewish journalist Vladimir (Zeev) Jabotinsky, who advocated the formation of a Jewish Legion under British auspices. In 1914, however, the War Office was not interested, though the next year it decided to enlist a supply unit, the Zion Mule Corps, from among Palestinian Jewish expellees in Egypt. After serving with credit during the Gallipoli operations the unit was transferred to England where it was disbanded when it refused to fight the Irish rebellion. Some 125 men chose to stay in the army, including Lieutenant Joseph Trumpeldor, a remarkable soldier who in 1904 had lost his left arm and won the Cross of St George fighting in the Tsar's army at Port Arthur. Jabotinsky had opposed formation of the Zion Mule Corps as degrading, but now he and Trumpeldor combined to agitate for a Jewish Legion. But in the first, as in the second world war, Whitehall was hostile to the idea of their being in existence a separate Jewish force, lest it establish political and moral claims contrary to imperial policy.

By 1917, however, with the Balfour Declaration in the offing, the War Office authorized the recruitment of two Jewish battalions, the 38th and 39th Royal Fusiliers, enlisted from Jews in England, Canada, and America. Together with a third battalion, the 40th, formed in Palestine after Allenby's conquest of Jerusalem in December 1917, the 'Jewish Legion', as it was popularly known, participated in the June 1918 offensive. Thereafter it was stationed at Sarafand Camp near Jerusalem pending demobilization. Many of the future leaders of the *Yishuv* served in the Legion. Perhaps the most important was Corporal Ben Gurion, who did not acquire much military expertise, but gained a lasting respect for regular army procedures which would become significant when he assumed a leading role in the defence affairs of the Jewish Agency and later the State of Israel.

The Balfour Declaration and the appearance of armed Jews in British uniforms with the Star of David and the Menorah as their insignia, convinced many Jewish settlers that henceforth the British would look after their security. Late in 1918 and in 1919 they voluntarily surrendered cartloads of arms to the new authorities. Under these circumstances the riots of 1920, a pogrom in British-controlled territory only two and a half years after the Balfour Declaration, came as a stunning shock. During the riots in Jerusalem's Old City, the Occupied Enemy Territory Administration, then governing Palestine, took a complaisant attitude towards the Arab attackers, in sharp contrast to the hard punishment imposed on Jewish legionnaires who had tried to organize a rudimentary defence. And later that year the British military did little to prevent incursions from Syria into the Upper Galilee, where isolated settlements came under heavy attack. Here Trumpeldor was mortally wounded at Tel Hai. For that matter, the military did not do much better during the 'disturbances' of 1921. That year Sir Walter Congreve, Officer Commanding British Troops in Egypt and Palestine, had sent a most unusual circular to his subordinate commanders. Normally, the letter stated, the army had no political preferences, but there were exceptions. 'In the case of Palestine', he pointed out, 'these sympathies are rather obviously with the Arabs.'[3]

The Jews, of course, were unaware of the circular, but the April 1920 riots led to the formation of a new self-defence organization. In June 1920 the newly founded Histadrut, the General Labour Federation, decided to allocate a fund to provide arms and to appoint a handful of permanent officers. After some further discussion it was decided that this new organization should be a broad-based workers militia and not a small elite body like the *ha-Shomer*. This was the origin of the Haganah (literally Defence), the major forerunner of the Israeli Army.

The going proved difficult at first. British opposition forced the organization underground, while some sectors of the *Yishuv* were apathetic and even hostile. The pious had little interest in defence; right-wing and religious Zionist groups disliked the idea of a 'red' militia and relied, somewhat optimistically, on the authorities to maintain security. The Haganah's main strength therefore came from the Labour parties and especially from the exposed collective settlements where arms could be stored and some elementary training conducted. But there was opposition even among the left-wing settlers, who refused to take military activities seriously. Some were opposed on pacifist principles; others relied on the international solidarity of the proletariat which, they felt sure, would spread to the Arab workers and peasants. For the time being, the Haganah remained a loose association of voluntary local defence groups, without any central authority.

Nonetheless, in the 1920s the Haganah produced some competent leaders, including Eliahu Golomb, an original tactician and future commander of the organization, and Yitzhak Sadeh, a burly Russian immigrant, Red Army veteran, master quarrier, poet, wrestler, and visionary, who in later years would become the founder of the Jewish strike forces. In the mid-1920s he conducted Haganah's first officer training course, first at the high school in the new Jewish city of Tel Aviv and later at a remote kibbutz.

The greatest problem, one that would dog Jewish military efforts for some decades, was the shortage of arms. Although readily available on the post-war markets, weapons had to be smuggled into Palestine piece by piece. With a very limited Haganah budget only a few went to the central arms caches at Kfar Gileadi, Geva, and Shekhunat Borochov; most went to individual settlements which paid for them out of their own meagre funds. At that the arms were of every conceivable make and calibre, a quartermaster's nightmare, and, even when supplemented by the few dozen 12-gauge shotguns issued in sealed cases to isolated settlements, few localities had enough to issue a weapon to every man. Tel Aviv, for instance, had the grand total of 50 pistols and a few cases of grenades in 1928. Overall military thinking was entirely defensive; there were no mobile reserves and reliance was placed on primitive works and barbed-wire fences.

The wave of violence sweeping the country in 1929 caught the *Yishuv* unprepared. Casualties were heaviest among the old orthodox communities who had no defensive capabilities whatsoever, but there were also heavy casualties in the ethnically mixed fringe areas between Jaffa and Tel Aviv, in Haifa, and Jerusalem. A number of Jewish quarters had to be abandoned, several rural settlements had to be evacuated, and many were not resettled until after the 1967 war. The Haganah had failed its first major test.

From Workers Militia to a National Defence Organization

Shaken by the events, the Histadrut recognized that it could not shoulder the burdens of defence alone. Responsibility for maintaining and expanding the Haganah was handed over to the Jewish Agency, requiring a change in the command structure. Supervision over the organization was vested in a civilian committee representing all Zionist parties. The committee in turn nominated a political National Command, the *Mifkadah Arzit*, with membership apportioned along party lines. The National Command controlled a small professional staff and for the first time there were funds to pay the permanent cadre and purchase additional arms. But unity did not last long. Though it tried, the National Command could not bridge the deep-seated differences over the nature of Zionist goals and the political struggle disrupted, not for the last time, military activities. The socialist parties, more nationalist in their own fashion than the bourgeois and religious groups, regarded the Haganah as the nucleus of a future army, while the non-socialists were content to perceive it as a mere auxiliary to the army and the police, designed to protect Jewish life and property when British protection failed. In 1931 the Haganah split and for the next five years the non-socialists maintained their own defence organization, the Irgun Zevai Leumi, or National Military Organization, popularly known as ETZEL.

Dividing severely limited resources was dangerous and the mass immigration beginning in 1933 stirred deep Arab resentments. By 1935 the storm signals were flying and on 15 April 1936, Arabs murdered two Jews in Jaffa, signalling the beginning of the Arab revolt. This time it was a more serious affair. For the first time the enemy were not the urban mobs, easily aroused by oratory but also easily dispersed, or villagers out for loot and plunder, armed mainly with knives and cudgels and only the occasional rifle. In the spring of 1937 there appeared major bands of irregulars, including a paramilitary formation led by a Syrian, Fawzi ed Din el Kaukji, an old friend of the Mufti. The British response was ambivalent and until 1938 limited primarily to static defence. Until the late summer of 1938 the bands were able to maintain themselves in the hill country and emerge to strike at Jewish settlements, road transport, and property. By the time the revolt assumed major proportions, the Haganah was reunited. In April 1937 about half of ETZEL returned, while the remainder, for the most part adherents of the revisionist movement which had broken with the World Zionist Organization, constituted a new fighting group. Led by Moshe Rosenberg and David Raziel, the new organization would soon make a name for itself; meanwhile the main burden of defence was carried by the Haganah. Although still weak, the Haganah managed to carry out its mission. No Jewish settlements were abandoned; on the contrary, in an effort to establish strategic positions linking Jewish areas, more agricultural communities were established than in any previous period. Military rather than economic considerations determined the location of these new settlements, though this did not change the prevailing pattern of the concentration of the Jewish population in the plains and the valleys.

The official position of the major Jewish bodies during these years was *havlagah*, a policy for self-restraint.[4] It was interpreted to mean that the defenders were allowed only to return fire, to hold their positions, and above all were forbidden to engage in counter-terror. The policy was based on the belief that the Arab masses did not really support the revolt and that retaliation would be counter-productive, coupled with the fear that an activist defence policy might provide a pretext for the authorities to close down immigration at this crucial time. And indeed, whatever the shortcomings of *havlagah* as a military posture, it seemed effective for a while.

For once the British authorities seemed willing to co-operate with the Jewish defence effort. Sir Arthur Wauchope, the High Commissioner, authorized the enrollment of Supernumerary Police Force, *notrim*, which eventually numbered 22,000 men. By far the largest group of these men received only basic musketry instruction and only 8,000 rifles were issued. Still, the Supernumerary Police Force served as a legal cover for the Haganah and with the assistance of British instructors the level of training of Haganah members was raised. Moreover, while most of the *notrim* performed static duties, beginning in the autumn of 1937 a mobile guard force, the Jewish Settlement Police (JSP) was authorized, employing both light trucks and armoured vehicles, and, though under British command, made a substantial advance towards the concept of a mobile Jewish force. Many of the *notrim* and practically all of the JSP were Haganah members and their presence relieved this organization, officially still illegal, from having to expose too much of its own still very limited store of arms – 6,000 rifles, 24 heavy and some 600 light and submachine-guns.

Despite the apparent success of this passive military policy, the new ETZEL wanted to answer terror with terror – an Arab life for a Jewish life. In 1937 it began a policy of retaliation causing a considerable number of casualties among Arab civilians. Ben Gurion and his socialist followers detested ETZEL on ideological as well as tactical grounds, but at the same time many elements within the Haganah were increasingly disenchanted with a purely static defence policy. To be sure, they did not want to engage in the killing of innocent bystanders, but they saw little sense in standing passively in their positions allowed only to return fire. Unless the meaning of restraint was changed there was the danger of a rebellion within the ranks.

After much soul searching the National Command decided to make restraint a more flexible concept. As early as 1936 a roving patrol, *ha-Nodedet*, had been formed in the Jerusalem hills by Sadeh and in 1937 he was authorized to form a mobile field force, known as FOSH, the abbreviation for *Plugoth Sadeh* or field companies. Organized late in 1937, and operational only for a short period the following year, FOSH was dissolved in February of 1939 because of the opposition from the right-wing parties to the existence of a predominantly left-oriented force.

FOSH's termination coincided with London's decision to put down the revolt. Early in 1938 substantial reinforcements arrived in Palestine and with them came a remarkable soldier, Captain Charles Orde Wingate, an intelligence officer of unconventional behaviour and brilliant mind, a devout Christian and a fervent Zionist. Ordered to protect the pipeline running from Iraq to Haifa, he formed nine small units of British and Jewish volunteers, the Special Night Squads (SNS), practising commando-style raids and ambushes which between May and the end of September 1938 secured the pipeline and pacified the Galilee. His political views, including the advocacy of a future Jewish army, were unacceptable to his superiors and he was ordered out of the country by 1939.[5] He did, however, leave behind a legacy, inspiring the Haganah to adopt a more aggressive outlook. Until Wingate had arrived, Jewish military skills, developed in secret weekend training sessions heavily influenced by men who had gained their military experience as soldiers and junior level officers in World War I, had been directed almost entirely towards a static defensive. Wingate's unorthodox fighting methods, his insistence on mobility and striking at the enemy where he least expected it were transmitted to the Haganah and eventually the Israeli Army by such officers as Yigal Allon and Moshe Dayan who had their first taste of this style of warfare in the SNS. To be sure, Sadeh already had expressed very similar ideas, but the National Command and Ben Gurion had been sceptical. When a regular British officer, however, advocated such concepts, Ben Gurion was willing to listen. And by 1939, Ben Gurion had become the ranking figure in Zionist Palestine and rivalled the ageing Weizmann in the World Zionist Organization.

One more important military development occurred before the outbreak of World War II created an entirely new situation. In 1937–8, when partition appeared a possibility, the National Command and its professional staff pondered on how to defend the *Yishuv* if the British actually left the country. They devised Plan 'Avner', a scheme to establish a defensive line all along the 280-mile frontier of the small Jewish state. At the same time, unreconciled to the loss of Jerusalem, a city which had had a Jewish majority since the mid-nineteenth century, the Haganah also worked out an alternate plan that involved the occupation of the city and parts of Galilee. To implement either scheme, so the calculations went, would involve at least 28,000 rifles, several thousand automatic weapons, mortars and armoured vehicles. Designed to protect the Jews against Palestinian irregulars and not against any regular army, the plans were detailed but unrealistic. Neither trained troops nor arms to execute either plan were available. Still, the mere conception of such plans showed that the Haganah was far removed from its beginnings as a workers' militia.

Uneasy Partners: The Haganah and the British, 1939–45

The partition proposal was abandoned in favour of the White Paper and the Arab revolt came to an end in the spring of 1939. Consequently, co-operation between the Jews and the British authorities ceased. Instead, as a prelude to implementing its new course, the government now attempted to disarm the *Yishuv*, striking not only at ETZEL but also against the hitherto tolerated Haganah. Arms searches and the arrest and imprisonment of members of Jewish defence organizations continued throughout World War II, the intensity and direction of the British effort being linked with the ebb and flow of the military situation in the Middle East.

When war came in September 1939, the *Yishuv* offered its support to Britain. Within days more than 130,000 men and women registered for national service and the Jewish Agency proposed to raise a considerable fighting force. But the government discouraged an independent Jewish role, motivated both by apprehension that this might establish a moral basis to revoke the White Paper and also that it would add to the *Yishuv*'s ability to oppose, perhaps by force, British post-war policy. Despite promising beginnings in 1940, the formation of a Jewish fighting force was repeatedly delayed. The authorities permitted individual enlistment, first to serve in pioneer companies, later in transport, engineer, and anti-aircraft artillery units. Smaller numbers were enlisted in the Intelligence Corps and after the fall of France as members of the 51st Middle East Commando. In addition, there was recruitment of ground crews for the RAF and a few Palestinian Jews were accepted for pilot training.

Jewish fighting units remained the most controversial issue. In 1942 the government authorized the enlistment of Palestinians – Jews as well as Arabs – in separate infantry battalions of the Buffs, but linked Jewish strength to raising an equal number of Arab units. Parity was abandoned only when it became clear that Arabs would not volunteer in appreciable numbers. Moreover, these units, retitled the Palestine Regiment, were trained and equipped for garrison duty only. It was not until September 1944 that the War Office, after considerable pressure from American public opinion, acceded to the formation of a Jewish Brigade Group. As Churchill told the House of Commons, the 'race which has suffered indescribable torment from the Nazis should be represented as a distinct formation among the forces gathered for the final overthrow'. Composed of the available infantry battalions and with a partial complement of Jewish gunners and transport, the brigade, its blue-white flag displaying the Star of David, was ready by the end of the year. By this time, the war in Europe was winding down and, inserted on the Italian front early in 1945, the unit saw little fighting. Still, it was the first Jewish experience with formations above the platoon level and with the use of heavy weapons. It would prove valuable within a few years. All in all, some 27,000 Palestinian Jewish volunteers served with the British forces during World War II.

During these years the Haganah grew, sometimes in co-operation but often in conflict with the British administration. Efforts to transport Jews from Europe to Palestine continued and even at the height of the war the Royal Navy could spare the ships to intercept the refugee transports and to deport them to far away Mauritius. As the German–Italian threat came closer, in mid-1941, the British made some informal arrangements with the Haganah.[6] With the very survival of the *Yishuv* at stake, the National Command already had decided to re-establish mobile field forces to replace the FOSH units dissolved in 1939. These new units, permanently mobilized, were the famed Palmach, *Plugoth Mahatz* or shock companies. By June 1941, the energetic Sadeh already had assembled a scratch force with hastily recalled FOSH and SNS veterans. The next month some of these units acted as a scout force for the invasion of Syria. Participating in these actions was Moshe Dayan, a future chief of staff of the Israeli Army, who had just been released from a long term of imprisonment for illegal military training. Hard-pressed, the British also utilized aid from ETZEL which also had agreed to a truce during the war. David Raziel, its commander, was sent on a mission to fight the pro-Axis Rashid Ali revolt in Baghdad and was killed there. His successor in command was Menahem Begin, who arrived in Palestine in 1942.

British–Jewish co-operation became even closer in 1942 when Rommel had defeated the 8th Army and penetrated deep into Egypt. Professor Yohanan Rattner and other members of the National Command devised the elaborate 'Carmel Plan', envisaging a last-ditch stand by the *Yishuv* gathered behind the mountain range in Haifa Bay. At the same time Major-General B.T. Wilson, commanding special operations in the Middle East, worked on stay-behind plans in the event of a German occupation in Palestine. Together with Haganah officers he established an intelligence network and plans for guerilla war by special Palmach units. Joint British–Palmach training headquarters were established at Kibbutz Mishmar ha-Emek, but after the tide of war turned at El Alamein in November, co-operation ended. Turning around abruptly, the British demanded the disarmament of all Jewish defence organizations and even confiscated Haganah arms used during the joint training. For its part, the Haganah had never quite trusted British intentions and even in the days of the closest co-operation had refused to disclose its personnel or arms. Now the Palmach went underground and in daring operations a few weeks later recovered the confiscated arms from British stores.

To be sure, some limited arrangements continued. Recruitment for the army was maintained by the Jewish authorities and a small number of agents continued in training to parachute into occupied Europe to assist Allied prisoners of war and to organize Jewish resistance. In the end, the British whittled down the number of parachutists to a mere handful. The authorities were not really interested in helping Europe's Jews to escape, while, following the lead of the Jewish political bodies who now emphasized the establishment of a state after victory, the Haganah began to lay the basis for converting from an underground force into a national army.

All this took place against the background of an internal debate in the *Yishuv* regarding defence policy, structure, and personnel. The main issue was the Palmach. One faction, mainly representing bourgeois parties, argued that enlistment in the British Army was the imperative national duty, while Labour groups asserted that it was necessary to keep an exclusively Jewish-controlled force on a permanent footing. While the controversy was going on, the Jewish Agency would appropriate no funds to keep the Palmach in being and its continued existence was doubtful. Finally, late in 1942, the kibbutz movement came up with a solution. Palmach units would be stationed in a number of collective settlements and they would alternatively train and work, earning their keep. There would be four battalions, one based on the settlements in the Galilee, one in the Jezreel Valley, a third in the kibbutzim of the Judean Mountains and the Negev, while the fourth battalion, including force headquarters and specialized naval, air, and reconnaissance sections, would be stationed in and near Tel Aviv.

Obviously the conditions of service in the Palmach – hard work and hard training, with neither the pay nor the recognition awarded the soldiers in wartime – attracted a special type of recruit. For the most part these were native-born sons and daughters of the old-established collective settlements and from families playing leading roles in the political life of the *Yishuv*. Unrecognized, unpaid, often short even of elementary necessities, the Palmach compensated by developing a collective personality of its own. It proudly considered itself more than just a military unit, but a living communal elite, a 'fellowship of fighters' as Sadeh once expressed it.[7] The special mission of the group demanded the surrender of individual interests to a higher ideal. Discipline relied heavily on social pressure and political awareness and it was significant that out of a total of 493 training hours given to Palmach squad leaders, 120 were devoted to ideological indoctrination. Essentially the Palmach, with about one-fifth of its members girls who participated in all actions, constituted a left-wing 'youth movement in arms', with its own egalitarian style, defiant both of bourgeois values and of external discipline as exemplified by the British Army. Its uniforms, if they can be so called, were khaki shirts and shorts, with the shirt commonly worn outside, supplemented by stocking caps and sweaters. The commanders were young. Sadeh, then in his early 50s was known affectionately as the 'old one', and in May 1945 Yigal Allon, 28 years old, assumed command of the organization. Rank conferred no privileges. There were no badges of distinction, all lived under the same conditions, ate the same food, and did the same work. The only special right accorded to commanders was that they were expected to lead during an attack and stay behind to cover a retreat – a concept that became embedded in the ethos of the Israeli Army.

Palmach training and doctrine stressed small unit operations relying on surprise, mobility, and resourcefulness rather than on frontal assaults and supporting fire. Initiative was encouraged – 'the smallest unit is the single man with his rifle' – and the Palmach was taught to take maximum advantage of darkness and closing rapidly with the enemy, fighting with short-range weapons, explosives and knives. This approach minimized shortcomings in weapons and numbers, combining the notions of Sadeh and the legacy of Wingate's SNS with Liddell Hart's concepts of the 'indirect approach', then coming to the attention of Haganah commanders.[8]

By 1944 it was evident that the Palmach could turn men and women into highly motivated fighters. Despite continued misgivings about the left-wing orientation of the force, the National Command decided to expand it by having members serve a two-year period and then return to their homes – subject to recall – while new recruits went through the training cycle. This built up a reserve and a pool of potential commanders. For all that the force remained small. Neither its special brand of discipline nor its fighting style were suited to large formations. Up to 1946 the Palmach rarely mustered more than 2,000 actives, raised to about 2,700, including 800 girls, in that year. When fighting broke out in December 1947, reserves and new volunteers provided a peak strength of about 4,000.

Palmach's superb spirit, unimpeded by the weight of a regular military tradition and with its troops above average in idealism and education, proved invaluable during the struggle against the British and in the first few months of the War of Independence. For the bulk of the Haganah, however, the war years were a period of stagnation. With many of the best instructors and commanders away in the British Army, training standards and attendance deteriorated. The return of veterans from military service raised the level of competence, though absorbing these men and women into paramilitary formations was difficult.

Haganah infrastructure improved. After the summer of 1938 the National Command once again was composed of proportional representation of the political parties of the Left and the Right, with a neutral, Professor Rattner, serving as its head. Financial support for security activities, and for those *notrim* paid for from Jewish funds, were placed into the hands of the community fund, the *Kofer ha-Yishuv*, also constituted by party formula. Only the revisionists and the small communist splinter groups remained outside this arrangement. In September 1939 it was realized that the small professional staff could not function as a real general staff to deal with technical problems, but the Right was reluctant to concede that such an agency was needed. In the end the left-wing representatives managed to have this concept adopted and a general staff, along conventional functional lines, was set up in Tel Aviv. Yaakov Dori, the Haganah's regional commander in Haifa, became chief of staff.

Efforts also continued to create field forces at the disposal of the National Command. FOSH had been dissolved in April 1939; in its place there arose HISH, *Chail Sadeh* or field force, enrolling the better trained Haganah members between the ages of 18 to 25. It was envisaged to raise 11 battalions with 450 men each, and though the number was exceeded, by the end of 1947 HISH, *Hail Sadeh* or field force, enrolling the better trained Haganah commands were reluctant to release these units to the National Command. The greater part of Haganah manpower remained in the loosely organized HIM, *Hail Matzav* or garrison force. This was a catch-all, about 27,000 men and women, with individual training at best, supposed to defend their own localities. In the major Jewish urban centres, in Tel Aviv, Haifa, and in Jerusalem, now with a Jewish population of 100,000, the membership tended to be perfunctory and far from universal; in the kibbutzim it was practically all inclusive. Finally, there existed several units of the GADNA, *Gedudei Noar* or youth battalions, serving as runners and in other auxiliary functions. All in all, on paper this underground army was substantial but it lacked the attributes of a modern fighting force.

Arms continued to be the most critical shortcoming. When the battles ended in North Africa, quantities of German and Italian arms remained scattered in lightly guarded dumps and the Haganah tried to seize the opportunity to upgrade its scanty arsenal. In March 1943 the mandatory government complained about a sharp increase of thefts of weapons and explosives from military stores and took stern measures to liquidate gun-running. In September there was a public trial before an invited press, attempting to prove that Jewish efforts to produce arms were interfering with the war effort. The trial ended with heavy prison sentences imposed on two defendants. Actually, the illegal arms trade was being carried on throughout the entire area and stolen weapons and ammunition were bought by Jews and Arabs alike. But the British fears of a Jewish revolt and considerations of imperial post-war policy determined that the emphasis in its repression should be against the Jews. In October and November 1943, troops and police staged arms searches at various locations. Few arms were discovered, but during a scuffle one settler was shot. These actions hit a vulnerable nerve. Every rifle, every cartridge was valuable to the *Yishuv* and increased chances for survival. The attempt to disarm the Jews contributed to the growing tension between them and the authorities.

The Haganah also tried to step up production in its underground workshops. For many years a simple type of grenade had been manufactured and arms repaired. During the war the production of entire weapons was undertaken for the first time. Of course, it was impossible to make precision products like rifles clandestinely, but simple weapons, mainly copies of the 9mm Sten submachine-gun and the 2-inch mortar were produced. Neither gun-running nor clandestine manufacture could provide weapons for an army. As late as the winter of 1946, Haganah arms consisted of only 10,500 rifles, 4,435 automatics, including 3,700 Sten guns, and some 300 light mortars. The rifles were of every make and calibre imported into the Middle East since before World War I and the same was true of the machine-guns. As for the Stens, these were unreliable and given to frequent stoppages. None of the arms were available in adequate numbers to equip units for mobile operations and, in order to escape confiscation, were dispersed in the secret storage facilities around the country. Even the elite Palmach was short. One American student at the Hebrew University, who had joined the Palmach in late 1946, remembered that his own company, about 100 strong, 'fielded in total about fifteen weapons, a museum of antique pieces, and no mortars or heavy machine guns'.[9]

As soon as the war in Europe ended, Ben Gurion, now chairman of the Jewish Agency executive, went to the United States to contact prominent Jews and ask them to prepare the shipment of arms and materiel and to provide funds for purchasing equipment. Unlike many other Zionist leaders – old-line socialists, liberals, and pacifists, who still put their faith in a political solution based upon British good will or the offices of the UN – Ben Gurion felt that a military confrontation was unavoidable. But in 1945 he came on his own and he did not have the unqualified support of the executive.[10] Still, the response to his request was good and from then on preparations for arms procurement were underway in America. In the end, however, though money and non-lethal supplies would be forthcoming, the United States embargo on weapons to the Middle East forced the Haganah to look for arms elsewhere. Ironically, they would come from Czechoslovakia, by then in the Soviet orbit.

The Struggle Against the Mandate: 1944–47

The uneasy truce between the *Yishuv* and the British began to unravel in 1943. In April that year the remnants of the Warsaw Ghetto staged a hopeless uprising against the Nazis. Soon thereafter, representatives of the Allied nations met in Bermuda to discuss possible havens for the European Jews. The British representative insisted that Palestine was out of the question; the White Paper was essential for 'stability in the Middle East'. Tension increased with the arms searches and with the approaching date, 31 March 1944, of the ending of all Jewish immigration. In February, ETZEL denounced its truce with the British. 'Four years have passed', ETZEL's wall posters stated, 'since the war began and all the hopes that beat in your hearts then have evaporated. . . . The British regime has sealed its shameful betrayal of the Jewish people . . . there no longer is an armistice between the Jewish people and the British administration. . . . Our people are at war with this regime.'[11]

ETZEL's 'declaration of war' had, to be sure, already been preceded by some violent incidents. In 1941 Avraham Stern, a brilliant scholar, and poet, and fanatic, who dreamed of restoring a Jewish commonwealth against all comers had broken away from ETZEL and formed his own group, *Lohamei Herut Israel*, LEHI, the Fighters for the Freedom of Israel – more commonly known as the Stern group. The Stern group refused to co-operate with the war effort (it even tried to make contact with the Axis powers) and it carried out a series of bank robberies to finance its activities. The police, assisted both by the Haganah and by ETZEL intelligence, acted with great vigour. In February 1942, Stern's hiding place was discovered and he was gunned down on the spot. For the moment LEHI was dead, though it was to rise again in 1944.

ETZEL's change of front was the beginning of a continual series of attacks on British officials, soldiers, and government installations by both extremist groups. In August there was an attempt to kidnap the High Commissioner, Sir Harold MacMichael, which failed. On 6 November 1944, Lord Moyne, the British Minister Resident in the Middle East, was assassinated in Cairo by two LEHI members. This act seriously strained relations with the British. Churchill angrily denounced the deed in the House of Commons and a frightened Jewish Agency decided to root out the terrorists. The Haganah and Palmach were ordered to track down suspected members of the two rival underground organizations; many were deprived of their jobs; students were dismissed from schools. Some LEHI and ETZEL fighters were taken as prisoners to remote kibbutzim, others were handed to the British. It was an ugly episode and its results negative. The operation, the so-called 'season' lasted from November 1944 to June 1945. It created bitter divisions and civil war was prevented only when Begin, showing himself more statesmanlike than Ben Gurion, refused to allow reprisals. There has been some debate about why Ben Gurion authorized the operation. Surely by November 1944 there was no longer any question that Whitehall had decided to liquidate its obligations to the Jewish National Home and the argument that the 'season' was undertaken to prevent an unfriendly turn in British policy seems hollow. It would appear that Ben Gurion acted to eliminate hated political and potential military rivals, enemies of long standing. But neither ETZEL nor LEHI were destroyed. Instead, persecution gained them considerable publicity and increased support and by mid-1945 they would resume their operations.[12]

Ill-feeling between the Haganah and the smaller underground groups remained, but it was temporarily submerged when late in 1945 the Haganah joined in action against the British. These meanwhile had heavily reinforced their position. In addition to the heavily armed Palestine Police – its numbers augmented by newly recruited British and Arab constables – there was the Transjordan Frontier Force (TJFF), originally constituted as a border patrol for the entire mandate. Also available was the British-officered Arab Legion. As for purely British fighting troops, the 1st Infantry Division had been stationed in Palestine since early 1945 and was joined in September by the 6th Airborne Division from Germany. Before the year ended the 3rd Infantry Division arrived from Germany. This was a formidable array, backed up by naval and air units. Bevin's statement that he would require additional troops to put down an Arab revolt if Jewish immigration was permitted does not appear to have been well-founded. On the contrary, it looked to many as if the government was preparing for a showdown with the *Yishuv*.

On the night of 31 October 1945 the Jews opened their offensive with a countrywide attack against communications. There were over 250 separate attacks: 153 breaches were blown in the railway lines, railroad yards at Lod

(Lydda) were damaged, and three police launches sunk, in addition to damage at the Haifa oil refineries. The Haganah, ETZEL, and LEHI co-operated in this operation and only one group of attackers was intercepted. British losses amounted to one soldier and one policeman, but life had not been the objective. The real purpose was to demonstrate that the Jews could not be prevented from military action despite the presence of more than three British divisions.

The year 1946 saw a continuous struggle between the British and the Jewish underground forces – 'altogether one of the most efficient, dedicated and dangerous enemies that the British Army was to face post-war'. Although numerically far inferior to the Haganah, until 1948 LEHI rarely had more than 150 fighters and ETZEL a nucleus of about 700, though with several thousand supporters, these organizations were the cutting edge of the assault. Haganah–Palmach operations still aimed at inflicting material damage, while ETZEL and LEHI were prepared to attack personnel, though they tried to avoid killing innocent bystanders. Facing what appeared to be a united Jewish resistance, the British struck back. On 29 June 1946 troops and police, backed by armour and air, staged raids all over the country, searching 27 settlements and taking into custody 2,178 persons, including top officials of the Jewish Agency and political leaders of the *Yishuv*. Operation 'Agatha', or the 'Black Sabbath' in Jewish annals, was a partial success. Some arms caches were discovered and the Jewish Agency was intimidated. Its executive ordered a continuation of efforts to bring in 'illegal' refugees until the detention camps were overflowing and the British decided to deport the detainees to special camps on Cyprus, but restricted armed operations to sabotaging installations specifically directed against refugee ships.

ETZEL and LEHI, however, were not willing to abide by orders from the Jewish Agency. They were determined to fight to the bitter end. On 22 July 1946, ETZEL units penetrated into the King David Hotel, headquarters of several civil and military government branches, planted explosives and blew up one wing. The government struck back eight days later. Operation 'Shark', carried out by a force of 16 infantry battalions, 3 armoured and 2 artillery regiments, supplemented by military police, Palestine Police, and support elements, cordoned off Tel Aviv. For four days, Tel Aviv, a city of 170,000 inhabitants, was under curfew, while troops and police tried to find ETZEL, LEHI, and Palmach commanders. Some 787 people were arrested, some arms caches were discovered, but no major figure – above all Begin – the main object of the operation – could be found.[13]

Palestine had become an armed camp. To be sure, the Haganah, perhaps fearful that further search operations would lead to the loss of vital arms needed, began to avoid armed clashes with the British, but this did not deter ETZEL or LEHI. Attacks on transports, camps, and installations continued.

In turn, the British were driven to more savage reprisals. Captured underground fighters were flogged and sentences of death were passed in more than 20 cases. LEHI and ETZEL retaliated in like fashion. By the winter of 1946, the British government evacuated all dependants and non-essential civilians, moving the remainder into fortified compounds, known derisively as 'Bevingrads'. On 14 February 1947, Bevin virtually admitted defeat when he informed Parliament that the government had decided to refer the entire Palestine problem to the UN. To be sure, violence continued and even escalated in Palestine, with the military and police turning to desperate methods, including the torture and killing of suspects. But the decision had been made and it was now only a question of time before the British would leave. To be sure, Whitehall had not resigned itself to the loss. Various British officials did much to encourage the Arabs to resist and hinted to the various Arab states that they would not oppose armed intervention. Britain's senior intelligence officer in the Middle East, Brigadier Clayton, predicted that the Arabs would handily win in any conflict and thus the cornerstone of Britain's future Middle East position – friendship with the Arabs – would remain intact. As Sir Alec Kirkbride, Whitehall's man in Amman noted in later years, the British were preparing to leave Palestine but at the same time were giving the Arabs the green light to intervene.[14]

In assessing the role of the various fighting organizations in bringing about the end of the mandate, the conventional version of history has been dominated by the Haganah, Mapai, and the Jewish Agency. The dissident underground groups have been 'relegated to a minor role as terrorists and the unsavoury and unproductive policies of the orthodox hidden away'. But thirty years later it would appear that their activities had more immediate impact on the British decision to give up than the more restrained and 'responsible' tactics of the Haganah.[15] Yet, both groups complemented each other. If ETZEL and LEHI were the immediate cause for Britain's decision, the Haganah and Palmach had over many years of patient labour laid the foundations for the army that would defend the *Yishuv* and the state. There was glory enough for all.

On the Eve of the War of Independence

While UNSCOP was preparing its report, there was talk of war in both the Jewish and the Arab camps. But once again commonly accepted versions of history need revision. Both advocates and detractors of Israel have claimed that the Jewish forces were ready to do battle. In reality, the opposite was true. The fact that partition was likely to be voted by the UN led to illusions among many Jewish politicians that there was no real danger of hostilities with the Arab states and there would be at most a resurgence of the guerilla activities on the pattern of 1936–9, with which the Haganah as then organized was prepared to deal. When the question of possible invasion was raised during the UN negotiations in the summer of 1947 and the Swedish chairman of UNSCOP told Major Aubrey (Abba) Eban, the Jewish Agency's liaison officer, that no matter what the justice of the case, 'we will recommend no state which you cannot defend', a strongly affirmative answer had been given.[16] But the Haganah was not then, and would not be for several months, much more than a part-time and partially trained static defence force.

In mid-1947, the organization could muster some 45,000 men and women, but the bulk of the HIM forces were inadequately trained and armed, and HISH was not much better. Besides the Palmach, about 3,000 strong at this point, the only permanent forces were some 400 men on the payroll as staff, instructors, and weapons-maintenance personnel, and also available, though still subject to British control, was the JSP with 1,800 men. Armament remained poor. Despite renewed efforts to bring in weapons, as late as December 1947 there were only 17,600 rifles, 775 light and 160 medium machine-guns, 670 two-inch and 84 three-inch mortars. The air service, established in November had 11 light planes. There were no combat planes, artillery, or anti-tank weapons, except for a few PIATs (Projector Infantry Anti Tank), a spring-loaded contraption, with the disconcerting characteristic that if it was pointed below horizontal, the bomb would slip out of the projector-tube.[17]

Moreover, there once again was political dissension within the ranks of the *Yishuv*. In September 1947, Israel Galili, appointed head of the National Command that spring addressed the National Council of the Histadrut. He pointed out that there was the danger of invasion from the Arab states, but even if this did not materialize, the Palestinian Arabs would fight and receive arms and volunteers from abroad. He asked that the Labour Federation authorize the Haganah Command to 'conscript any member for guard, command, and training duties'. At the same time he warned against any provocation of the Arabs, called for renewed self-restraint, and urged action against the extremists. Galili, it should be noted, was a prominent member of the Achdut ha-Avoda party, a left-wing movement which had split away from Mapai in 1944. He was still thinking in terms of a workers militia and of small battalions on the Palmach pattern. For that matter, most of the Palmach commanders and many of its members belonged to the same political grouping. These illusions, however, were not shared by Ben Gurion, who had been named director of the Jewish Agency's security affairs late in 1946. He foresaw a major war, not a guerrilla campaign and therefore advocated a general mobilization and the establishment, albeit still underground, of forces organized along conventional military lines.

But it was hard to make the psychological switch. Arms were still purchased
in penny packets and it was not until November that the first emissaries went
abroad to seek large-scale supplies in America and Europe. Mobilization was
even more difficult. The *Yishuv* was war weary; to mobilize the veterans just
returned from the British Army was difficult, and it was not until a few days
before the UN vote that the Jewish Agency and the *Vaad Leumi* consented to
partial mobilization of six HISH brigades. Moreover, activation of such large
formations could not be concealed from the British, still entrenched in great
force in the country and, despite UN instructions, unwilling to countenance
the establishment of Jewish or Arab militias to preserve order. If anything, the
British presence was unfavourable for the Jews. While British forces did little
to block the influx of quasi-regular and irregular Arab forces, allowing them to
take up strategic positions and quarters in the Arab community, they did much
to hamper Jewish operations by continuing to bar the entry of immigrants, and
the importation of arms. Politically divided, with false strategic assessments,
and hampered by an unfriendly major power still in occupation of much of the
country, the Jewish forces would face a difficult time during the first months of
the War of Independence.

2

The Army of the War of Independence: 1947–49

'And fight for your brothers, your sons and daughters, your wives and your homes.'

Nehemiah 4: 8

The War of Independence began in December 1947 and fighting, interrupted by a series of cease-fires, continued into January 1949, the longest and bloodiest war fought by the Jewish forces and the Israeli Army. Despite the hostility of the Foreign Office and repeated turnabouts in the attitude of the State Department, and without any effective help from the UN, the Jewish community in Palestine established its state and defended it first against guerrilla attack and then against the onslaught of five regular Arab armies. Initially hard pressed, after July 1948 Israel was able to take the offensive, only, and not for the last time, to be deprived of a decisive victory by an imposed truce.

The Arabs Attack: December 1947 to April 1948

The Haganah, like most armies, looked to past experience. In summing up the situation in October 1947, Galili foresaw an initial pattern of hostilities resembling that of 1936–9. The Palestinian Arabs, he noted, had made no preparations for war on a large scale 'such as the training and conscription of forces and staff planning'.[1] He warned Haganah commanders against retaliatory actions which might escalate the conflict, cautioning them that there would be real danger if intervention occurred by the regular Arab armies.

Basically his assessment was correct. The Palestinian Arabs had made no major preparations, but nonetheless had substantial military assets for a guerrilla war of attrition. They had at the outset a marked superiority in numbers, were well equipped with small arms, and could count on the benevolent neutrality of the British government and on the active support of the Arab states. Although their level of training was indifferent, the Arabs

39

esteemed martial qualities and almost every adult male had a weapon and knew how to use it. Over the years many had served in the Palestine Police, some 6,000 had served in the British Army, and when in January 1948 the government dissolved the TJFF, most of the 1,700 troopers joined the guerrillas. Finally, a few of the Mufti's followers had received training in the German *Wehrmacht*.

The Palestinian Arabs would be supported by volunteers and materiel from the Arab states. Overestimating Jewish strength at 50,000 well-equipped men, the Arab states decided that initially they would not challenge the Jews or the UN openly, but limit themselves to support the guerrilla war with men, arms, and supplies.[2] Almost immediately after the UN partition resolution individual fighters and volunteer units, with titles such as the 'Lions of Aleppo' and the 'Heroes of Homs' departed for Palestine. Iraq dispatched small volunteer units from its regular armed forces, while from Egypt the fanatic Moslem Brotherhood sent several hundred fighters. In December 1947 recruiting stations opened in Damascus and Beirut for the Arab Liberation Army (ALA) and soon Arabs, but also a sprinkling of foreign volunteers – Moslems from Yugoslavia, German SS men, Polish adventurers, and the occasional British deserter – flocked in for the war against the Jews. The Arab League entrusted command of the ALA to Fawzi el Kaukji, who had returned after spending World War II in Germany, and it became the largest volunteer formation.

The various Arab volunteer groups could also count on two paramilitary youth organizations in Palestine, the *Nejada* and the *Futuwa*, largely recruited among the urban youth, and on temporary local volunteers from the villages. Although numerous, the guerrilla forces had only a primitive military organization. Political rivalries between the Arab governments, family and clan feuds in Palestine, made local co-operation difficult and an overall unified command practically impossible. In the opening stages of the war some control was exercised by the Mufti, who had evaded arrest in post-war Germany and now was living in Cairo, and by the Arab Higher Committee. Most of the fighting, however, was done by local bands of widely differing size and relatively little staying power. In early 1948, two major guerrilla forces emerged. Abdel Kader el Husseini, a relative of the Mufti and perhaps the ablest and most charismatic leader of the Palestinian Arabs, led a well-armed and highly motivated force, some 5,000 men at its peak, recruited from the villages around Jerusalem and from the towns of Hebron, Ramallah, and Jericho. A second major grouping was that commanded by Hassan Salameh, who had been trained in Germany and had parachuted into Palestine late in the war. His force, about 3,000 at most, operated in the Jaffa–Lod–Ramleh area. On 20 January 1948 the ALA, some 4,000 organized in five regiments and supported by armoured cars and artillery, crossed the Jordan and entered the Nablus–Jenin area. Iraqi volunteers infiltrated into the Jerusalem region and into some of the major cities, while Moslem Brotherhood volunteers appeared in the Negev and the Judean hills. Overall the number of Arab pararegulars, irregulars, and volunteers can be estimated at 25,000 to 30,000 men.

Although there was little co-operation between the various groups and many lacked training and discipline, these qualities were not required for a guerrilla campaign. In outline the Arab plan was simple but effective. Enjoying the advantages conferred by the initiative, they would carry out terrorist attacks in urban areas and assault isolated settlements. But these actions were primarily diversionary. The main targets would be the vulnerable Jewish lines of communications. The UN partition plan allocated to the Jews the eastern Galilee, the upper and most of the central Jordan Valley, the valley of Jezreel, Mount Carmel, the coastal plain between Haifa and Tel Aviv, and the major parts of the Negev, containing the bulk of the *Yishuv*. Thirty-three settlements were located in areas assigned to the Arab state, while Jerusalem with a Jewish population of 100,000 was designated a UN-administered enclave. The zones had been delineated with expectations of peaceful co-existence; they had no boundaries which were natural barriers and at three points communications ran through narrow bottlenecks. Even the most thickly populated Jewish areas were interspersed with Arab settlements and the Arabs held most of the high ground dominating the roads. The Jewish state to be was wide open to attack and it seemed likely that systematic strangulation of communications would inflict enough damage so that plans for a Jewish state would have to be abandoned.

From December on there was sniping, bombing, and occasional clashes in the mixed cities and along the Tel Aviv–Jaffa boundary, but the main issue was the 'battle of the roads'. In early 1948 travel from Haifa to the Jezreel Valley became hazardous; communications between Haifa and the Galilee were interrupted; there was interference with traffic from Haifa south to Tel Aviv and from Tel Aviv to the Negev. Traffic had to proceed in convoys escorted by HISH and Palmach troops. Suggestions to evacuate the most remote settlements and consolidate positions were made to Ben Gurion, who increasingly came to dominate the direction of the Jewish efforts, but he refused to permit any pull-backs. Every settlement, however remote, would be held, even though efforts to reinforce and supply such locations were expensive in lives and materiel. Only a policy of standing fast, Ben Gurion was convinced, would provide the morale necessary for the *Yishuv* to survive and to establish the state.

The most crucial line of communications was the road from Tel Aviv to Jerusalem. Although the city was outside the area assigned to the Jewish state,

Ben Gurion was not prepared to surrender it to the Arabs. The fall of Jewish Jerusalem, he maintained 'would be a fatal blow to the Jewish community and break its will to stand before the Arab aggression'. In this battle, however, the Arab held most of the tactical advantages. The 30 miles of road from Tel Aviv to Jerusalem went through terrain principally controlled by the Arabs. For the first part of the journey, convoys could be rerouted on an alternate route through Hulda south of the main road, but from the Latrun crossroads on, all traffic had to ascend the Bab el Wad, Shaarha-Gai in Hebrew, a defile with wooded slopes where boulders offered natural sniper positions and the Arab villages on the heights constituted strong points. Many of these villages, above all Kastel near Jerusalem,became bases for Abdel Kader's forces and foreign volunteers operating against the road.

To protect convoys on the last 16-mile stretch was difficult and costly. At first young men and women, armed with Sten guns and pistols, acted as escorts. In a firefight, to be sure, these weapons were outranged by the Arab rifles, but they had to be used because the British, though making little effort to keep the route open, still searched the convoys, confiscating weapons and sometimes arresting the guards. By March, British interference diminished, but Arab methods became more sophisticated. They progressed from sniping to mines and roadblocks, and fell on halted convoys with massive flank attacks swamping the escorts, usually two or three sections, dispersed throughout the column. After losing a number of convoys, new Jewish tactics evolved out of bitter experience. Home-made armoured trucks, the so-called 'sandwiches' were introduced, consisting of a box-like structure on a truck bed, protected with two sheets of soft steel separated by a thin layer of poured concrete. These armoured vehicles had no turrets, but they had firing slits and provided some protection. From late February on the vehicles would be concentrated to punch their way through an ambush while a mobile reserve of armoured vehicles at the rear of the convoy dealt with sorties against the unprotected supply trucks. If troops were available, a Palmach or HISH company would be deployed in suspected ambush areas. In March, when the situation along the road became even more difficult, Haganah engineers came up with an armoured truck-dozer designed to clear road obstacles, but it was ruled an offensive weapon by the British and on occasion they would not permit its use.

In fact, the Jews contended with British as well as Arab hostility. Since the days of the White Paper it had become British policy to align themselves with the Arab interests and the new Labour government continued this long-standing course. It considered the establishment of a Jewish state a disaster undermining British influence in the oil-rich Arab world and therefore refused to aid in the implementation of partition. The onset of the Cold War also played a role. Moscow, it was feared, would have considerable influence in the

Jewish state and threaten the conservative Arab monarchies. These considerations were shared by important elements in Washington, where the State Department, the Defense Department, and the oil interests all opposed the Jewish cause. Therefore the British pursued a policy in Palestine, outwardly neutral, which was actually designed to produce chaos. Although they announced that they were determined to maintain order as long as the mandate lasted, they refused to take any effective steps to halt the fighting. In fact the more intense the violence and the confusion in Palestine, the more probable it became that many members of the UN would reconsider partition and instead substitute a temporary British trusteeship. Failing this scenario, the British believed that the Arab Legion of the newly independent Kingdom of Transjordan, British-officer and trained, would take over all, or at least most, of the country. 'It seems', Foreign Secretary Bevin told King Abdullah, 'the obvious thing to do.'[3]

Jewish efforts to procure arms abroad were dealt a heavy blow by the State Department which 'in view of the current disorders' embargoed military exports to the Middle East. Although this embargo applied to Jews and Arabs alike, it actually was discriminatory since the neighbouring Arab countries continued to obtain arms and munitions from British sources. On 15 January 1948 Bevin signed an agreement with Iraq speeding up the supply of arms and ammunition already ordered, and providing additional automatic weapons. At the same time, support for the Arab Legion was stepped up. It received additional armoured vehicles and 25-pounder gun-howitzers, and an ammunition reserve adequate for 30 days' fighting.

In the UN, Great Britain declared herself unable to open a port for the Jews as recommended in the partition resolution. On 21 January 1948, Sir Alexander Cadogan objected to the 'Jewish story that the Arabs are the attackers', explaining that the Arabs were merely demonstrating that they would 'not tamely submit to partition'. Viscount Montgomery, Chief of the Imperial General Staff, declared that 100,000 men would be required to enforce the UN resolution and no such force was available. Therefore, the British made no attempt to close the land frontiers of Palestine, allowing men and arms to enter freely from the adjoining Arab states, while at the same time the Royal Navy continued its blockade of the coast, seizing Jewish immigrants for internment on Cyprus and blocking the importation of arms.

Throughout the spring of 1948 the General Officer Commanding in Palestine, Sir Gordon Macmillan, deployed over 50,000 troops, including such seasoned units as elements of the 6th Airborne Division, Royal Marines and Commandos, and they could easily have dispersed the ALA and the bands and safeguarded communications. But these were not his instructions. Macmillan was ordered to see to the removal of some 210,000 tons of stores and to the safe evacuation of British troops, police, and the huge retinue of colonial administrators. Troops were to be engaged only when necessary to protect the evacuation routes, otherwise a neutral stance would be maintained. In practice this meant that, until March, British troops and police continued to interfere with Jewish defence organizations, while sharply curtailing their activities against the Arabs. On the Jerusalem–Tel Aviv road, for instance, twice a day a British armoured car patrol went quickly up and down, while the Arabs carefully refrained from firing. The road was then declared secure. Moreover, as the British began to evacuate non-essential positions, subordinate officers were free to make their own choices. Frequently they handed over strategic points to the Arabs and turned a blind eye as munitions were transferred to the irregulars. To be sure, there were officers and men who favoured the Jews, and others who tried to be even-handed, but the attitude of the majority was summed up by one writer, a former British officer. 'Gay, courteous, and endearingly incompetent', he recorded, the Arabs 'differed in every respect (except bravery) from their scowling foe and it was hard for the British to conceal which side they preferred.'[4]

On several occasions this preference took dark and ugly forms. On 12 February 1948, for instance, a British military patrol arrested Haganah men in an exposed sector of Jerusalem, disarmed them, and then set them free in an Arab area to be butchered by an excited mob. Ten days later British personnel were believed implicated in the Ben Yehuda Street bombing in Jewish Jerusalem which killed 54 persons. Neither of these provocations nor a score of lesser incidents were officially countenanced. The bombing, in fact, was the work of British deserters in the Mufti's pay, but henceforth the Haganah ordered that future British attempts to disarm the Haganah or to enter into major Jewish areas were to be resisted. 'I blamed the British', one Haganah officer with a distinguished record in the Canadian Army explained, 'no less than the Arabs,' and, he continued, 'I now felt no hesitation about confronting the British Army.'[5] For that matter neither ETZEL nor LEHI ever placed much trust in British intentions, though since December 1947 they had restricted themselves to arms-acquisition raids; now they retaliated against individual soldiers and heightened animosities.

The Haganah took a calculated risk by ordering its men to resist arms confiscations. But the British faced their own dilemma: that of demonstrating to the UN and world opinion that on the very eve of their withdrawal from the country they were engaged as participants in a full-scale war, and on the side of the Arabs. Whatever the ultimate designs entertained by his superiors, General Macmillan had no desire for such a development. By the end of March he deployed his forces for final evacuation. Only token units were left in the Galilee; the army withdrew from Tel Aviv and its environs, as well as from the

Arab regions around Nablus, Jenin, and Tulkarem. The Arab Legion, still officially part of the imperial forces, was redeployed south and east of Jerusalem, closer to its main base at Zerka across the Jordan. Uncertainty about British intentions remained and Jewish calculations could never exclude armed intervention. Only the most desperate circumstances, Ben Gurion ruled, would compel the Haganah to commit large forces before the end of the mandate.

Such desperate circumstances materialized late in March 1948. That month Colonial Secretary Creech Jones told the House of Commons that the Palestine situation was 'rapidly becoming insoluble', while Washington reversed itself and on 19 March proposed that the UN rescind partition in favour of a trusteeship. Only the Soviet Union, surprising in view of what was to happen later, remained constant in support of partition. Moreover, the Jews seemed to be doing as poorly on the military as on the diplomatic front. In late February and March the Palestinian Arabs and their allies launched an offensive that inflicted heavy casualties in Jerusalem, Haifa, and the Tel Aviv area, while in the battle of the roads a number of convoys, armoured vehicles and all, were ambushed and suffered severe losses. The Arabs hardly appeared to be 'endearingly incompetent', and one seasoned British officer concluded that the 'Jews had a difficult time ahead'.[6] Jerusalem was being systematically strangled, the Jewish Quarter in the Old City under direct attack, and supplies were running out. It was a desperate situation requiring desperate measures.

The Jews Fight Back: December 1947 to 14 May 1948

Neither Arab hostility nor British passivity came as a surprise to the Jewish leadership. In October 1947, Sir Alan Cunningham, the last of the British High Commissioners, had told Ben Gurion that 'if troubles begin, I fear . . . we shall not be able to protect you.' Except for Ben Gurion and some Haganah commanders, however, most of the Jewish establishment in Palestine was trying to continue business as usual. Still, by December 1947, the Haganah for the first time had a substantial budget, its National Command had been reorganized to allow the professional staff to operate as a general headquarters (GHQ), and four regional commands were operational. The Palmach was mobilizing and HISH battalions were gradually called to active duty. In February 1948 the HISH battalions were grouped into six brigades – Alexandroni, Carmeli, Etzioni, Givati, Golani, and Kiryati, while the original four Palmach battalions had been expanded to ten and formed into three small brigades – Yiftach, Harel, and Hanegev – with their own countrywide headquarters.

Initial mobilization, involving all men and women between the ages of 17 to

25 encountered difficulties. As late as February not all Haganah members had been called up, while non-members would not be mobilized until March and April. In part this was because of the risk of British intervention, and in part it was caused by the shortage of uniforms, blankets, boots, and canteens. Then too, the newly formed National Administration was not yet a government and had to enforce conscription by social pressure. This was no problem in the collective settlements or for that matter in Labour movement-oriented towns such as Haifa, but it was more difficult in Tel Aviv and even more so in Jerusalem, where many of the ultra-pious and some of the Oriental Jewish community remained indifferent to defence preparations. In Jerusalem, moreover, ETZEL and LEHI were relatively strong, while the local Haganah commander, David Shaltiel, a former sergeant in the French Foreign Legion, was not the man to unite the divided factions. As a result, Jerusalem's military position was weak. While its citizens displayed great fortitude in the face of constant shelling and deprivations, operations here continued to suffer from lack of co-ordination among the various fighting groups.[7]

Jerusalem, and indeed the entire Jewish defence effort, still suffered from a grave lack in arms and munitions. Many of the arms caches had to remain concealed; weapons still could not be shifted freely from one region and one units to the other, and as late as March, the Haganah was not able to arm all of its 21,000 mobilized men and women. But on this score at least, the outlook was brighter. Small quantities of light arms were dribbling in from resistance veterans in France and Italy, and in December 1947, the Haganah had found an unexpected source of major supplies. Czechoslovakia was willing to sell arms in quantity, though how these could be brought to Palestine remained an unresolved problem.

While the Haganah was mustering, Ben Gurion worried about its command. Not a single Haganah or Palmach officer, including the veterans of the Jewish Brigade, had experience with formations above the company level. The old Haganah hands, Galili, Dori, Rattner, Shaltiel, and others were too oriented towards positional and defensive fighting and too accustomed, Ben Gurion thought, to the limitations of a clandestine army. The young Palmach officers, on the other hand, emphasized mobility and offensive tactics, but Ben Gurion was not convinced of their competence in handling large units and he was uneasy about their political orientation. With the state in the offing, Ben Gurion turned away from the partisan traditions of the underground and from the volunteer and egalitarian mystique of the Palmach. He did not believe that this tradition could be successfully transferred to a mass-based national army. Perhaps overrating the value of professional military education, he looked for senior commanders outside of Palestine. Major-General Ralph C. Smith, a former US Army divisional commander was approached, but turned down the offer to head the Jewish forces. On a lower level Colonel David 'Micky' Marcus, a West Point graduate who had served on General Eisenhower's staff was more receptive and very briefly, from 28 May to 11 June, commanded on the Jerusalem front. For all his good intentions and symbolic value, Marcus had little field experience and had little impact on the army. More effective, if less well known, was Ben Dunkelman, formerly a major in the Canadian infantry, a long-time Zionist, and an experienced combat officer. He had lived in Palestine in the 1930s and returned in March 1948, served on the staff of Harel Brigade and commanded the 7th Brigade from 5 July to the end of the fighting.

The failure to recruit a truly senior outsider forced Ben Gurion to rely on local talent, usually men in their thirties or below, many native sons rather than immigrants, and all lacking formal training in handling large formations. With the establishment of the proto-government National Administration, followed by the provisional government after 14 May, the political National Command was redundant. Galili became deputy defence minister and Dori was appointed Israel's first chief of staff. But Galili soon drifted into the background, while Dori fell ill and could not carry out his duties. His chief operations officer, Yigael Yadin, then barely 31 years old, took over effective control of the IDF field units. Other commanders were equally youthful. Allon, perhaps the outstanding senior field commander of the War of Independence was barely 30; Yitzhak Rabin, commander of the Harel Brigade, was 26, and Shmuel Cohen was 25 when he took over Yiftach Brigade. Moshe Carmel was considered old at 37, and Sadeh, who first continued at GHQ but eventually received command of the 8th Brigade, was the oldest field commander – 58 years old. Of the 12 brigade commanders, six had learned their trade in the Palmach and they made up for any lack of professional education by personal leadership, initiative, daring and originality. Without detracting from the contributions made by Jewish volunteers from abroad, the failure to secure senior commanders outside the country was highly beneficial to fostering confidence and self-reliance in the fledgling Israeli Army.

At the outset of hostilities the Haganah adopted a defensive strategy. Though Galili had argued that 'we have to wean ourselves and rapidly too from the assumptions on which our defence plans were based between 1936–9,' the National Command still worried about the morality of actions that might take the lives of innocent bystanders. Therefore, the Haganah was limited to operating against the most direct targets only, though as the fighting escalated, measures were taken to ambush Arab irregulars, demolish their bases, and intercept their supplies. To counter invasion by regular armies, GHQ prepared a new operations plan, 'Daleth' – a combination of defensive objectives and offensive action. When the danger of British intervention had passed, the field brigades were to consolidate communications among the Jewish areas, move into certain areas held by the enemy, and occupy positions blocking the most likely invasion routes. But in March, even though the British were still in the country, the situation demanded action. With Jerusalem on short rations and support in the UN fading away, Ben Gurion authorized Operation 'Nachshon', the first brigade-scale operation.

The objective of 'Nachshon' was to break the blockade of Jerusalem by siezing the commanding heights by joint operations from Tel Aviv and Jerusalem. During the last days of March a three-battalion provisional force, 1,500 men, assembled near Hulda, but there were not enough arms. Only the arrival of the first major shipment from Czechoslovakia saved the operation. On 31 March, *Balak* 1, the first of an airlift of some 100 flights, touched down on an abandoned RAF airstrip carrying 40 ZBG-34 medium machine-guns and 200 Czech (P-18) Mauser rifles. Two days later a ship unloaded 200 more machine-guns and 4,300 rifles.[8] On 3 April, Palmach units from the Jerusalem end of the road took Kastel and though the village changed hands several times, held it during the critical period. Nachshon Force moved east on 6 April, seized the village of Saris, commanding the Bab el Wad, and by 17 April a number of convoys had partially resupplied Jerusalem. During the fighting for Kastel, Abdel Kader was killed and many of his followers, discouraged by his death, returned to their homes. The same day, 9 April, LEHI and ETZEL forces made a diversionary night attack against the village of Deir Yassin, inflicting heavy civilian casualties. Although still disputed, the affair was denounced by the Haganah and provided grist for Arab propaganda.[9] But the immediate result of the affair was a blow to Arab morale and the exodus of Arab civilians from the fighting areas, already underway since January, assumed massive proportions.

While Nachshon, temporarily at least, opened the route to Jerusalem, the Arabs suffered several other setbacks. During the first week of April the ALA mounted a major artillery-supported attack against Mishmar ha-Emek, some 20 miles south east of Haifa in the Jezreel Valley, but was outmanoeuvred by the Haganah and forced to withdraw to Jenin. On 12 April a determined assault by a Druze battalion against Kibbutz Ramat Yohanan in the Galilee was repulsed. Impressed, the Druze, an Arabic-speaking religious minority, withdrew from the fighting and some weeks later the Druze villages in the Galilee switched sides and joined the Jews. By mid-April the military situation had been stabilized.

During the next month the Haganah was able to implement most of the objectives of Plan 'Daleth'. Although these operations were carried out under brigade control, there were no continuous fronts and the struggle revolved around towns and strategic vantage points, fought over by units rarely exceeding battalion size and lacking support weapons. Tiberias, the capital of the Lower Galilee, was captured by elements of the Golani Brigade on 18 April. After some fighting, the Arab positions collapsed and some 6,000 soldiers and civilians fled the town. In Haifa, Palestine's major port, with a population of 130,000 about equally divided between Jews and Arabs, large-scale fighting erupted after the British garrison withdrew to the port on 21 April. In 31 hours of savage street fighting the Carmeli Brigade broke Arab resistance. In Haifa the Jews did their best to induce the Arabs to stay, an effort attested by British accounts, but, apparently on orders from the Arab Higher Committee, the Arabs left during the next few days.[10]

Towards the end of the month three brigades – Alexandroni, Givati, and Kiryati – were engaged in mopping up the areas facing Tel Aviv and the Plain of Sharon. For the moment, however, GHQ did not intend to deal with Jaffa, a purely Arab town with a British garrison still in place. Firing from Jaffa had exacted a heavy toll in the streets of Tel Aviv and on 25 April, ETZEL took matters into its own hands. Although only 600 fighters and a few mortars could be mustered, Amihai Palgin, an able commander, penetrated into the town, inching forward from house to house with much sapping and mining.[11] When ETZEL seemed ready to break into the centre of Jaffa, the British intervened on 28 April with tanks and commandos brought in from Malta and Cyprus. The tanks were halted, but ETZEL suffered heavy casualties and transferred its positions to Haganah control. Until the last British troops left there was a stand-off, but on 13 May, the town – almost entirely deserted by its defenders and population – formally surrendered. The central sector had been consolidated, but the next day, 14 May, GHQ missed a golden opportunity on the road to Jerusalem. After Nachshon Force had been disbanded and its units returned to their parent brigades, the Harel Brigade had taken over responsibility for the route. It managed to bring in several more convoys, but then was diverted to stabilize the situation in Jerusalem and the road once again was closed. On 14 May, however, the British evacuated the police fort at the Latrun crossroads and no major Arab forces were in position at this time. Unfortunately, GHQ was unable to divert troops to exploit this opening.

On 14 May all available units were fully engaged. In the Upper Galilee the ancient Jewish community in Safed had been under siege for some time and when the British withdrew they handed over important tactical positions to the Arabs. On 10 May, Operation 'Yiftach', with Allon commanding two Palmach and one Golani battalion, defeated substantially larger Arab forces and lifted the siege by a bold combination of indirect approach, frontal assault, and bluff. He exploited his success by securing the exposed finger of the Galilee while Golani cleared the Lower Galilee and part of the Jordan Valley. Also in the north, just before the British departure, the Carmeli Brigade re-established land communications with settlements in the western Galilee and isolated Acre, which fell on 17 May.

In Jerusalem, the last city held in force by the British, Jewish positions in the New City were consolidated. British interference, however, and the lack of co-ordination between the various elements, prevented both the occupation of the Sheik Jarrah quarter leading to Mount Scopus and a permanent link-up with the isolated Jewish quarter in the Old City. Finally, in the south, last-minute action reopened communications with settlements in the Negev and some reinforcements were sent to help delay the expected advance of the Egyptian army.

An era ended on 14 May when the British departed from Jerusalem and central Palestine. One armoured column moved north to Haifa, where an enclave was retained in the port until 30 June; the second column staged through Latrun and then south to Gaza on the coast road to the Suez Canal. Neither Jews nor Arabs paid much attention to the departing troops; they were engaged in a race to occupy abandoned strongholds, an affair in which the Jews generally succeeded. But that morning, south of Jerusalem, the 6th Regiment of the Arab Legion overwhelmed the last defenders of the Etzion bloc and here surrender was followed by a massacre. As both sides braced for the larger conflict, the British column moving south of Gaza on 15 May encountered an Egyptian brigade going north on the same road. Evidently the Egyptians were jittery because the 2nd Battalion of the KRRC was attacked by Egyptian planes flying cover for the advancing column and suffered one man killed and three wounded.[12] That day Arab Legion elements advanced in Jerusalem while others swung south to Latrun, and Lebanese, Syrian, and Iraqi units began to attack Jewish settlements from the north and east. Also that day, Egyptian planes bombed Tel Aviv. The struggle for Palestine was over; the war for Israel had begun.

The Jewish State at War: 14 May 1948 to 11 June 1948

The Arab governments had hoped that the Palestinian Arabs, aided by several thousand armed and trained volunteers, would be able to take over the country without the intervention of regular armies. The fighting in April had revealed that the Jewish forces were too strong and too determined to be defeated in this fashion. Aroused, the Arab masses pressed their governments for action. In mid-April the Arab League's Political Committee decided on armed interven-tion and the chiefs of staff met later that month to settle details. Dynastic rivalries and political differences between Egypt and Transjordan prevented agreement on a unified command or an effective combined strategy. This, however, did not unduly disturb the generals. The near success of the guerrillas convinced them that regular forces, equipped with planes, tanks, and artillery would easily wipe out Jewish resistance. Field Marshal Montgomery and for that matter the US Secretary of State, former General George C. Marshall, tended to agree. On 15 May the Arab governments announced that their armies had entered Palestine to 'restore order', and Azzam Pasha, Secretary General of the League declared that 'this will be a war of extermination and a momentous massacre which will be spoken of like the Mongolian massacres and the Crusades.'

The Arab armies looked formidable to the Jews and to the Palestinian Arabs who were abandoning their homes in the expectation of a triumphant return, but they were not as strong as they appeared. The five Arab states did indeed have some 80,000 to 90,000 soldiers, but they woefully underestimated Jewish capabilities and grossly overestimated their own, and committed initially less than 30,000 men to help the ALA and the Palestine Arabs – 10,000 Egyptians, 6,000 Jordanians, 4,000 Iraqis, 4,000 Syrians, 1,500 Lebanese, and small contingents from Saudi Arabia, Yemen, and Morocco. The Egyptian, Transjordanian, and Iraqi units were organized and equipped on the British pattern; the Syrians and the Lebanese followed the French model. The best-trained force was the Arab Legion, commanded by war-experienced British officers, transformed at the stroke of midnight, so the Foreign Office insisted, from servants of King George to servants of King Abdullah. It was organized in two brigades with 25-pounder gun-howitzers, 6-pounder anti-tank guns, 3-inch mortars, and supported by a fleet of over 50 Marmon-Harrington armoured cars. Egyptian and Iraqi brigades were equipped to similar scale. The Egyptians had no armoured brigades, but their mechanized regiments were equipped with surplus British Locust, Valentine, and Sherman tanks, a motley collection of lighter vehicles and armoured cars, and hundreds of open-tracked Bren-gun carriers. Syria and Lebanon had French materiel, including some light tanks and field guns. Altogether the Arabs fielded 152 field guns, 140 to 160 armoured cars, 40 to 60 tanks, and 60 combat aircraft.[13]

Although most accounts have stressed the imbalance of national resources, the 'few against the many', a population of some 650,000 Jews facing millions of Arabs, the most acute problem for the IDF was not intolerable numerical superiority on the battlefield, but overwhelming firepower. On the day of the invasion, not counting HIM units, GADNA battalions, auxiliary services, ETZEL or LEHI fighting groups, the mobilized Jewish forces numbered close to 30,000 men and women. Their training, to be sure, left much to be desired. The Palmach had at least one year of training for each fighter, but HISH troops averaged only 50 days, and HIM even less.[14] But the gravest problem during the first four weeks of the war was firepower, especially the almost complete lack of anti-tank and anti-aircraft artillery.

In April 1948 the Haganah had received its first guns, 20 Hispano-Suiza anti-aircraft cannons from French sources, and five ancient 65mm mountain guns, dubbed 'Napoleonchicks', arrived on 15 May. Moreover, there were some additional PIATs and some obsolete anti-tank rifles, but there was little ammunition. The small-arms situation improved as additional *Balak* flights arrived from Czechoslovakia, though until the first armistice there were only a total of 30 flights carrying 107 tons of supplies, including four dismantled ME-109 fighters. During the first weeks of the war, from 15 May to 11 June, the Arabs had a good chance of overrunning forces not yet fully operational and poorly armed, and with their best units, the Palmach brigades, depleted by casualties suffered in the war against the irregulars.

Time was needed to build an army and time was provided by the stiff-necked resistance of the settlements in the path of the invading armies, by the sacrifices of the Palmach, and the staying power of HISH. The stand of frontier settlements like the two Deganias against the Syrians, of Yehiam against the Lebanese, and of Nirim and Yad Mordechai which delayed the Egyptians, to name but a few, was truly remarkable. Usually settlement defences consisted of some light-weapon emplacements, hastily dug communications trenches, a few mines and strands of barbed wire. Their armament, moreover, was inadequate. Kibbutz Nirim had 1 medium machine-gun, 1 Bren gun, 4 Stens, 10 Lee-Enfield and 7 Carcano rifles with 200 rounds for each machine-gun and only 40 rounds for the other weapons, but it stood off an attack by an Egyptian battalion. Yad Mordechai, on the road to Tel Aviv, with 24 assorted rifles, 4 submachine-guns, 2 medium machine-guns, and 1 PIAT with 3 rounds, and a garrison of 70 combatants including women, held out for six days, from 19 to 25 May, against an Egyptian brigade and then was evacuated. Fighters in other localities showed the same determination. The will to live, the feeling that after a long history of pogroms, persecutions, and betrayals, they again faced a 'war of extermination', infused uncommon unity and an almost fanatic spirit among the Jews. 'We fight because there is no alternative' was a common saying in 1948, to be repeated in 1956, 1967, and 1973.

Jewish defence profited by Arab mistakes. The Arab war plan assigned the Legion responsibility for the central front from the sea up to Bethlehem, while the Syrians and the Iraqis, supported by the Lebanese, the ALA, and 800 Moroccan volunteers, would deal with the Upper and Lower Galilee. But instead of using his highly mobile Arab Legion for a thrust to the sea, Abdullah ordered it to 'liberate Jerusalem'. It overran the weakly defended and isolated Jewish Quarter in the Old City, but lost much of its trained manpower in an attempt to break into the New City. Other Legion elements, however, moved eastwards to occupy Lod, Ramleh, and Latrun, only a few miles away from Tel

Aviv. Advancing through Arab-held areas, the Egyptians and Iraqis also managed to come within a short distance of the centre of Israel. The Egyptians, delayed by the resistance of the settlements, advanced to within 23 miles of Tel Aviv and were halted only by an unexpected Jewish air strike on 29 May; a second Egyptian column reached Bethlehem and from there joined the Arab Legion guns in bombarding Jerusalem. Iraqi troops established themselves in the Tulkarem–Jenin area and from there menaced the coastal strip north of Tel Aviv, though the hard-pressed IDF prevented a breakthrough. In the Galilee the situation was easier. The Syrians and the Lebanese managed to seize only a few square miles of territory, while the ALA remained no more than a nuisance.

Neither side had enough strength to hold a continuous line and it was standard strategy for both to place strong forces in a commanding position and attempt to stop the enemy as he tried to capture it. This was well illustrated at Latrun, once again blocking the Jerusalem road. The Legion held this junction against a series of assaults supported by 65mm field guns and improvised armour. During the last attack, the newly formed 7th Brigade, with many fresh and only semi-trained immigrants in its ranks, was repulsed with heavy losses. Yadin had opposed this action but had been overruled by Ben Gurion, who insisted that the road to Jerusalem had to be opened. In the end, just before the first truce went into effect on 11 June, a bypass to the city avoiding Latrun, the so-called Burma Road, was found through the Judean hills.

Israel had survived a desperate holding action. Some territory had been lost, a few settlements had been overrun, others were besieged and Jerusalem was cut off. Perhaps most grievous was the loss of the Jewish Quarter in the Old City and it would remain the object of repeated attempts to recover it. Casualties had been high. The Palmach brigades and Givati, especially, had suffered almost 50 per cent losses, with a disproportionate number of officers and non-commissioned officers, a pattern repeated in all subsequent wars. New arms were arriving and new manpower was being levied, but time was needed to make these operational. On the Arab side, the dream of easy conquest was shattered. The Legion also had heavy casualties which it found hard to replace; ammunition was depleted and the fighting vehicles required maintenance. The one-month truce declared by the UN was welcomed by both sides.

Operations from 8 July to January 1949

Both sides utilized the truce to strengthen their positions, but the setbacks suffered during the initial campaign had shattered Arab command unity. Once this was realized, the IDF GHQ was able to concentrate forces and defeat individual enemies in detail. During the truce the IDF obtained additional weapons and equipment, mobilized more manpower, and formed new brigades, the 8th (armoured) Brigade and the 9th Oded Brigade. Also, albeit not without serious conflict, it absorbed ETZEL units and reorganized its command and control system.

When fighting resumed for ten days on 9 July, Allon – now commanding a strike force of almost four brigades – launched Operation 'Dani', which removed the Legion from Lod and Ramleh and relieved pressure on Tel Aviv. An attempt to take Latrun failed once again, but communications with Jerusalem were improved and secured. In the Lower Galilee the revitalized 7th Brigade under Dunkelman took Nazareth, defeating the ALA and the Iraqis, while Syrian and Lebanese counter-attacks were defeated, the Israeli Air Force (IAF) going into action for the first time on this front. However, after several days of fighting, armies on this front largely retained the positions they had held when the truce began. On the southern front, the IDF took a defensive posture against the Egyptians and there was little action. In the Jerusalem area, Jewish forces captured a number of positions, narrowly failing to retake the Jewish Quarter of the Old City. As Sir Alec Kirkbride remarked, 'there is little doubt that, but for the assistance to the Arab defenders which was afforded by the medieval city wall, Jerusalem would have been captured by the Israelis.'[15] The IDF was prepared to continue its offensive when a second truce, this time of unlimited duration, was forced by a United States threat to propose sanctions in the Security Council.

During the uneasy truce that prevailed until October, the IDF became even stronger, though Count Bernadotte, the UN mediator, was hostile to Israel and did his best to impede efforts. He incurred the hatred of many and in September 1948, was assassinated by persons believed to be close to LEHI. When, early in October, a series of Egyptian provocations permitted the IDF to resume fighting, this new power was demonstrated in three major operations, two in the south and one in the north. The Egyptians were driven from the Negev, the Syrians from the Galilee, and IDF units penetrated into Lebanon up to the Litani River. The ALA was destroyed and disappeared. During these operations the IDF grouped several brigades under one command, the so-called 'Fronts'.

Chronologically the first major operation was 'Yoav', involving three, and later four, brigades, a tank battalion, eight batteries of field artillery, one battalion of heavy mortars, as well as air support. Allon, front commander in the south, launched his operation on 15 October and, encountering stiff Egyptian resistance in the western section, rapidly shifted his forces towards Beersheba and captured the town and surrounding area. One Egyptian brigade remained behind in the so-called Faluja pocket and maintained itself until the end of the war. Fighting ended on 22 October when the UN imposed yet

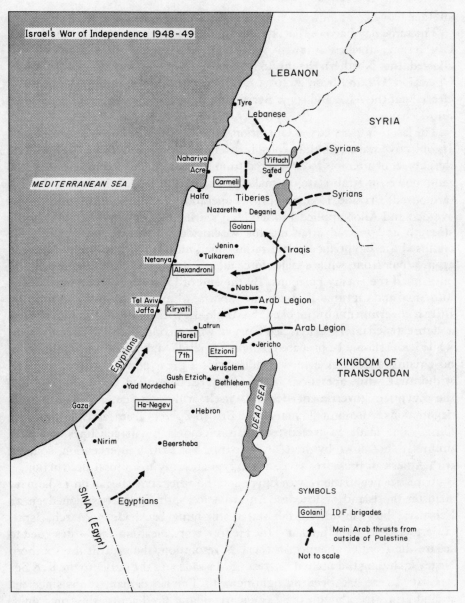

Israel's War of Independence 1948–49

LEBANON

SYRIA

Tyre

Lebanese

Nahariya
Acre

Yiftach

Safed

Syrians

Carmeli

MEDITERRANEAN SEA

Halfa

Tiberies

Syrians

Nazareth

Degania

Golani

Jenin

Netanya

Tulkarem

Iraqis

Alexandroni

Nablus

Arab Legion

Tel Aviv
Jaffa

Kiryati

Latrun

Arab Legion

Harel

7th

Etzioni

Jericho

Jerusalem

KINGDOM OF
TRANSJORDAN

Gush Etzioh

Bethlehem

DEAD SEA

Yad Mordechai

Egyptians

Gaza

Ha-Negev

Hebron

Nirim

Beersheba

SINAI (Egypt)

Egyptians

SYMBOLS

Golani   IDF brigades

Main Arab thrusts from
outside of Palestine

Not to scale

another truce.

The same day Fawzi el Kaukji, who did not consider himself bound by any UN action, attacked a Jewish settlement near the Lebanese border. This allowed the Northern Front to become active in a lightning campaign, Operation 'Hiram', from 29 to 31 October, during which four IDF brigades cleared out the ALA and some Syrian and Lebanese elements and penetrated into Lebanon.

The last major stroke was Operation 'Horev', which began on 22 December. Its objective was twofold: to consolidate Israel's control over the Negev – still the subject of attempts to be severed from the state – and to compel Egypt, the most powerful Arab state, to make peace. Five brigades, including the 8th (armoured) Brigade, took part in this operation, in which frontal assault was avoided and Allon applied Liddell Hart's principles of avoiding the enemy's strength and instead attacking his weaknesses in unexpected ways.[16] He confused the Egyptians by infiltrating small mobile units in his rear, feinted against their front, while a major force moved along an ancient desert track and outflanked the enemy positions. By the end of December, Allon had broken into Sinai and captured El Arish, an important Egyptian base. A disconcerted British government now invoked the Anglo–Egyptian Defence Treaty of 1936 and threatened intervention. Ben Gurion, whose axiom then and later was that, while Israel should be prepared to fight any or all Arab armies, it should under no circumstances risk armed conflict with a great power, ordered an IDF withdrawal, while operations in the Gaza area continued. On 6 January 1949 the Egyptian government declared itself willing to enter into armistice negotiations. Also on 6 January, five British fighters from bases in the Suez Canal Zone made an armed reconnaissance over the Israeli lines and were promptly shot down by the IAF. The threat of British intervention, coupled with American pressure, saved the Egyptian army from total destruction.

Armistice negotiations with Egypt and the other states began on 11 January 1949 on the island of Rhodes. An armistice with Egypt was signed on 24 February, but the other Arab states still hung back. On 7 March, Israel undertook Operation 'Uvdah' – the Hebrew word meaning 'fact' – designed to secure the frontier assigned in the UN resolution, the area in the southern Negev including the ancient fortress of Massada and the outlet to the Red Sea at Eilat. There had been no fighting with Transjordanian troops since the second armistice, though the Legion frequently fired across the truce lines. Even now neither side wanted an armed collision and the Jordanians withdrew at the approach of an Israeli column across the Gulf of Eilat to Akaba. On 10 March 1949 the Israeli flag was hoisted at Eilat. Lebanon signed an armistice on 23 March, Jordan on 3 April, and Syria on 29 June. Iraq, however, refused to sign any agreement and merely withdrew her troops. The various areas still held by the contestants now were evacuated up to the agreed lines. Egypt retained control of the Gaza Strip, while Abdullah formally annexed the remainder of Arab Palestine in 1950, ending prospects for a Palestinian state. Israel had been victorious, though the cost was high: over 6,000 were killed, almost 1 per cent of her total population.

Evolution of IDF Command, Control, and Manpower Structure

The army that emerged from the first war for Israel was a far cry from the oddly assorted companies of idealistic youths, middle-aged home guards, and raw immigrant recruits, many of whom, as observers despairingly noted 'did not know one end of a rifle from the other'. By the end of 1949, though still poorly equipped by standards of major contemporary armies, the IDF had become the strongest force in the region. But the change from underground to regular army status had been difficult and on occasion painful.

During the War of Independence the IDF grew from a motley collection of units with widely varying fighting capabilities to a centralized national defence establishment of 12 brigades, support and auxiliary services, and air and naval elements. Its effectives rose from 21,000 men and women in March 1948 to 30,000 by the end of May, and at its peak, at the time of 'Yoav', numbered over 80,000. This mobilized strength comprised well over 10 per cent of the total Jewish population, the highest mobilization ratio in modern times. Most were recruited within the country, a task made easier after the establishment of the state. On 26 May the provisional government promulgated Order No. 4, establishing the 'Israel Defence Force, consisting of ground, air, and naval forces'. All soldiers were to take an oath to the state and the existence of any other armed formation was prohibited. Conscription was extended to the middle-aged and the young, both men and women. The youth battalions established a good record in the fighting for Jerusalem and women also participated in combat. From June on, however, they were gradually withdrawn from combat duty, though girls remained in vital support roles with front-line units.

Foreign Jewish volunteers did not play a major role in this war and their actual numbers fell far below Israeli expectations. There had been hopes that thousands of Jewish–American war veterans would come to the aid of the threatened Jewish state, but all in all, MAHAL, foreign volunteers from abroad as they were designated, numbered at best 5,000, while the official history placed their number much lower, 'approximately 2,400'.[17] The higher number seems to be more likely. There were some 1,500 volunteers from the United States and Canada, about 500 each from France and England, 300 from South Africa, and the balance from Latin America, Scandinavia, and other

The Army of the War of Independence: 1947–49

Haganah and IDF strength 1947–8

This table has been prepared from various and conflicting sources
and represents the author's best estimate

	December 1947	15 May 1948	12 October 1948
Mobilized manpower	4,000	32,500	80,000
Mobilized field units	4 battalions Palmach	3 Palmach brigades: Yiftach, Hanegev, Harel	3 Palmach brigades
	No formed HISH units above company level	6 HISH brigades: Golani, Carmeli, Alexandroni, Kiryati, Givati, Etzioni	9 HISH brigades: as of 15 May plus 7th, 8th, Oded (9th)
Weapons by type: Guns, field and AA	0	6 65mm mountain, 10 20mm	250 incl. 60 75mm
Mortars 120mm	0	0	12
6 inch	0	0	33
3 inch	50?	105	389
2 inch	650	682	618
Davidka	0	12	22
PIATS and AT rifles	10?	75	675
Machine-guns – light and medium	775	1,550	7,550
Rifles, all types	10,500	22,000	60,000
Submachine-guns	3,700	11,000	22,000
Tanks*	0	3 inoperative	10 H-35, 1 Sherman, 2 Cromwell
Planes	12 light planes	10	10 ME-109?, 14 Spitfire, 3 B-17, 1 DC-3, plus others
Warships	0	0	3 corvettes

*A variety of 2-pounder armed armoured cars, about 50 in running condition.

countries. Proportionally, the small Finnish Jewish community – less than 2,000 souls – provided the largest number, 29 volunteers. Late in the summer of 1948 there were unsuccessful efforts to form a Jewish volunteer brigade in Czechoslovakia and other countries of the Soviet bloc. Ben Gurion refused to have a combat unit under the control of officers whose primary allegiance could be doubtful, and the Czech government, pressed by the United States, changed its mind. In the end, some 600 volunteers from behind the Iron Curtain arrived in late autumn, but saw limited action and did not fight as a separate unit. It was not the first time that Ben Gurion had refused to permit formation of a foreign unit. In May he had turned down a request by Dunkelman to form English-speaking volunteers into a separate brigade, though one battalion of the 7th Brigade was nicknamed the 'Anglo–Saxon' battalion.

Although disappointingly small in numbers, the foreign volunteers provided valuable expertise, not so much in command – where the new Israeli commanders proved quite able to handle large formations – but in technical skills. In the IAF most pilots and a large proportion of the ground technicians were 'Anglo–Saxon' volunteers, and MAHAL was prominent in the navy and the medical service. Perhaps the fairest assessment of MAHAL is that its importance 'did not lie in their numbers but in the qualifications and experience of its members'.[18]

Immigrants who arrived in Israel after the establishment of the state were subject to conscription and designated as GAHAL, overseas conscripts. Again, immigrants came from the displaced persons camps in Germany, from eastern Europe, North Africa, and the internment camps on Cyprus. Some were sick, others destitute, and few had military experience (obtained in the Soviet Army and the partisan movement). Since 1947, the Haganah and ETZEL had provided training in the camps, but its level was not high. Then too the UN-imposed restrictions on the number of immigrants of military age permitted the British to retain large numbers of young men in their internment camps.

The overwhelming bulk of IDF manpower was composed of the men and women from the *Yishuv*, with both the strengths and shortcomings of this closely knit community. By and large, their military qualities were surprisingly high. An American officer who observed them described the Israeli as 'a good soldier. If the war continues he will be a much better one. He has courage, intelligence, initiative, resourcefulness, and endurance.'[19] Their greatest weakness was lack of discipline, never a virtue of the individualistic Jews. The new army had been built on the framework of the egalitarian Haganah where there had been little distinction of rank except by individual merit. Now many disparate elements had to be welded into a single fighting force and egalitarianism, based on shared ideals and common background, no longer was adequate. Badges of rank had been unecessary as long as all leaders were known and respected by their men, but during Operation 'Nachshon', when units had been drawn from different brigades, it had been necessary to provide commanders with distinctive insignia, a blue ribbon on their shirt epaulets. And during the first engagements of the Harel Brigade, expanded by an influx of new recruits, there had been occasions when orders had not been obeyed because men did not recognize the officers. As Dunkelman put it, 'the outcome was a costly confusion intolerable under combat conditions.'[20] The problem was aggravated by the tendency of Palmach brigade commanders to disregard instructions if they conflicted with their own ideas.

Lack of individual discipline and divergent loyalties up and down the chain of command were symptomatic of the continued infighting among the various political factions in Israel, each suspecting the other of trying to wield too much influence in the new army. Political disputes raged at all levels, including GHQ and the cabinet. At issue were questions of command, discipline, and the relationship of ETZEL and the Palmach – both claiming special status – with the central command.

Combining the posts of prime minister and minister of defence, both in the national administration and in the provisional government, Ben Gurion, the leader of the left-centre Mapai Party, was acutely aware that many Palmach and other senior officers belonged to the newly formed Mapam Party, a merger of various leftist groups, while ETZEL's political orientation was to the right. The prime minister favoured an apolitical army organized along conventional lines, but by necessity political considerations affected decisions. On 2 May 1948, he had abolished the position of Head of the National Command, a political post held by Galili, a leftist who remained, however, in the new government as deputy defence minister. Political considerations also were involved when Chief of Staff Dori suffered a stroke and no longer could carry out his duties. Normally Sadeh, his deputy, would have taken over, but Ben Gurion considered him too much committed to the Palmach and too unorthodox in his approach to war. Yigael Yadin, the head of the Operations Branch at GHQ, basically apolitical, became the *de facto* chief of staff, though he retained his old title. Sadeh was eased out and took over command of the newly formed 8th Brigade.

During the first truce Ben Gurion set up a highly centralized command system. From his office orders were to emanate through GHQ to the four regional commands, North, Centre, East, and South, functioning as operational fronts with brigades assigned according to need. Ben Gurion was determined to personally direct the war effort and conducted himself in what Yadin regarded a high-handed, and on occasion wrong-headed, fashion. The two men already had clashed over the Latrun operation, when Yadin had recommended an indirect approach and Ben Gurion had insisted on a frontal attack by the 7th Brigade, repulsed with heavy casualties. When the army was reorganized in June, Ben Gurion, who preferred British-trained officers, tried to appoint Shlomo Shamir, who had not distinguished himself at Latrun, and Mordechai Makleff to high command. This created a crisis at GHQ. Yadin took his case to the cabinet and complained about the prime minister's interference in operational and personnel matters. A special ministerial committee headed by Yitzhak Gruenbaum, the interior minister, was set up to conduct an investigation during which both Ben Gurion and Yadin threatened to resign. In the end, however, they compromised. Carmel obtained command of the North with Makleff leading a multi-brigade formation; Shamir rose to command the East Front, while Allon obtained command of the critical Central Front during Operation 'Dani'.

In addition, Ben Gurion gained his points on issuing standard uniforms for the army, with military courtesies, badges of rank, and separate messing facilities for officers and men. Much resented, the new arrangements were obstinately boycotted in the fighting units until the end of the war, but, much to Galili's displeasure, the old egalitarian structure of the Haganah, at least in principle, was broken. These innovations were, of course, most fiercely disliked by the Palmach, but though this angered Ben Gurion, Palmach prestige was too high and its fighting capabilities needed so that it retained its autonomy until November.

If Ben Gurion was concerned about the Palmach, he positively disliked, even hated, the right-wing ETZEL and LEHI. On 12 May 1948 he had informed the national administration that he could not remain responsible for defence affairs unless all armed forces would be controlled by duly constituted authority – the prime minister and the minister of defence. For a time it appeared as if this question could be resolved easily. After the proclamation of the state, Begin had offered to place ETZEL at the disposal of the government and following promulgation of Order No. 4, both ETZEL and LEHI agreed to disband and join the IDF. But integration took time and they continued to exist as distinct units with their own officers. Moreover, the agreement did not apply to Jerusalem, legally outside the territory of the state, where relations between Shaltiel and the right-wing fighting groups deteriorated steadily. For his part Ben Gurion was determined to eliminate any and all remnants of separatism in the army, left or right, but he could not yet move against the Palmach. No such inhibitions existed with regard to ETZEL. The situation came to a head on 20 June 1948 when the SS *Altalena*, a landing ship outfitted by ETZEL in France, tried to unload a cargo of 5,000 rifles and 100 machine-guns on the Tel Aviv beach. When Ben Gurion demanded that these weapons, destined for ETZEL units in the IDF and Jerusalem, be handed over, ETZEL refused. Ben Gurion regarded this as a clear challenge to government authority. The Alexandroni Brigade cordoned off the beach and Palmach units were brought in. Firing broke out and the ship was set afire, with some two dozen men on both sides killed.

Civil war seemed near. But once again Begin refused to permit a war among the Jews. Although he had enough men in Tel Aviv to contest the government, he called off his troops and agreed to their complete integration into the IDF.[21] LEHI alone could not maintain a separate existence and dissolved its units. After the assassination of Bernadotte in September, the government arrested a number of leading LEHI figures and the organization disappeared from the military scene.

At the end of September, Ben Gurion moved against the Palmach. By this time the army had doubled in size; many of the Palmach cadres had been dispersed as officers and sergeants to the n℮ ℮v formations. At first Ben Gurion tried to reason with the Palmach commanders. In a series of meetings he pointed out that the state required an army organized on regular lines and that under the new circumstances there was no justification either for a separate Palmach identity or a separate headquarters. Few commanders were convinced. On 29 September, Ben Gurion instructed Dori to issue orders disbanding Palmach headquarters and to place its brigades under direct GHQ control. Dori complied, but tried to soften the blow by explaining in his directive that all details would be worked out by joint agreement between GHQ and Palmach leaders. Almost a month passed before further steps were taken and during this time there were protest meetings, angry editorials, and some resignations. The Palmach, its advocates argued, not only was the elite of the army, but also the repository of the agricultural pioneering spirit of the Zionist Labour movement. Ben Gurion disagreed. Although, he declared, he always would be prepared to fight for the Zionist Labour movement, he never would accept 'any barrier or organizational distinction between one Jew and another . . . in the army'. Pioneering, he maintained, ought not to remain the monopoly of a select elite, but should be the responsibility of all military units.[22]

Once again, Ben Gurion prevailed. Although Palmach members commanded six out of the 12 operational brigades, and its national commander, Allon, now headed the key Southern Front, there was no threat of overt dissidence. The three Palmach brigades were the first to be demobilized and Palmach veterans, just like former ETZEL fighters, found some avenues of promotion closed to them in the army.

Arming the IDF

Ben Gurion had hesitated because of the Palmach's close identification with the pro-Soviet Mapam Party. Although the Soviet bloc had been the only large-scale source of small-arms and aircraft during the war, Ben Gurion now was looking towards peace, reconstruction, and the absorption of millions of immigrants. The financial support necessary for this could come only from the West, especially from the American Jewish community. Moreover, Ben Gurion was only too well aware that Soviet policy in the Middle East was highly pragmatic. For nearly 30 years the Soviet regime had outlawed Zionism and persecuted its adherents as 'agents of British imperialism'. Only when they discovered the Jews in revolt against British rule did they become more sympathetic and provide strong and consistent support in 1947–8. But, as Ben Gurion realized, all this could change overnight, depending on the requirements of Soviet foreign policy.

The Soviet Union provided aid through diplomatic activity in the UN and through the sale of arms from Czechoslovakia. Contact with Czech military officials and arms manufacturers actually had started in December 1947 but continued after the Communist take-over the next spring. Czechoslovakia needed hard currency and deliveries were paid for at prevailing prices in cash. At a time when no Western European government, nor the United States or Canada, would sell arms, the Czech connection provided the infantry weapons that saved Israel – 24,500 rifles, 5,015 medium and 880 heavy machine-guns, 57 million rounds of 7·92mm and 1·5 million rounds of small-arms ammunition, aerial bombs, and even twelve 120mm mortars, bought by the Prague government in Switzerland and transferred to Israel.[23]

Bringing the arms from land-bound Czechoslovakia to Israel was difficult. Some shipments went by sea from Yugoslavia and Rumanian ports, but the bulk of the weapons, including some disassembled fighter planes, were flown out of the Czech air base at Zatec, code-named 'Etzion', first by chartered aircraft and later by Israeli C-46s and one Constellation, all smuggled out of America. There were some 100 *Balak* flights before the United States pressured Prague to suspend operations at Etzion at the end of August 1948. Before the Czech connection closed down, it also had provided Israel with an air force. It sold 49 ME-109 fighters, more properly AVIA C-199s, Messerschmidt airframes with Junker-211 engines. These modified planes had severe shortcomings. One Israeli pilot remembered that they were hard to fly and unreliable, but they were the IAF's first real combat planes. The Czechoslovak government also sold Israel Spitfires, which had belonged to the Free Czechoslovak fighter squadrons with the RAF, and these were excellent aircraft, combining superb performance with high firepower.[24] Together with two Spitfires assembled from downed Egyptian planes and from the scrapheaps of abandoned RAF airbases, Israel by October 1948, had 25 Spitfires, about a dozen ME-109s, three B-17s, four P-51s (smuggled crated out of New York), some Beaufighters boldly flown out of England, as well as various other aircraft of many different types. Maintenance and spare parts proved a problem and only about half of the Spitfires and fewer of the Messerschmidts were operational at any one time. By July 1949, the official end of the war, 68 aeroplanes of various types had reached Israel from the United States, and a further 17 had been brought from the US Occupation Zone in Germany. But 182 planes had come from 'Etzion', 13 had been flown out of Great Britain, and 8 from South Africa. Finally, two Egyptian Spitfires had been salvaged.

Although Israel now was a recognized state, only Czechoslovakia would provide arms on a government-to-government basis. The planes procured from the United States – transport planes as well as bombers and fighters – had to be smuggled out of the country under the watchful eye of the FBI and the customs service. In addition to the planes several hundred Browning machine-guns from surplus dumps in Hawaii, some explosives, and some arms-manufacturing machinery were smuggled out of America. The Brownings lacked mountings, but were useful in planes and vehicles, and the rifle-producing machinery eventually served as the first major equipment for the Israeli armament industry. But for the most part, items shipped from the United States were limited to clothing, boots, communication equipment, and some trucks. The FBI even interfered with shipments of barbed wire and overall the United States vigorously enforced its own as well as the UN embargo, even pressuring other countries not to provide arms for Israel.

There were chinks in the embargo. For a price, artillery could be bought in Mexico and aid also came from France. In the post-war period, the French government was largely composed of former Resistance members who sympathized with the Jews and also detested the British, who had squeezed France out of her former possessions in the Levant. Although officially the French government could not afford to antagonize the United States, politicians such as Georges Bidault, Jules Moch, and Robert Schumann were glad to turn a blind eye to the flow of small arms to the Haganah and ETZEL in 1947–48, and the first IDF guns, the 20mm Hispano-Suiza cannon, and later some 75mm field guns, were procured in France. The French also permitted the acquisition of some H-35 light tanks, relics of bygone days, which arrived in Israel early in June 1948 and allowed planes on their way to Israel to refuel on Corsican airfields.[25]

The French H-35s, together with one Sherman M-4 and two Cromwells 'liberated' during the last hectic days of the British evacuation constituted Israel's first tank battalion which, beginning with Operation 'Dani', saw action in the remaining campaigns, though with little success. Its first commander, Major Felix Beatus, who had served with the Polish division in the Soviet Army, had trouble communicating with his men, about half of them English-speaking, and little experience with maintenance. He was soon replaced by Shaul Yoffe who, in addition to the available tanks, received some Sherman M-4 hulks bought in Italy which, their cannon having been removed, had been armed with 75mm field guns. These tanks too had little success during the War of Independence.

Mechanized forces, armed jeeps, armoured White M-3 half-tracks, and various makes of armoured cars, home-made, captured, and some imported, did much better. At Latrun, Chaim Laskov's home-made armoured cars, the 79th Battalion, had done well, and during 'Dani' a mechanized commando battalion led by Dayan, largely equipped with armed jeeps but with one captured Legion armoured car, the 'Terrible Tiger', had been highly effective at Lod. Mechanized forces, supported by some captured anti-tank guns and PIATs had held their own against an Egyptian attack spearheaded by Locust tanks during Operation 'Horev'.[26]

Artillery was relatively unimportant during the War of Independence. The obsolete 75 and 65mm field guns had neither the power nor the range to be effective, except during the opening days of the war when, coming into action for the first time, they had scared the Egyptians at Degania. But they had not been effective at Latrun or against the solid walls of the Egyptian-held police fort at Iraq Manshieh. Mortars, on the other hand, had excelled as support weapons. Available in sufficient numbers, these relatively simple weapons had already been manufactured by underground establishments and after the British left, local industry was able to turn out a sufficient quantity of these pieces, progressing to the heavier 3-inch model.

Finally, during the first few weeks of the War of Independence, the IDF activated a small navy, like the air force subject to GHQ control. At best it was a matchbox navy. Its major vessels were three superannuated corvettes rusting in Haifa harbour since having been seized by the British as refugee transports. Barely reconditioned, and armed with field guns bolted to their decks, the small force prevented major Egyptian naval action against the Israeli coast, shelled enemy positions in the south and the port of Tyre in the north, and managed to sink the flagship of the Egyptian navy, the *Emir Farouk*, during Operation 'Yoav'. But its operations were marginal and for over a decade, the Israeli Navy would remain the stepchild of the defence establishment.

Reflections on the War of Independence

Despite the contributions of air, armour, artillery, and naval elements, the War of Independence remained mainly an infantry war, fought by small units. 'The performance of the lightly armed, hard hitting, fast moving footsoldier', an American military observer noted, 'has been an interesting one to watch.' The

Israeli infantryman, he thought, had accomplished much with very little. Better support, above all heavier field artillery, howitzers rather than light field guns, would have made his job a lot easier, but he had managed to do without it. 'He takes his rifle, thanks his stars for mortar support, and goes ahead.' Amidst the increased importance of crew-served weapons and armour, the Israeli soldier, he wrote, had taught military men a valuable lesson: one should not 'place so much reliance on push-button gadgets that we forget the importance of the little man with the little rifle'.[27] The foot soldier had won the war for Israel.

The assessment needs only slight modification. Against determined and well-led regulars in fortified positions, Israeli infantry, lacking adequate fire support failed at Latrun, Jerusalem, and Iraq Manshieh. Then too, during the War of Independence crew-served weapons still played only a supporting role and on the strategic level Arab firepower was inadequate to prevent the IDF from concentrating troops and executing approach marches. But on the tactical level, it sometimes proved overwhelming. Making a virtue out of necessity, the IDF fell back on the 'indirect approach', avoiding firefights and the stage of 'fighting to the objective'. Instead, taking maximum advantage of darkness and surprise, it tried to go directly to the stage of 'fighting on the objective', at which point the Israelis faced the Arabs in close combat and superiority in crew-served weapons no longer mattered.[28]

Armour was available only in very small amounts, most of it obsolete and poorly handled. It was in effect relegated to an infantry support role and even here often failed to perform according to expectations. By contrast mechanized and motorized infantry did better. The greatest weakness of IDF infantry lay in the low number of effectives and the lack of well-trained reserves. When employed in sustained combat, brigades often exhausted themselves within a few days. Towards the end of the war, with many of the most highly motivated and qualified soldiers gone, and even the Palmach brigades diluted by new drafts, there was a marked decline in the mobility of the infantry and on occasions a nearby objective was not taken as infantry became more dependent upon transport.

The appearance of the IAF gave a psychological boost, but did little to change the outcome of the war. Strategically, though Tel Aviv was bombed 15 times, with several hundred civilian casualties, its population proved as resilient as that of Jewish Jerusalem. After June, the IAF to a substantial extent maintained control of the air, though the Arab air forces retained a numerical superiority. There were no more Egyptian air raids against Tel Aviv; instead the IAF made a few bomb runs over Arab capitals, but the bomb weight dropped was inconsequential. During the autumn and winter, the IAF maintained its superiority and bombed Egyptian forward airfields in Sinai. Air support encouraged IDF infantry and discouraged the enemy, though as one authority has pointed out, 'effective cooperation with the ground forces was the exception rather than the rule'.[29]

Throughout the war there was constant improvement in the effectiveness of Israeli command and control. Ben Gurion's overall direction, though faulty on occasion, sometimes taking great risks and sometimes hesitant, proved more effective than that of the quarrelling Arab leadership. At the same time, the establishment of front commands allowed greater flexibility, exploiting the existing predisposition among Israeli commanders to act independently.

Much, of course, was improvised and improvisation, especially during the first few weeks, might not have succeeded if there had not been an extraordinary will to fight. Both the realization that his life and that of his family literally were at stake, and keeping the esteem of his comrades, especially important in a small country like Israel, provided motivations not only for the closely knit Palmach, but also for the HISH brigades and the new formations. Memories of the holocaust in Europe and the fear that it could happen in Israel, fuelled by the pronouncements of Arab politicians about a 'war of extermination', stiffened the will to fight.

3

The New Army: 1949–53

'Of every tribe a thousand throughout all the tribes of Israel
ye shall send to the war.'

Numbers 31: 5

During the months following the armistice agreements optimism prevailed in Israel. It was believed that the Arabs would sign permanent peace treaties and that the nation could return to its original priorities – absorbing immigrants and building the homeland. But Arab hostility, all the more bitter because of defeat, continued undiminished and the requirement for a strong military establishment became only too clear. Even so, the straitened economic and social circumstances and the dispute over the shape of the future Israeli Army made this a difficult transition period. Fortunately the political disarray within the Arab states, coupled with the British–French–American Tripartite Declaration of May 1950 'guaranteeing' the territorial *status quo* and limiting arms transfers to the area, provided Israel with a few precious years to create a new army.

The Geostrategic Position

In 1948 Israel had achieved victory by mobilizing its entire resources while its more numerous enemies had been able to utilize only a fraction of their potential. But the new state could not continue to devote 10 per cent of its population, over 20 per cent of its work force, and an even greater proportion of its national product to defence. As Ben Gurion, since January 1949 premier and defence minister of a duly elected government, pointed out to Israel's parliament, the Knesset, the country was 'but a small section in the midst of a gigantic territory inhabited completely by Arabs'. Israel, he continued, was a small nation, and 'even if our numbers should increase, we shall remain a tiny minority in the midst of an Arab sea.'[1] A substantial military establishment as well as an active diplomacy seeking peace agreements through direct negotiations were required. But prospects for such a settlement receded when the Arab governments refused to negotiate with Israel, claimed that a state of war continued, engaged in economic warfare and even refused to recognize the state's right to exist at all. And hopes of a partial settlement vanished when King Abdullah, the only ruler who had shown any inclination toward negotiations, was assassinated.

For the foreseeable future then, Israel's security would have to depend on an army strong enough to deter attack and to defeat it if deterrence failed. The problem was complicated by the small size of the country and its long frontiers, for the most part lacking topographical obstacles. Wedged in between the Mediterranean and its four hostile neighbours, Israel shared 330 miles of border with Jordan, 165 with Egypt, 47 with Syria, and 49 with Lebanon. Although the position was somewhat improved in comparison with the fragmented areas proposed in 1947, Jordanian-occupied Palestine, the West Bank, constituted a bulge menacing Israel's heartland, the narrow coastal strip between Haifa and Tel Aviv. Three-fourths of its population and industry were located in this strip, 25 miles at its widest near Haifa, 14 miles wide near Tel Aviv, and shrinking to a mere 9 miles at Netanya. From their positions atop the mountain ridges along the coastal strip, the Jordanians threatened Israel's north–south communications, while their hold on the hills around Jerusalem and its approaches enabled them to interdict access to the city. Almost all of Israel's population centres and military bases were within reach of medium artillery and all of Jewish Jerusalem was within small-arms range, a nightmarish situation relieved only by the fact that Jordan was relatively weak. Control of the bulge by any other Arab army, however, was regarded by Israel as a mortal danger requiring an immediate military response and the creation of a unified Jordanian–Egyptian command in 1956 and 1967 was among the prime factors leading to war.

Frontiers with the other Arab states offered little more security. The Egyptian-held Gaza Strip approached within 30 miles of Tel Aviv, posing another threat to the heartland as well as a base of operations against the Negev communications. Lebanon, to be sure, was not an active menace, but Syria, with guns emplaced on the Golan Heights dominating the settlements of the Jordan Valley, was potentially dangerous. To the rear and east and west was the second echelon of hostile states: Iraq which had refused to sign an armistice agreement, Saudi Arabia, and others. The Mediterranean coastline, 117 miles long, exposed some of Israel's major cities to naval attack and all of the country was within minutes of Arab air bases. From Damascus to Haifa it was seven minutes by jet, ten minutes from Egyptian airfields in the Sinai to Tel Aviv.

The lack of strategic depth and the shape and topography of its borders did

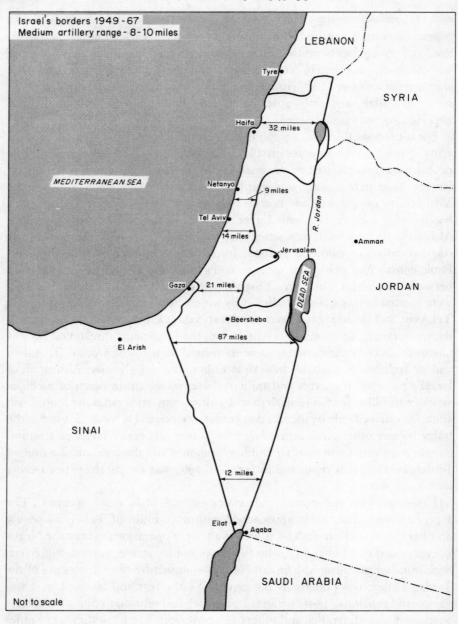

Israel's borders 1949-67
Medium artillery range – 8-10 miles

LEBANON

SYRIA

MEDITERRANEAN SEA

Tyre

Haifa   32 miles

Netanyo   9 miles

Tel Aviv   14 miles

Jerusalem

R. Jordan

•Amman

JORDAN

DEAD SEA

Gaza   21 miles

Beersheba

87 miles

El Arish

SINAI

12 miles

Eilat
Aqaba

SAUDI ARABIA

Not to scale

not permit Israel to adopt a purely defensive strategy. At the same time, economic and demographic considerations precluded maintenance of large standing forces. Israel solved this problem by developing a military posture tailored to her special requirements in the Defence Service Law adopted in 1949.

The Defence Service Law of 1949

During the summer of 1949 there was a heated debate over the shape of the new army. Still smarting over the dissolution of the Palmach, the small but politically influential left wing of the kibbutz movement and its political party, the Mapam, resurrected familiar arguments. In particular they opposed reliance on a conventional conscript army based on conventional discipline. Instead, Mapam defence intellectuals and commanders advocated a 'people's army', combining highly motivated and politically schooled mobile formations on the Palmach pattern, with territorial defences based on the collective settlements, and backed by a popular militia. The proposal was doctrinaire and elitist, but carried appeal because the idea of an Israeli Army without the Palmach, already revered in story and song, was unthinkable to broad sections of the public.

Ben Gurion strongly opposed such ideas. Party politics and doctrine, he asserted, had no place in the Army. The security of the state should never be in the hands of a restricted elite answerable to a party rather than to the elected government and the people. Moreover, the social and political integration of the great immigration that within two years would more than double Israel's Jewish population, bringing in Jews from Asian and African countries as well as the European survivors of the holocaust, demanded that the Army serve as the school of the nation, 'not only as the fortress of our security . . . but as an educational force for national unity'. Jews from Yemen and Morocco, from Persia and Poland, of many different shades of skin and conflicting cultures would be taken into the Army and made into Israelis, 'friends and partners with the native born'.

In co-operation with Yadin and Dori, Ben Gurion sponsored the Defence Service Law of 1949, which, enacted by the Knesset on 8 September, and repeatedly amended and consolidated, provided the framework for the new IDF. Its essence was the intensive exploitation of the entire national manpower pool through the universal conscription of men and women, coupled with a long reserve obligation, and the utilization of almost all state-supported activities: transportation, hospitals, communications, and construction, for dual military–civilian functions. Conscription, Ben Gurion powerfully argued, was essential because the smaller army proposed by the opposition could not possibly defend Israel against the potential masses of the Arab enemy. The legislation, he told the Knesset was designed 'to prepare the entire people for defence; to give the youth – Israeli born and immigrant – pioneering and military training, to maintain a permanently mobilized force adequate to withstand a surprise attack and hold out until the reserves were mobilized.'[2]

Under the new law recruits normally were inducted at age 18, though for new immigrants liability to conscription extended up to 29 years. After completing their active duty, conscripts were assigned to a reserve unit and called for refresher training or other duties one month a year. Actual length of active and reserve duty as well as the age limits have changed from time to time. Amendments to the original legislation provided that tours could be extended or shortened to conform with the military situation.

There were few exceptions. Married women and mothers were exempted as were full-time students in rabbinical academies. Pious girls were provided with the right to ask for alternative service or total exemptions. Non-Jewish citizens of the state, Arabs and Druze, were excluded from compulsory service, but allowed to volunteer. There were only a small number of Arab volunteers, though some Bedouin tribes provided trackers and scouts, several of whom distinguished themselves in action. The Druze, however, came forward in large numbers and in 1956, at the request of their elders, conscription, widely regarded as the passport to Israeli society, was extended to the male Druze.

The Israeli Army was, and is, comprised of four major elements: a 'permanent' cadre of career officers, non-commissioned officers, and specialists, the annual conscript contingent, the reserves, and the territorial defence units. The active forces consisted of the career soldiers and the conscripts. Reflecting the technical requirements of the air force and the navy, career soldiers constituted a larger percentage in these corps than in the Army overall. The active Army performed a dual role, carrying out ongoing training and, together with the fortified frontier settlements, acting as the covering force while the reserves mobilized.

Despite his opposition to a politically motivated 'people's army', Ben Gurion had by no means abandoned his Labour Zionist beliefs and ideals. He too wanted to fuse military, economic, and Zionist goals, 'pioneering' in the language of the movement, but in contrast to the Mapam proposals, he intended that the entire Army, not just an elite, would become farmer-soldiers. To this end Article F of the Defence Service Law stipulated that 'after completion of basic military training, 12 months of the recruit's tour of active duty will be devoted to agricultural instruction.' In the same vein, the law regularized the establishment of the Fighting Pioneer Youth, *Noar halutzi lohemet* or NAHAL, which since November 1948 had enabled members of the various Zionist youth movements to join the Army as integral groups combining agricultural preparation and military service.

The farmer-soldier scheme and NAHAL were concessions to the socialist wing of Zionism, but Ben Gurion also made concessions to the religious. While many of the earliest settlers in Palestine had been pious Jews, they had shown little interest in defence, and secularists had set the tone in the Haganah. Ben Gurion, though a secularist, believed that the Bible occupied a central place in the life of the Jewish people and that a Jewish state would have to come to terms with its observant minority. Already in 1947 he had indicated that the future state would continue to keep the Sabbath, retain religious controls in matters of marriage, and observe the dietary law in its official institutions. Except for a zealot fringe, the religious in turn made accommodations, supported the establishment and defence of Israel, and provided the margin of votes for passage of the Defence Service Law in the Knesset.

At this point it became necessary to settle the issue of religion in the new Army. There had been suggestions that special 'religious' units be formed, but Ben Gurion, always concerned about national unity, had refused to permit this. Instead Chief Rabbi Colonel, later Major-General, Shlomo Goren, a veteran of the battle for Jerusalem, reconciled Jewish observant law, *halacha*, with military requirements. Regulations provided for kosher kitchens, observance of the Sabbath, and time for prayers. These special provisions were operative only in peacetime. During an emergency they were automatically suspended. Saving of life overrides all religious injunctions and Rabbi Goren ruled that the protection of Israel made it permissible to fight and operate certain types of equipment even on the Sabbath and given the ongoing threat, even in peacetime. What emerged was a complex, on occasion contradictory system, but it worked. Many pious young men and women, especially those belonging to the collective settlements of the religious Poale Agudat Israel, made it a point of honour to serve in the Army and in later years they were joined by students from some of the most prestigious rabbinic academies. Only the issue of exemptions for religious girls remained a sore point, occasionally raising heated arguments between secularists and observant Jews. Overall, however, in the Army, if not in civilian life, the controversies between the secularist and the pious, between the Ashkenazi and the Sephardic branches of Judaism were reconciled. All were Israeli soldiers, training, working, and if necessary, dying together.

But other provisions of the Defence Service Law remained controversial and its adoption did not terminate objections. Both the Right and some senior officers criticized the farmer-soldier concept. Agricultural training, they argued, was incompatible with the requirements of a modern army and would reduce combat readiness. This provision, in fact, remained very much a dead letter. From the outset it was not applied in the air force or the navy, and within a year the defence minister obtained authority to postpone or eliminate it entirely when he thought it advisable. The Right, and some senior officers also, did not like the NAHAL scheme and for that matter they questioned the effectiveness of the territorial defence concept. The older kibbutzim were cohesive and included many veterans in their membership, but these factors were lacking in the new immigrant villages. Moreover, the soldiers pointed out that in a future war fought with more advanced weapons, armed settlements did not have much resistance capability.[3] The objectors were right. Although there were exceptions, especially the paramilitary NAHAL settlement, territorial defence based on small agricultural communities was fast becoming a romantic anachronism, important perhaps for maintaining the pioneering mystique, but a liability and not an asset in the face of a major attack.

The Left was dissatisfied with the law for just the opposite reasons. It resented the relatively low priority given to defence settlements and insisted that they be allocated a larger role. Mapam did not like the proposed Army organization; especially it warned that the career cadres would become a militaristic elite. Finally, as staunch and aggressive secularist, leftists objected to the religious compromise in the Army and to the exemptions from military service granted to the pious. But neither the objections from the Right or the Left would change the major thrust of the legislation.

Civil–Military Relations: 1949–53

Always a firm believer in the supremacy of civilian authority over the military, Ben Gurion had directed the War of Independence assisted by a small group of trusted senior officers and advisers. The Defence Service Law did not designate a commander in chief and made no formal division of authority between the defence minister and the chief of staff. The law also gave the defence minister far-reaching powers, including the all-important responsibility for deciding on calling out the reserves. Many observers have concluded that this *de facto* made him the head of the Israeli armed forces, but the interim report of the Agranat Committee published in 1974 stated that 'the Defence Minister is not *ipso facto* a super Chief of Staff.'[4] The relationship between the defence minister and the chief of staff was not institutionalized and as long as Ben Gurion held that office, 1947–53, 1955–63, usually in combination with the office of prime minister, decision making remained in the hands of a small circle. Only the prime minister, the defence minister, and the chief of staff received the sum total of all the country's intelligence estimates and therefore only they were in a position to make important decisions.

In theory a decision to call out the reserves or undertake a major military operation had to be ratified by the Foreign Affairs and Security Committee of the Knesset, which could confirm it, rescind it, or bring it before the whole house for debate, but in practice this was not done. Ben Gurion, a powerful politician, prevailed because he had established his own supreme authority and he wielded it to the fullest extent. To be sure, once he had brought the IDF firmly under the control of the legitimate government deriving its authority from the electorate, he rarely interfered in questions of military doctrine, though, together with the chief of staff, he determined the major outlines of national security policy. Ben Gurion, however, practised a highly personalized leadership and sometimes had difficulty in distinguishing between devotion to the state and allegiance to himself. Moreover, though the Army was rapidly becoming professional and depoliticized, at least in the sense that it no longer had any ties with political movements and parties, the overriding importance of national security policy decided jointly by the defence minister and the chief of staff, made it inevitable that political loyalty, or at least conformity with the overall orientation of the government, became a prerequisite for appointments to the highest military office. And these criteria continued to be applied under Ben Gurion's successors. After Dayan became defence minister in 1967, he observed that 'it was clear to me that I could not propose as chief of staff an officer who was not acceptable to the prime minister.'[5]

Although the intrusion of political considerations into military appointments was in part inherited from the underground organizations and in part stemmed from legitimate security considerations, it nonetheless was a dangerous legacy. Dangerous not because of military interference with the political process – no senior officer between 1948 and 1973 meddled in politics or used his prestige while in uniform for party advantage – but dangerous because there was the danger that politicians would exert undue influence to the detriment of military efficiency. None of the ten chiefs of staff of the IDF up to 1978 – Yaakov Dori, Yigael Yadin, Mordechai Makleff, Moshe Dayan, Chaim Laskov, Zvi Zur, Yitzhak Rabin, Chaim Bar-Lev, David Eleazar, and Mordechai Gur – could have been promoted to the post if they had been considered opposed to the overall political direction of the government, dominated until 1977 by the Labour Party and its allies. All these were able men, but in the late 1960s there were charges that even more promising officers, including Ezer Weizman and Arik Sharon, had been passed over because of their political affiliations with the opposition. The election of Menahem Begin in 1977 constituted, in this as in many other matters, a new departure, when Gur, appointed by the previous government was confirmed in office and his term extended for a fourth year.

After the passage of the Defence Service Law, Ben Gurion had to face the problem of what to do with the leftist Palmach veterans holding senior positions in the Army. Out of 45 colonels, 20 were Palmach veterans, while over 40 per cent of all lieutenant-colonels and majors came from the same background. In co-operation with Yadin, Ben Gurion retired the most prominent and passed over several others in making new appointments. Allon, head of the Southern Command, was relieved in October 1949 and replaced by Dayan, Ben Gurion's protégé, and at the same time Galili, the ideological father of Mapam, then serving as deputy defence minister, was removed from the cabinet. These measures opened old wounds. For some officers the dissolution of their parent organization in late 1948 had been a hard blow. Rehavaam Zeevi, then a captain who eventually did become a general, remembered the feeling that 'my whole world had collapsed. The Palmach meant everything to me, home, family, and friends.'[6] He decided, however, to soldier on as did many of his comrades. When Dayan arrived at his new command he found many of his staff officers, almost all of them ex-Palmach, perturbed by Allon's summary dismissal, but managed to persuade most of them to remain on active duty.[7] Even so, there was a considerable exodus of well-trained and combat-wise officers. Ben Gurion made no effort to persuade them to stay. Their departure, Colonel Makleff one of his military advisers commented, lost valuable experience, but it ended the continuing internal controversy about organization, tactics, and the relationship of the military to politics and society and allowed the new Army to get on with the job of reorganization.

Yadin and the New Army

On 9 November 1949, Yigael Yadin succeeded Dori as chief of staff and became the architect of the post-war IDF. He took office at a difficult time. During the first three years of statehood, Israel's Jewish population almost doubled, but the majority of the immigrants were penniless and unskilled. Few of them could speak Hebrew and many were in need of special care. Their absorption strained the economy, resulting in austerity, shortage of services, and unemployment. Food, clothing, and building materials were all strictly rationed and the Army did not escape these hardships. Pay was low, rations barely adequate, troop housing sub-standard, and uniforms of poor quality with expensive items such as overcoats lacking. Weapons and equipment were wearing out and could not be replaced. Understandably, morale was at low ebb.

Yadin's goal was to rebuild the cadres, improve troop morale and effectiveness, elaborate staff and service agencies, reorganize the active and reserve formations, and develop appropriate strategic and tactical doctrines. He was assisted by his deputy, Colonel Makleff, who also functioned as head of the General Staff (Operations) Branch at GHQ and by Colonel Chaim Laskov, head of the Training Branch, and one of the Army's most versatile and original thinkers. During Yadin's term, ending prematurely in 1952, not all of these objectives were met, but much was done and a framework was created, surviving in many essentials to the present time.

The new IDF retained the unitary centralized command structure of the War of Independence, a single GHQ working under the chief of staff, holding the rank of *rav aluf,* then the equivalent of major-general. Administratively GHQ was organized into branches, Manpower, General Staff, Quartermaster, and until 1953, Training. In addition, the commanders of the Northern, Central and Southern Commands, replacing the four fronts of 1948, and the commanders of the air force and the navy also were permanent members of the GHQ.

Given the ongoing nature of the Arab threat, intensifying after 1954, accurate intelligence, both strategic–political as well as tactical, was indispensable. The Haganah's original intelligence service, SHAI, became the nucleus for five intelligence organizations – the Central Intelligence and Security Agency, also known as the Institute or *Mossad*, the Security Service, *Shin Beth*, an internal police agency analogous to the FBI or the Special Branch, and two minor bodies, the Research Section of the Foreign Ministry and the Special Intelligence Section of the Police. The fifth organization was Military Intelligence which, despite some setbacks, had greatly expanded during the War of Independence. Originally Military Intelligence relied heavily on the human element, but in the early 1950s it began to receive electronic equipment and began to eclipse the other agencies. A section of the General Staff Branch until 1955, it became an independent branch that year.

Because the chief of staff, until now always chosen from the ground forces, was responsible for all operations, no separate ground forces commander was appointed. The three area commands had dual functions, acting both as administrative and operational headquarters, with their commanders controlling all troops stationed or assigned to their areas. Air and naval units, however, were excluded from their jurisdiction. Although the air and naval commanders, holding the rank of *aluf,* theoretically were on the same level as other branch chiefs and their forces were not considered separate services but corps, comparable to infantry or artillery, in practice their special functions gave them functional autonomy. Both the IAF and the IN maintained their own countrywide operational headquarters, co-operating with, but not under the control of, area commanders. Also reporting to GHQ were various inspectorates and specialized agencies. Among the agencies were the Judge Advocate General and the Army Rabbinate, while the inspectorates were responsible for training, discipline, and administration of arms, branches, and corps including artillery, engineers, infantry, signals and others, as well as the Women's Army Corps (CHEN), NAHAL, and GADNA.[8]

Relations between the agencies and inspectorates, on the whole, were harmonious and did not pose any special problems, but a major challenge to the unitary IDF structure came from the air force. Aspiring to independent status, its 27-year-old commander Aharon Remez asserted that 'the air force is not an auxiliary of the ground forces. It is a decisive force. Air superiority will decide the battle.'[9] He demanded a separate air force, not merely functional autonomy, and preferential treatment in promotions, pay, and housing for his airmen. Yadin refused to consider this. He could not see why a pilot or a radar operator should be treated differently from a rifleman or a tank driver and believed that IAF aspirations were far in excess of what its past performance and existing capabilities warranted.

During the War of Independence the IAF had been useful, but it had not provided the decisive margin of victory. In his summary of the major factors contributing to Israel's victory, Yadin did not mention airpower, but he had listed unity of command as all important.[10] Remez challenged this basic concept at a time when the IAF was not impressive. A handful of ageing Spitfires, some Mosquitoes and P-51s, three B-17s, and a collection of transport and training planes did not constitute an impressive force. Ben Gurion, always somewhat of a visionary, did try to mediate a compromise between the two commanders, but failed. Budgetary constraints, coupled with Yadin's threat to resign, compelled him to decide against Remez who was removed from his post in mid-1950.

Yadin's choice as the next commander of the IAF clearly signalled the, albeit temporary, defeat of any air power aspirations. Shlomo Shamir, a ground officer then serving as commander of the navy succeeded Remez. It was not a good choice. Shamir had good qualities as an administrator, but he had little feel for handling his men and within a year he was replaced by Chaim Laskov. Although Laskov, too, was a ground commander, he was a truly remarkable man. Appointed in 1949 to develop new combat doctrines, he had suggested mobile armour units supported by air power and during his two-year term, from 1951 to 1953, he laid the foundations for converting the IAF from a propeller to a jet air force.

Even so, only an air officer could really gain the confidence of the airmen and much of the burden for maintaining IAF morale and cohesion fell on men like Ezer Weizman, a former fighter pilot and now serving on the small air staff. He tried to imbue his men with the feeling that they were an elite and that the air force was a living community where pilots, ground crews, and their families worked towards an important common goal. His greatest problem, perhaps, was pilot retention. Most of the MAHAL pilots had left and many of the remaining pilots were kibbutz members who were being called home. Repeatedly Weizman had to visit settlements and convince sceptical kibbutz general meetings that their boys were not becoming militaristic mercenaries, but were needed for a special and vital mission to protect Israel. One of the pilots he personally recovered was Motti Hod, commander of the IAF in the Six Day War.[11]

Israel's second specialized corps, the navy, headed after Shamir's departure by Mordechai Limon, did not present GHQ with any difficulties. The naval service, too, had suffered from the return of the MAHAL volunteers to their homelands, though there remained an Israeli nucleus able to carry on after a fashion. It was a time for organization, training, and gaining much needed experience. At the same time, the force remained small and lacked any real punch. In 1950 there arrived three ex-Canadian River-class frigates, and these, together with two corvettes from the same source, and with the restored relics of the War of Independence formed the backbone of the IN until 1955.

In 1951 a naval presence was established in the Gulf of Aqaba and three 40-ton torpedo boats, acquired from Italy, were hauled overland to Eilat. Already during the War of Independence the IN had employed naval commandos, frogmen, explosive motor boats, and demolition teams, and these had done extremely well. Naval commandos, cheap to maintain and requiring no major equipment, remained on the naval establishment and became one of the most elite combat units of the IDF.[12]

The crux of Yadin's problems, however, were the ground forces, suffering from a shortage of junior officers and severe morale problems. The shortage of junior officers was especially serious because the new mass-based Army required large numbers of junior officers to train and lead the new formations. By 1950, one estimate placed the shortage at over 10,000 lieutenants and captains. Some, to be sure, had resigned for ideological reasons, but the majority had left because conditions of service were unattractive. Within the limits of austerity and in the face of grumbling that he was destroying the basic egalitarian structure of Israeli society, Yadin set out to improve conditions for officers. He could not provide more pay, but despite vociferous objections from the Left, he tried to give career soldiers both psychic and material compensations – smarter uniforms, more status, separate messing facilities, and family housing on military bases. Even then, compared with other military career establishments, the Israeli officer retained an austere style of life and it was patriotism, rather than material rewards, that held men in the Army.

Above all, the new career officers did not form a closed corporate entity. Unlike other armies, the IDF did not establish special military academies to train and indoctrinate new generations of career officers. There were, and still are, no educational requirements for commissioning; all officer candidates have to begin their service in the ranks and are selected by tough screening procedures. In 1952, Yadin proposed that Israeli high schools should offer special military curricula for future officers, but this proposal ran counter to the egalitarianism then still strong in the country, and was opposed by educators and many politicians. In the end there emerged a much watered down programme. Boarding students at two high schools, the Reali in Haifa and the Herzlia in Tel Aviv, could elect to take special military courses, but only as a supplement to the regular curriculum. Moreover, they were not automatically commissioned on graduation, but entered the Army as conscripts and underwent the common selection process. Overall, though the programmes survived, they had but little impact on the officer corps.

At the same time, Yadin also had the problem of providing uniform instruction for officers of all grades. The IDF had fought the War of Independence with commanders from diverse backgrounds – Haganah, Palmach, British, Canadian, American, and other training, and it was vital that all be taught the same procedures and basic doctrine. Already in 1949, Laskov had begun to develop courses for junior officers and battalion commanders, and by 1951 even senior officers were required to take the standard course. There were objections. Dayan, for one, refused to accept the idea that there were standard solutions for tactical problems and argued that operations could not be conducted by the book. The same feeling was expressed by senior officers who were sent abroad for more advanced training. Most of them went to British or French staff schools where they found the reception 'correct but cold' and the doctrines taught altogether too rigid and not suited to Israel's special circumstances. Weizman, sent to attend the RAF Staff and Command College, departed with great expectations, but came back convinced that 'we must not learn from others.' Dayan's experience at the British Army Senior Officers' School at Devizes was very similar and he too concluded that 'correct' school solutions were not applicable to IDF problems.[13] A distinct preference for doing things their own way, for originality, inventiveness, and improvisation, remained characteristic of the IDF and served it well.

Yadin's second major preoccupation, perhaps even more serious than with the officers, was the condition of the rank and file. The new recruit intake often lacked motivation and the desirable standard of education; many could speak but little Hebrew. The technical corps and services, above all the air force and the navy, but also the signals and engineers, received the pick of recruits, usually of native or European origins, while the infantry battalions, still the bulk of the army and its main fighting element, had to make do with conscripts coming in large part from the squalor of the immigrant camps. Leaving behind their families in shanties, tin huts, and tents, these men had difficulty in accepting military service. Pay was nominal. Between 1950 and 1953 the estimated annual outlay for a soldier's maintenance was $600, inadequate for them to assist their impoverished families and it was not uncommon to find rifle companies where almost 70 per cent of the troops qualified as welfare cases. Not surprisingly, morale was low and the soldiers' hearts were not in the Army. To turn these men into good fighting material was difficult, though in time it was done. For the moment, however, standards declined even further when during the harsh winter of 1950, the Army was called upon to deal with tasks that the civilian agencies could no longer handle. Ben Gurion called upon the military to administer and maintain the immigrant camps. While the investment of manpower and equipment to this effort produced long-range benefits, it placed another burden on an already strained military establishment.

NAHAL units presented different kinds of problems. Highly selected and motivated volunteers, they were regarded by some as successors to the Palmach and sometimes have been described as a commando force. In reality, however, NAHAL groups were supposed to be nuclei for agrarian collectives, and also used to reinforce exposed settlements, and therefore more closely related to territorial defence units than to mobile shock troops. Only their political consciousness was similar to the Palmach and this did not make them necessarily more combat effective. During the early years some NAHAL units were poorly disciplined, and those affiliated with Mapam youth movements displayed an overt pro-Soviet ideology which, in one case at least, forced GHQ to disband the unit. Critics of the organization, including Dayan, claimed that NAHAL merely provided an opportunity for middle-class youths to avoid regular military service, giving them false glamour and the illusion of pioneering. Few of its members, he charged, had any intention to become permanent settlers and meanwhile NAHAL drained off the cream of the recruits from other units.[14]

The indictment was too strong. To be sure, NAHAL did not come even close to the goal of founding 200 new settlements set by Ben Gurion in 1949. Yet, it performed some useful duties. When civilian contractors baulked at building a road along the western shore of the Dead Sea, NAHAL troops, undeterred by climate, distance, and Arab marauders, constructed this strategic link. Other NAHAL units established the first settlement at Eilat and cultivated the arid ha-Arava region between the Dead Sea and the Gulf of Aqaba. In all, it founded some 40 settlements. After 1954, the corps shifted its priorities to conform with the changing needs of the Army. Although still entering the service as a group, NAHAL units spent less time on agricultural training and more on military duties, on occasion sending their members to serve in regular combat formations. In 1956 and again in 1967, NAHAL units fought very well.

By accommodating itself to changing circumstances, NAHAL managed to survive as a separate corps, providing special opportunities for volunteers from the various Zionist youth movements and constituting a living link with old traditions. It did not, however, as some had hoped, become a major element in the Israeli Army.

On the other hand, the reserve components were the most essential part of Israel's military establishment and the organization of a highly effective reserve system must be considered Yadin's major accomplishment in the post-war period. While in other countries reserves were used to bring first line active units up to war strength, or when serving as independent second-line formations, would be ready for action only weeks or even months after being called up, Israeli reserves were supposed to take the field within 72 hours, a vital component of the IDF, in fact the flesh and muscle around the bare bones of the active Army.

During the debate concerning the Defence Service Law and even after its passage, critics warned that the entire concept was faulty. The extended reserve obligation would place too great a burden on the economy while at the same time the reserves would neither be able to mobilize nor be combat ready. Yet, given the overall situation, both Ben Gurion and Yadin, supported by Makleff and Laskov, felt that it was the only possible way in which a force of adequate size could be maintained and they looked for ways to make the scheme work.

From the outset Yadin and his staff discarded the idea of organizing the reserves according to age groups, except that the older veterans in the already existing reserve pool would be used to reinforce the static defences. The younger men and women, between 20 and 39, and those coming into the reserves from active duty would be organized into field brigades equipped with all ancillary services. After visiting Switzerland in 1949, Yadin and Makleff opted to adopt the Swiss system of forming these brigades on a proximity basis, permitting faster mobilization. Unlike the Swiss, however, the Israeli reservist did not keep his weapon at home. Instead, mobilization stores were dispersed and special depots for each reserve formation created. Initially there were doubts whether reservists could adequately fill the more complicated command and staff positions, but with career officers in short supply, formations entirely composed of reserves became the rule.

These formations were not disbanded, but maintained on a reduced level at all times, becoming fully operational when their reservists were called up for their annual tours of duty. Yadin once declared that he regarded the Israeli reservist as a regular soldier who happened to be on leave 11 months of the year. The statement aroused an immediate negative reaction. The average Israeli remained a fierce individualist and a determined civilian, who, facing a clearly perceived threat, would submit to military discipline. Far from being an army of regulars temporarily on leave, it probably was closer to the truth that the mobilized IDF was a host of civilians temporarily putting on uniforms.

To speed up mobilization and make it more flexible, two types of call-up were introduced. The first, silent mobilization, summoned officers and key personnel by telephone or messenger and they in turn contacted their men. The second type utilized the radio. Code names such as 'Open Window', 'Eternal Spring', 'Men of Work', 'Lovers of Zion', would mobilize the men of a particular unit, each soldier responding only to his own unit's designation. Mobilization could be carried out in various stages. Key personnel could be called, selected units could be mustered, or a general mobilization could be ordered. When broadcasts read out the code names, youths and men rushed to pre-arranged assembly points where buses would take them to their depots. Gradually refined and tested by partial call-ups, the system could by 1951 provide over 100,000 men and women, combat-ready active and reserve soldiers in less than three days.

Sceptics still remained dubious whether the system would function during total mobilization and some predicted that it would break down in utter confusion. To test the scheme, Yadin, overcoming powerful opposition of the Finance Ministry, which claimed that the economy could not stand the expense, obtained Ben Gurion's permission to hold three large-scale man-oeuvres involving over 100,000 soldiers. The first, Manoeuvre A, in 1950 tested the call-up system, while Manoeuvres B and C, held in 1951, actually deployed reserve formations in the field. Manoeuvre B tested the system under the assumption that Israel had suffered a surprise attack, while C assumed that the state had launched a pre-emptive strike.

The manoeuvres, directed by Laskov, proved that the system worked and that reserve formations performed as well as active force units. To be sure, there were complaints that the manoeuvre rules were too schematic and paid too little attention to armour and air capabilities, but there was consensus that mobilization had been fast and effective. By 1952, Yadin was able to make refinements. As the reserves pool grew, additional units were formed and older reservists shifted to non-combat tasks.

Reserve obligations imposed, and still do, considerable hardships on individuals. To provide some relief, in 1952 the Knesset passed the Reserve Compensation Law giving pay to all persons serving for more than three consecutive days on active duty. It was, however, only a small relief. Yet, reserve duty did not cause much resentment. For many it was a distinct and perhaps welcome break from the stresses of everyday civilian life; it brought together men and women from different social classes and origins, and within a few years reserve units began to develop their own corporate spirit.

With the establishment of the reserve system Yadin had founded the new Army on a simple and effective organization, but at the same time there were pressures on the government to shift priorities. The continuing unrest and disunity in the neighbouring Arab states made a massive attack, though not small incursions, unlikely and critics now argued that by cutting defence spending much needed social programmes could be implemented. In response, Ben Gurion ordered a slash in IDF strength and a reduction of the defence budget from 50 to 40 million Israeli pounds. Yadin accepted the decision. He insisted, however, on making the necessary savings by a selective reduction in force rather than by disbanding entire units as the prime minister demanded. When no agreement could be reached, Yadin resigned on 22 November 1952.

Makleff and Dayan

Yadin's successor was his 33-year-old deputy, Mordechai Makleff. Born in the small village of Moza near Jerusalem, where his entire family had been killed during the 1929 riots, Makleff had joined the Haganah at an early age, served with Wingate's SNS, and during World War II had reached the rank of major in the Jewish Brigade. At the time of Yadin's resignation Makleff was studying political science and economics in London, preparing for his retirement. A studious and reserved man, he agreed with Ben Gurion about the need to reduce military expenditures. A weak economy and a dispirited civilian population, he believed, would endanger an effective military posture. A determined disciplinarian and a staunch advocate of professionalism on the British model, Makleff was quite prepared to settle for a smaller but more efficient force. He carried out the cutbacks ordered by Ben Gurion, eliminating many administrative and support units, and ruthlessly weeded out officers who did not measure up. Because of the haste in which the new Army had been created, he wrote, 'we had absorbed a high proportion of incompetents' and these were discharged.[15]

Makleff, however, differed with Ben Gurion regarding the selection of a deputy chief of staff and head of the General Staff Branch. His personal preference was Rabin, but Ben Gurion, who had not forgotten Rabin for being one of the leaders during the public protests attending the dissolution of the Palmach, refused to countenance this. Instead the prime minister insisted on Dayan, his personal protégé, a member of the Labour Party, but with no strong political ties. Dayan even then had the reputation of being extremely bold and venturesome, but by the same token a wilful commander.[16] He had no interest in administration and accepted the post with the proviso that he would act as Makleff's deputy only when the chief of staff was out of the country. Moreover, he insisted that the General Staff Branch would assume the senior position at GHQ. Surprisingly, Ben Gurion and Makleff accepted these terms and Dayan now entered into the decision-making circle.

Makleff and Dayan did not make a good team. Dayan did support Makleff in his efforts to get rid of inefficient officers and to reduce non-fighting units. 'Better bayonets than stoves', he remarked. On the other hand, however, Dayan delegated all administrative responsibilities to Colonel Meir Amit and he did not support Makleff's efforts to make the Army look more 'military'. While Makleff was a stickler for order, discipline and a smart turnout, Dayan cared little about appearance. He never bothered to check if soldiers were properly dressed or smartly turned out, as long as their weapons and equipment were in good order. Relations between the two men, never cordial, soon soured.

In addition to having serious differences with his senior officer, Makleff also had trouble with his civilian superior, acting defence minister Pinhas Lavon. In late August 1953, Ben Gurion, tired out and in need of rest, decided to retire for a few years and in preparation asked the cabinet for a two months' leave of absence. Pinhas Lavon, a labour organizer and Ben Gurion's picked choice, acted as defence minister throughout the later part of 1953. Lavon had been a dove, scornful of the military, and reluctant to provide funds for the Army, but as defence minister he changed completely. He proposed a much more activist policy regarding the increasing number of Arab incursions and also wanted to reorganize the military establishment by making the Ministry of Defence responsible for manpower and supply, functions it now shared with the Army. Makleff, who disliked Lavon from previous encounters, regarded this as an attempt to undermine the Army, while Dayan approved the scheme because it would free the Army for its major purpose – to wage war. Increasingly isolated, Makleff decided to retire and when Ben Gurion actually stepped down, he too handed in his resignation. On 6 October 1953, as his last act before leaving office, Ben Gurion appointed Dayan as the IDF's fourth chief of staff.

Force Structure, Arms Procurement, and Fighting Doctrine

In January 1951, Ben Gurion told the Knesset that if necessary Israel could field 200,000 armed combatants.[17] This figure, however, was exaggerated and perhaps designed for external consumption. It represented the total mobilization of all man and woman-power, excepting only a few key workers in essential services, and even in the dire circumstances of 1973 Israel did not resort to this extreme. A more accurate estimate for that time would place the active Army at about 30,000 career soldiers and conscripts, backed by 70,000 to 80,000 reservists.

With less than some 5,000 in the air force and the navy, the overwhelming majority belonged to the ground forces, where the main fighting formations consisted of 11 brigades. The active Army comprised of one armoured and two infantry brigades, and there were 8 reserve infantry brigades. In addition, GHQ disposed of one active paratroop battalion. The infantry brigades were heavy, formed according to Laskov's doctrines as independent brigade groups. Each was organized into three rifle battalions, a jeep-mounted scout company, and headquarters and support units. Every brigade group also had one or more additional combat elements attached. All possessed one heavy, 120mm mortar battalion, sometimes supported by a field artillery or anti-tank artillery unit. Laskov had hoped to assign some armour to each of the brigade groups, but limited funds and even more limited access to equipment had made this impossible.

Arms and equipment were another worry for the IDF in the early 1950s. The British–French–American Tripartite Declaration of 25 May 1950, aiming to maintain an arms balance in the Middle East, was interpreted by each power according to its own interest. While Great Britain, declaring herself bound by treaty, continued to supply Iraq and to a lesser degree Egypt, the United States was maintaining a modest flow of arms to Saudi Arabia. None of the three powers was willing to supply the IDF. 'We have turned', Ben Gurion reported to the Knesset at the end of 1951, 'to all countries from whom it is possible to obtain our requirements. Not from a single country did we receive all our needs.'[18] As a result, IDF ordinance remained a mixture of what had been and still was available. Infantry was equipped with Czech or British bolt-action rifles, supplemented by locally made submachine-guns. By 1953 the unreliable Stens were replaced by the Israeli-designed and manufactured Uzi, a most effective short-range weapon. Mortars also were available in sufficient quantity; medium machine-guns, however, dated primarily from the War of Independence and more were needed. Artillery, finally, was definitely obsolete, inadequate in number and lacking hitting power.

Israel was forced to shop in many places to obtain a modest amount of more up-to-date weaponry. When Deputy Defence Minister Shimon Peres tried to purchase medium machine-guns in Great Britain he was refused, and then turned to Canada. The Canadian cabinet, largely composed of men with World War I experience, regarded machine-guns as offensive weapons and also refused to permit their export. To Peres's surprise, however, the cabinet was willing to authorize the sale of war-surplus 25-pounder gun-howitzers to replace the pre-1914 vintage IDF field guns. 'It's your luck', a Canadian official told Peres, 'that they did not go over the top carrying 25-pounders.'[19] At about the same time the United States, though both the State and the Defense Department were still ambivalent about supporting Israel, was willing to sell a few ·30 calibre Browning machine-guns and a few bazookas.

Acquisition of armour was even more difficult. To maintain its modest inventory of some 50 plus Sherman M-4 tanks in running order, vehicles had to be bought as scrap from as far away as the Philippines. Purchased as demilitarized scrap, they were refitted with assorted guns of dubious quality, the best being some 76mm rifles taken off 1943 US M-10 tank destroyers. Laskov originally had planned for a force composed of armoured and mechanized infantry brigades, but the small number of tanks and the 200 M-3 half-tracks available permitted only the partial mechanization of three brigades. Engineer, ordnance, and supply units were short on specialized equipment and in the event of mobilization had to rely on requisitioned civilian vehicles.

Material shortcomings also hamstrung the air force and the navy. As commander of the air force Laskov had attempted to phase out the motley array of bombers, fighters, and fighter-bombers in favour of one all-purpose type. He and the air staff favoured fighter-bombers. But it was impossible to obtain up-to-date planes, especially jets. Until 1955, the IAF had to rely on its ageing Spitfires, supplemented by P-51s and Mosquitoes, many of which were rebuilt from scrap.

The navy, finally, was perhaps the worst off. Its few ships were of World War II vintage, but their armament was even older. All had been acquired without guns and fire-control equipment and during the War of Independence they had been armed with field guns lashed to their decks. Unable to purchase modern naval weapon systems, Israel finally found a source of naval arms supplies. The Italian Navy was only too glad to clear out its ordnance depots and sold Israel some 120 and 102mm guns dating from World War I with fire-control instruments of the same vintage. Rearmed with these old pieces, the frigates were somewhat more potent, though they still lacked all anti-submarine capability and their radar was of the primitive SG type.

Considering Israel's armament, it probably was just as well that the Army was not called upon to fight a major action during this period. Given the geostrategic situation, IDF strategic planning remained committed to the rapid counter-strike, carrying operations as soon as possible into the enemy's territory to gain a convincing victory before outside pressures compelled a halt. This strategy required highly mobile, armoured or at least mechanized, formations, supported by strong tactical air arm, but neither of these was available at this time. Even so, in working out its tactical doctrines the new IDF stressed the offensive, fighting on the move with a combination of the aimed fire taught by the British and the suppressive moving fire embodied in German and Soviet doctrine.

Both the state of armament and the training of the troops were inadequate to carry out such tactics during Yadin's and Makleff's terms as chief of staff, but with the Arab armies operating under similar constraints this did not become a threat to Israel's immediate security until 1955.

Border Raids and Retaliatory Operations

Until the Czech–Egyptian arms agreement of 1955 upset the balance of forces, the actual threat to Israel's security came from a renewal of Arab raids and the patent decline in the effectiveness and morale of her Army. In 1950, already, Dayan had been very unhappy with the performance of the 7th (Armoured) Brigade in the Southern Command. On this occasion the Jordanians, claiming that the road to Eilat infringed on their territory, had blocked it for several days. Dayan had given orders to clear the road and though this was done, he was 'not at all pleased with the dithering, indecisive way' the task had been carried out.[20] And as head of the General Staff Branch he witnessed even worse failures. In early May 1951 units of the Golani Brigade failed to drive Syrian intruders off a hill, Tel Mutilla, near Lake Kinneret and only succeeded after being reinforced by elements of a Druze volunteer battalion. The Golani commander, Major Zeevi believed that his conscripts, mainly recent Yemenite and Bulgarian immigrants, had shown stamina and determination, but GHQ considered the affair a grave setback.[21] Less serious but demonstrating poor morale, was an incident in December 1952 when a group of soldiers carrying supplies to Mount Scopus was fired on, dropped their loads, and ran. But the worst failure was the Falama affair. On 22 January 1953, a conscript infantry company, employed in a retaliatory action, crossed the armistice line to demolish some houses in Falama, a small hamlet north east of Tel Aviv. When engaged by the local militia, the unit, having suffered only one fatality, retreated without carrying out its mission. Dayan, present on the scene, was furious. He relieved the company commander on the spot and directed that in the future any officer whose unit failed to carry its objectives would be dismissed unless his troops had suffered over 50 per cent casualties.[22]

But Dayan also realized that it was not just the failure of individual commanders. The malaise went deeper. No longer primarily oriented towards fighting, the IDF had become too much engaged in social action and too little in realistic training. Too many infantry companies were composed of new immigrants and these units, where officers often did not understand the mentality of their men, could not cope with actual fighting. A solution to this problem was vital.

The Falama incident highlighted the issue of the Arab incursions which had never ceased entirely. At the outset many of these incidents were trivial, involving the theft of livestock or irrigation pipe, but before the end of 1950, they had escalated to sabotage and the murder of civilians, becoming ever more brutal and bloody. In 1950, Israel had 19 citizens killed and 31 wounded by these acts; 48 were killed and 49 wounded the next year, and in 1952 casualties rose to a combined total of 182. All of the victims were civilians, many women and children. Altogether incidents numbered in the thousands, 1,751 in 1952.

Protests to the Mixed Armistice Commission were of no avail. The 50-odd UN observers compiled reports, but could do little about such violations of the truce agreements. Clearly, the government of Israel had to protect its citizens and, failing to achieve this by diplomatic means, it resolved to use force, short of war. Armed reprisals seemed the answer, both for military and psychological reasons. As Ben Gurion stated, 'the Jews in this land will not be like lambs led unto the slaughter.'

In 1952 he authorized retaliatory raids. Small active Army units went across the armistice lines, mainly into Jordanian-occupied Palestine, to blow up houses suspected of being infiltrator bases. Many of these missions failed; Falama was just one example. By 1953 out of 85 such actions only 15 were considered successful. Many times the raiders returned unable to find their objective; on occasion they were repulsed. In the summer of 1953, Makleff decided that drastic action was needed and, overriding Dayan's objections that all Army units ought to be capable of carrying out such raids, he established a special unit for such missions – Unit 101. Never numbering more than 45 volunteers, dressed and armed according to their personal preferences, the unit carried out a number of raids with surgical precision. Still, actions could backfire. After Arab raiders murdered a mother and her two children near Tel Aviv, Lavon and Makleff authorized a major raid against the village of Kibya. On 12 October 1953, Unit 101 and elements of the 890th (Independent) Paratroop Battalion struck. Despite standing orders to safeguard civilian lives, the action resulted in the death of 69 Jordanians, about half of them women and children.

Although international reaction to the killing of Israeli civilians had been remarkably muted, the world press reacted angrily to Kibya. The Israeli government promptly disclaimed all responsibility and stated that the raid had been carried out by 'outraged private citizens'. Few believed the story. Nonetheless, the government decided that it had no choice but to continue retaliatory actions, though instructions were issued that all future raids would be against military targets only. Attacking military bases raised the stakes in future confrontations. Yet by 1953 it appeared necessary. Up to this time neither the Egyptian Army nor the Arab Legion had rendered much assistance to the infiltrators, but since 1952 there was a new situation. That year King Farouk of Egypt was overthrown by the military and the new government, at first under Colonel Naguib, but actually directed by Gamul Abdel Nasser, embarked on a programme of escalating the ongoing hostilities with Israel. In late 1953 and early 1954 the Egyptians formed the infiltrators, mainly Palestinian refugees, into paramilitary units, *fedayeen* or self-sacrificers, and actively aided their incursions from the Gaza Strip. In Jordan, meanwhile, King Hussein, uneasy on the throne of his murdered father, could do no less.

Arab hostility began to assume a more active and menacing stage. In Israel many felt that the ring was closing and that a second round was becoming unavoidable. A few days after becoming chief of staff, Dayan expressed this siege mentality in an address to the graduates of an officers' training course. World opinion, he told the graduates, always was only too ready to condemn Israel for defending herself, but 'when the time comes to fight for the capital of Israel . . . you alone will bear this responsibility.'[23] And Dayan was resolved to prepare the Army for the coming challenge.

4

Moshe Dayan and the Suez War: 1953–57

'Hear oh Israel, this day ye are approaching the war against
your foes. Do not let your hearts grow faint!'

Deuteronomy 20: 3

Any leader who wishes to impress his own spirit on a whole army faces a
formidable task. In the case of General Dayan, however, there is no doubt that
he made an impression on the Israeli Army out of all proportion to his actual
ability, considerable as it was, as a strategist. Unlike his two predecessors,
Chief of Staff Dayan concerned himself less with organizing a 'regular' military
establishment, but with moulding a tough and aggressive-minded fighting
force. He divested the IDF of most of its civilian functions, reduced its tail
elements, and revived the combat spirit of '48.

To do this he de-emphasized outward appearance, ceremony, and formal
discipline and instead stressed the primacy of its combat mission. He enlarged
the raiding force to set the style for the rest of the Army. Following the large-
scale acquisition of Soviet arms by Egypt in 1955, he oversaw the transformation of the IDF from predominantly individual to crew-served weaponry and
directed it during Operation 'Kadesh', the Israeli part of the Suez War, the
first of the Arab–Israeli conflicts featuring major air battles, armoured
encounters, and massive firepower.

The Paratroopers and the Revival of the Army

Dayan was 38 years old when he became chief of staff. He had held a number of
appointments with competence and distinction and had gained a reputation as
a determined pragmatist, a quality that recommended him to Ben Gurion.
Even so, he did not reveal his remarkable gifts of leadership, eventually coming
to exemplify the bold 'follow me' type of Israeli commander, until he assumed
the highest post in the Army. He was an inspiring combat leader, convinced

that boldness usually paid off in battle, and boldness required that officers set a personal example. 'Officers of the Israeli Army', he told a graduating cadet class, 'do not send their men into battle. They lead them into battle.'[1] Commanders did not have to be insured against becoming casualties; the most important thing for any unit was to attain its combat objective.

Up to 1953, however, this primary objective had not always been achieved. On the contrary, Dayan was troubled by the evident decline in the Army's fighting spirit for which he blamed changes in officers' conceptions of their role and a general reluctance to suffer casualties in a time of supposed peace.[2] To improve performance, he issued instructions to assign better qualified and motivated conscripts to the infantry. This, in time, would produce results, meanwhile, however, there remained the problem of dealing with the Arab incursions, escalating in number and intensity. Dayan favoured continuing reprisal raids, but realized that the new policy initiated after Kibya of striking only at military targets required a larger force than Unit 101. Such a force was created by combining the Independent Paratroop Battalion with the raiders.

When the formation of a special raiding force had first been proposed, Dayan had not been enthusiastic. He was sceptical about the creation of a 'private army' as he saw it and feared that it would raise all the special problems barely laid to rest with the dissolution of the Palmach. The exploits of the raiders had changed his mind and he now believed that the unit not only could carry out its specialized missions, but also had the potential to set an example for the faltering Army. As constituted, however, Unit 101 was too small to execute the new policy of military targets only, while essentially a small partisan band rather than a military formation, it could not provide a model for the rest of the Army. By contrast the paratroopers lacked fighting experience, but were a thoroughly 'professional' unit, excelling in smart turnout, drill, and hand-to-hand combat demonstrations. Dayan decided to combine the best qualities of both units by merging the raiders with the paratroopers. Amalgamation, carried out in January 1954, created difficulties. Unit 101 veterans preferred their own partisan style, while many of the paratroopers objected to the loss of 'professionalism' as they saw it. Feelings did not improve when Dayan passed over Lieutenant-Colonel Yehuda Harari, the Paratroop Battalion's commanding officer, and instead appointed Major Ariel (Arik) Sharon, the 25-year-old leader of the raiders to head the new formation, designated Unit 202.[3]

If the merger nonetheless succeeded beyond all expectations, credit belonged to Sharon and his inspired band of young officers, including Majors Rafael Eytan, Aharon Davidi, and above all 21-year-old Captain Meir Har Zion, a daring leader of small units and a legend in his own time. Their enthusiasm, battle skills, and gallantry forged Unit 202 into a fighting brotherhood consciously emulating the mystique of the tough paras of the French Army. Everyone was a volunteer and all took jump training, though normally the paratroopers fought as assault infantry going into action on armoured personnel carriers or on foot. For almost two years they monopolized retaliatory actions and almost invariably succeeded. Within a short time the paratroopers replaced the fabled Palmach in popular esteem and their red berets and silver jump wings became coveted badges of honour. Qualified volunteers came forward in large enough numbers to expand the unit into a three-battalion brigade. To identify the Army at large with the new fighting spirit, basic parachute training became a prerequisite for all senior officers in the combat branches. Dayan took the course in 1954 and even Rabbi Goren, the chief chaplain, earned his jump wings.

The paratroopers practised a special style of night fighting, abandoning the traditional fire and movement sequence in favour of closing rapidly with the enemy. Hesitation, Sharon drummed into them, was fatal and until detected, the assault should be carried out silently. Once on the objective, the paratroopers would split up into teams and fight the enemy with submachine-guns, grenades, and knives. These tactics were well suited to night attacks, producing a maximum of surprise and psychological shock. Coming to close quarters with the enemy also obviated the need for artillery support which, severely restricted in an effort to prevent civilian casualties, was provided only under the most exceptional circumstances. Officers, of course, were expected to lead the assaults and their casualties were severe. 'I do not think', Dayan recorded in 1956, 'that there is a single veteran officer in the paratroopers who has not been wounded in one of their actions.'[4]

Retaliatory actions, both along the armistice line with Jordanian-occupied Palestine, in Sinai, and the Gaza Strip normally were carried out by small forces, platoons and companies; even the largest operations did not involve more than a battalion. Despite the small numbers involved, these exploits signalled the revival of the Israeli Army's martial spirit. They provided combat experience and restored confidence. Dayan had expected this, though he must have been aware of the risk that the rest of the ground forces, left out of the action, might come to feel that they could never match the paratroopers and deteriorate even further. As it turned out, however, the 202nd Brigade became an example for others. By the end of 1955, when hostilities sharply escalated, Dayan felt confident enough to have other units join the paratroopers in action.

The first such joint operation took place on 2 November 1955. In October, regular Egyptian forces had established themselves in the demilitarized zone around El Auja in northern Sinai. Their presence there, in violation of the armistice agreement, could not be tolerated and when UN protests proved unavailing, Ben Gurion, who had returned as defence minister in February

1955, gave orders to evict them. The operation was carried out by a joint force of paratroopers, infantry of the Golani Brigade, and NAHAL units. One month later, on 5 December, Ben Gurion, who now had also reassumed the post of prime minister, authorized an operation to silence Syrian guns that had fired on Israeli fishermen on Lake Kinneret. Once again Golani infantry fought alongside the paratroopers, demonstrating a new spirit.[5] Even so, until the Suez campaign, there remained the question whether reservists, the bulk of the Israeli fighting force, would manifest the same high level of combat performance.

The Debate over the Reprisal Policy

Critics regarded the last two actions evidence of the failure of the reprisal-raid policy. Their purpose had been twofold. Long range, they were to project the image of a Jewish state determined to defend itself, while immediately, with Israel's long frontiers quite indefensible against infiltration, the reprisals were to exact a price so high that the various Arab governments would decide not to pay it. By 1955, however, the *fedayeen* had come under the official sponsorship of various Arab governments, primarily Egypt, and increasingly regular troops were stationed close to their bases to counter the expected Israeli reprisals. And this, of course, turned minor forays into ever larger encounters. Between September 1955 and October 1956 the *fedayeen* raids intensified. There were almost daily incidents and in 1956 the death toll of Israeli civilians approached 400 with many more seriously wounded. At the same time, reprisal raids were met with increasingly better prepared resistance, escalating into battalion-sized engagements.[6]

With the UN hopelessly deadlocked between the United States and Russia, little could be done in the Security Council. Still, in April 1956 UN Secretary Dag Hammarskjöld paid a surprise visit to the Middle East and arranged a border truce. Conditionally accepted by Israel, the arrangements collapsed when Egyptian-sponsored *fedayeen* renewed their incursions from the Gaza Strip. In July fighting flared up again along the Jordanian line and after some particularly serious incidents Ben Gurion personally authorized large-scale reprisals. Between 12 September and 10 October the IDF mounted four major attacks against fortified Jordanian positions. The last, an attack on the Kalkilya police fort, resulted in heavy casualties on both sides. The Jordanians, familiar with the now stereotyped night-raiding tactics, trapped the Israeli blocking force positioned too far out. Efforts to extricate it lasted into the next day and required medium artillery support. When it was all over, Israeli losses stood at 18 killed, including 8 officers, and 50 wounded, including 14 officers. Raids were becoming too costly and Dayan concluded that the Army had 'reached the end of the chapter of night reprisal actions'.[7]

For some time now Israeli critics, headed by Moshe Sharett, foreign minister and prime minister during Ben Gurion's leave, had argued that the raids were counter-productive and that Israel should instead seek to negotiate with her Arab adversaries, rely on the UN and the great powers. Unfortunately these suggestions had little base in reality. The Arab governments, following the Egyptian lead, assumed a more aggressive stance, broadened their economic war against Israel and openly supported the *fedayeen* proclaimed as national heroes. The UN, of course, remained powerless, and the great powers either hostile or at best indifferent. The Soviet Union now espoused the Arab cause, while Great Britain, though no longer on cordial terms with Egypt, still was allied with Jordan and Iraq and busy sponsoring schemes to placate the Arabs by forcing Israel to cede the Negev. And United States policy, as revealed in State Department documents published in 1977, was dominated by pro-Arabists and the oil lobby.

The Lavon Affair

Recognizing that her freedom of action was drastically limited, fear and frustration led Israel into some desperate expedients, notably an attempt in 1954 to spoil American–Egyptian relations by sponsoring attacks on American offices in Alexandria and Cairo. Poorly conceived and executed, with suspicions that the Israeli operator in charge was a double agent, the attempts failed. There were bitter charges and counter-charges regarding responsibility for this fiasco. Defence Minister Lavon charged that the whole affair had been deliberately rigged by certain senior officers to discredit him, while Military Intelligence claimed that the minister had acted on his own. A commission of inquiry, consisting of former Chief of Staff Dori and Chief Justice Yitzhak Olshan, concluded that it was not possible to assign blame. When Sharett refused to back Lavon, the minister resigned in anger. It was at this point that Ben Gurion had returned as defence minister.

The 'unfortunate affair', which would continue to haunt Israeli domestic politics for several years, illustrated the difficulties inherent in the un-structured relationship between the IDF and the defence minister. Ben Gurion had the prestige and the knowledge to control all defence matters, while Lavon lacked his expertise and status. Regardless of his involvement in the Egyptian sabotage affair, senior IDF officers resented Lavon's proposals for the creation of a mixed military–civilian national security authority. A throwback to the political National Command of Haganah days, such a body would have turned the IDF into a battleground for the various parties and endangered the unified and depoliticized Army. Ultimately, Lavon's ouster was the outcome of this clash. Still, relationships between the chief of staff and the defence minister remained basically unresolved and would again reach a crisis point after October 1973. Beyond this, the Lavon affair highlighted the growing apprehensions and fears in Tel Aviv, where frustrations about the state's diplomatic isolation were reinforced by the steady growth of Arab military power.

The Arab Build-up

In the final analysis, Israeli defence planners were most directly concerned with the steady build-up of the Arab armies and military capabilities. While they recognized that, seen from the Arab side, the growth of the IDF, coupled with the tough reprisal policy, projected an equally threatening image, they held that Arab military preparations were not, as Nasser once claimed, a direct reaction to Israeli raids. Instead, they believed, and Arab rhetoric seemed to confirm it, that the Arabs had not given up hopes of reversing the verdict of 1948. The raids contributed incentive to the Arab build-up, but revenge was the most important motivating factor, followed by inter-Arab rivalries, and internal security problems. Finally, both Great Britain, and to a lesser degree the United States, supported this development by supplying arms to Egypt, Iraq, and Jordan, hoping to reduce the intrusion of Russian influence into the Middle East.

Between 1949 and 1956 Iraq's armed forces increased from 38,000 to about 50,000, organized in five understrength divisions, including one armoured, equipped with 42 British Centurion tanks and 30 M-8 Greyhound armoured cars from the United States. Her air force gradually was re-equipped with British jets: 36 Venoms, Vampires, and Sea Furies. Much of the Iraqi Army, however, was absorbed in the perennial war against the Kurdish minority and Israel considered its combat effectiveness low. Still, Iraq had never signed an armistice with Israel and Israeli government spokesmen frequently announced that entry of Iraqi forces into Jordan would constitute a *casus belli*. Israel also had relatively low regard for Syria, perhaps the most belligerent of her immediate neighbours. Although Syrian forces tripled from 15,000 to 45,000 between 1950 and 1956, constant internal turmoil, poor equipment, and low levels of supply reduced their potential.

By contrast, Israeli soldiers held a high opinion of the British-trained and officered Jordanians. Until 1956 Jordanian forces comprised two distinct and separate elements. Considered potentially unreliable, the newly acquired Palestinian subjects formed a loosely organized and poorly equipped National Guard, designed for local defence duties only. Its maximum strength was 30,000, with about one-third on active duty. More important was the expansion of the Arab Legion, now designated the Arab Army. By 1956 it comprised 25,000 long-service soldiers, organized in three motorized and one armoured brigades. In 1955 Jordan had received a number of the newest British tank-destroyers, Charioteers, 20-pounder guns on Cromwell tank chassis, augmented by 150 armoured cars. Artillery was re-equipped and organized in one medium field regiment and a mixed regiment, consisting of one battalion anti-tank and one of anti-air artillery. Finally, Jordan acquired a modest air strength, a squadron of Vampire jets.

Political turmoil, disputes between Bedouin and Palestinian elements, and between factions favouring Syria against Egypt, and between dynastic loyalists and radicals, hampered the effectiveness of the Jordanian forces. Dayan and the Israeli general staff did not consider the Jordanian armed forces alone as a major threat. They were, however, concerned about Jordan's geostrategic position, menacing Israel's heartland and about possible joint operations with the Egyptians.

Then as now Egypt was the largest and the most important of the Arab countries. Since the military coup of 1952, she had steadily improved her armed forces. Nasser repeatedly proclaimed that the destruction of Israel remained his major objective and in pursuit of this aim Egypt had acquired arms and military equipment from every possible source. Some had come from Italy and France, though even after being expelled from the Suez Canal Zone, Britain continued to supply arms – 41 Centurion tanks, 200 Archers, tank-destroyers with a 17-pounder gun mounted on a Valentine tank chassis, Vampire and Meteor jets, some heavy bombers, and two Z-class destroyers. The latter, sold in 1955, were, however, matched by the same number sold to Israel.

These arms acquisitions were of course nothing compared with those received by Egypt under the Czechoslovak–Egyptian arms purchase treaty announced by Nasser on 27 September 1955. Since the spring Egypt had got, or was getting, some 300 medium and heavy tanks, T-34/85 and JS-3s, 200 armoured personnel carriers, BTR-152s, 100 SU-100 assault guns, 500 medium field guns and howitzers, 200 57mm anti-tank guns, 134 anti-aircraft-guns, 1,000 recoilless rifles, together with large quantities of scout cars, small-arms, trucks, and other military equipment. To provide air power, there were 50 twin-engined IL-28 jet bombers and 120 Mig-15 fighters, as well as 20 transport planes. In addition, the Soviets sent two Skory-class destroyers, 15 fast mine-sweepers, several submarines and scores of torpedo boats. All this equipped an Egyptian military establishment expanded from 65,000 regulars in all services in 1950, to 90,000 regulars and 10,000 reservists, and a 100,000 strong National Guard by 1956, forming five infantry divisions, three armoured brigades, and a number of independent formations.[8] With the Russian equipment, of course, there came numerous Russian experts, instructors, and technicians to augment the German instructors who had been at work on the Egyptian Army for some years.

For Israel, Egypt's Soviet connection, and the arms build-up and intensification of pressure, presented a palpable threat. The build-up was especially worrisome when seen in the light of the deployment of her armed forces in the Sinai Peninsula. The German advisers had proposed that Egypt's major defences should be sited in the western part of the peninsula, some 25 miles east of the canal on the hills that run north to south in the Bir Gafgafa area controlling the major east–west axes and the Mitla and Giddi passes. The recommendations were sound. Nasser, however, rejected them because he was not primarily concerned with defence. He wanted his main positions and bases as close as possible to the Israeli frontier to serve as a springboard for a future offensive and to defend the *fedayeen* camps in the Gaza Strip. Accordingly the major Egyptian bases were located in the Rafah–El Arish–Abu Ageila triangle, with a strong blocking position east of Abu Ageila at Um Katef. Further south, Kusseima, hard on the Israeli border, guarded an important road junction and was strongly fortified, while in the centre and south there were fortifications and garrisons at Kuntilla, Thamad, Nakhl and at Ras Nasrani and Sharm el Sheik on the Gulf of Aqaba.

Israel's general staff and intelligence assumed that the Egyptian deployment in the Rafa approaches could only be intended for a large-scale conventional offensive, though its exact timing remained a matter of speculation and discussion. The date would depend both on Egypt's relations with the great powers and on her ability to assimilate the new war materiel. As Nasser's policy unfolded, he allowed guerrillas to operate against Israel from Egyptian territory and allowed the government-controlled press to increase its strident rhetoric for war. In this context, the closing of the Straits of Tiran to Israeli shipping, combined with the continued denial of peaceful transit through the Suez Canal, was taken in Israel as the final straw in a cumulative process which would culminate in full-scale attack unless it was promptly scotched. From November 1955 on, Dayan and his senior officers started to make plans for a pre-emptive strike into Sinai and exerted every effort to acquire arms abroad.

The Rise of Israeli Armour and the Reorganization of the Ground Forces

It had always been recognized that reprisals could at best provide only temporary security. Long-range security, Ben Gurion and the military leadership realized, could be provided only by a combination of diplomacy, industrial development, and military power. Diplomacy, however, had failed, military industries were still primitive, and the massive Soviet arms shipments to Egypt, introducing new and sophisticated weaponry, made improvizations no longer feasible. Israel's security rested on the actual capability of her army to wage war with highly mobile, armoured or mechanized, forces.

Tactically, although infantry-oriented, Israeli commanders realized that tanks, combining mobility, firepower, and protection, were ideal for her defensive–offensive strategy. But there were few Israelis with armour experience, no technical manuals in Hebrew, and no accepted doctrine. Moreover, there still was the feeling that the rigid discipline, conformity, and technology required for armoured warfare ran counter to the socialist-egalitarian ideals of Israeli society.

Nevertheless, the formation of true armoured units had already begun under Yadin and continued under Makleff and Dayan. Training courses conducted with translated manuals and much experimentation, produced tankers and mechanics who regarded tanks no longer as mysterious machines imported from abroad, but as vehicles to be used, repaired, and even modified. There remained, however, the problem of actually acquiring tanks. As of 1953 the IDF still had but one armoured brigade, the infantry heavy 7th, consisting of one battalion of 50 Sherman M-4 tanks, one infantry battalion on half-tracks and two battalions on trucks. This undersized and technologically obsolescent force fell far short of actual requirements.

Israel would have liked to purchase British or American tanks, but was refused. On the other hand, relations with the French military, if not the diplomats, remained cordial and late in 1952 talks were conducted regarding the sale of AMX-13 tank-destroyers. Although agreement was reached the ever-cautious French Foreign Ministry, still hoping to mend relations with the Arabs, delayed deliveries until 1954. A total of 100 AMX-13s, light mobile tanks with a medium-velocity 75mm cannon, were acquired, together with some 150 extra guns, 150 renovated US M-3 half-tracks, and 60 French M-50 105mm howitzers. The additional equipment enabled the IDF to activate two new armoured brigades, the 27th and the 37th, both reserve formations. In 1955, when even the Foreign Ministry realized that Nasser was actively promoting the Algerian revolt, France sold Israel another 60 Shermans and in 1956, just before the Sinai Campaign, additional tanks were delivered in French naval tank-landing ships to deserted Israeli beaches. The last shipments were composed of modified Shermans M-4A3 E8s, with improved suspensions and wider treads, and mounting the long US 76·2mm tank gun. The Israelis, meanwhile, had cannibalized some of their old tanks to install the new 75mm cannons, though this required extensive reworking of the turrets to accommodate the long breech and recoil mechanism. In 1956, therefore, IDF armour consisted of four types of Sherman: the French modification designated as M-50, the Israeli modification, known as the M-51, together with various older models of the M-4, some still with the original short 75mm guns and others with the short 76mm cannon. In addition, there were about 100 AMX-13s and between 400 and 500 half-tracks. It remained an open question, however, how well the modified Shermans could stand up to the heavier-gunned Egyptian T-34/85s.[9]

Recognizing the increased importance of armour a Headquarters Armoured Corps, actually an inspectorate on the same level as infantry, was established in 1953 and two additional brigades, the 27th and the 37th, both reserve formations, were activated. During the Sinai Campaign none of these formations had the same table of organization and all fielded an astonishing variety of vehicles. The 7th comprised of two armoured battalions, one with Shermans and the other with AMX-13s, one mechanized and one motorized infantry battalion, a towed field-artillery battery, and supporting elements. The 37th Brigade had a similar organization, except that it had only one company of AMX-13s instead of a full battalion, while instead of a towed battery it had a troop of self-propelled M-50 howitzers. Finally, the 37th Brigade had a total of only four tank companies, one mechanized and one motorized infantry battalion, and a jeep-mounted reconnaissance company equipped with recoilless rifles. Moreover, before going into action, the brigade had to detach 25 of its Shermans to reinforce the 11th Infantry Brigade. In fact, many Israeli infantry formations were reinforced by a few attached tanks, violating the cardinal principle of massed armour.

These curious dispositions in part were field expedients, tailored to specific mission requirements, but they also reflected the unresolved dispute over the proper role of armour in the IDF. During the immediate post-war period the handful of ageing and poorly maintained tanks were widely considered to be inferior instruments to mechanized infantry. This belief was challenged by armour enthusiasts. As early as 1952, Lieutenant-Colonel Uri Ben Ari, operating his 7th Brigade as part of the 'blue' forces directed by Dayan in Manoeuvre B, penetrated to the rear of the opposing 'green' forces disrupting their communications. Yadin, who had planned an orderly infantry-based exercise was much put out. The armoured brigade was ruled out of action and in the post-manoeuvre critique Ben Ari was told in no uncertain terms that the proper role of armour was to support infantry. Unabashed, Ben Ari repeated his manoeuvre the next year and this time the umpires did not rule against him. Moreover, Ben Gurion, present during the exercise, was much impressed when the charge of armour unnerved defending infantry, sending it flying to the rear, and thereafter he supported the acquisition of additional tanks.[10]

But even Ben Gurion's very considerable leverage could not budge thinking at GHQ or provide sufficient funds in a time of austerity. Although Dayan had backed his subordinate in 1952 and favoured swift penetrations into the enemy's rear, he belonged to the mechanized infantry school. Tanks, he believed, were too expensive and mechanically unreliable for extended operations. Deep penetrations could be carried out cheaper and more efficiently by armed jeeps, half-tracks, and armoured cars. Tanks should be carried forward on their transporters and unloaded only at the last possible moment to provide suppressive fire.

General Laskov, who at Ben Gurion's insistence had become head of the General Staff Branch in 1955 and, disliked by Dayan, had then been shunted to command the Armoured Corps in the summer of 1956, had opposed this fragmentation. Tanks, he asserted, were not merely infantry support vehicles, but 'the crucial weapon of the ground forces'. Their primary role was to fight massed against enemy armour. The dispute between Dayan and Laskov continued until September 1956 when Ben Gurion was called in. The issue was complicated because the Egyptian deployment in the Sinai did not feature heavy armour concentrations. Instead, there were a number of strong hedgehog defences, with armour either dug in as anti-tank artillery or held back in reserve. Dayan, backed by Ben Gurion, held that armour should not assault these positions directly. The typical assault formation, he ordered, would consist of 'an infantry battalion, plus a tank company, plus artillery support'. Armour was to act as part of a combined arms team to breach the defences and enemy armour would not necessarily be its main objective.[11] In the end, however, Dayan modified his original instructions. One armoured brigade, the 7th, was allowed to remain concentrated, though assigned a subordinate role.

There also was expansion, reorganization, and a limited amount of re-equipment in the other branches of the Israeli ground forces. Altogether, including air and naval forces, the active Army in the mid-1950s comprised 45,000 men and women, constituting on mobilization 16 brigades, including 1 paratroop, 3 armoured, and 13 infantry brigades. The increase in the overall number of brigades was partly the result of a larger number of reservists entering the system and to the streamlining of the brigade structure. Dayan cut the size of these units to about 3,500 all ranks for armour, 4,000 for paratroop, and 4,500 for infantry brigades. Organization, however, remained flexible. The Jerusalem Brigade, for instance, holding an exposed sector and largely composed of local residents and students from the Hebrew University, had a larger establishment than normal.

Infantry brigades were organized on a triangular basis, three rifle battalions providing the main strength. Supporting elements included a heavy mortar company, a reconnaissance company, a signal platoon, an engineer platoon, and usually an anti-aircraft platoon. With Israel as yet unable to manufacture heavy weapons and with artillery difficult to procure, normally artillery was not integral to the brigade and the heavy mortar company, if necessary expanded to a full battalion, was the main support weapon. After 1954 France provided some self-propelled 105mm howitzers as well as a small number of 155mm field guns, but artillery did not catch up with the rapid development of the other IDF corps for some time.

At a lower level each rifle battalion was organized into three companies with three platoons each, with company fire support furnished by a medium mortar section, a number of light mortars, and medium machine-guns. Individual weapons remained a mix of submachine-guns, rifles, and light machine-guns. Purchase orders had been placed in Belgium for automatic FN rifles chambered for the NATO cartridge, but few had been received by the time of the Sinai Campaign. The majority of Israeli infantry fought with bolt-action Czech and British rifles, supplemented by submachine-guns.

Suitable transport remained in short supply. As late as September 1956, Dayan noted that 'a check of our logistic material makes us more aware than ever what paupers we are' and among his most urgent requests to Paris was the immediate delivery of several hundred 6×6 trucks. Even so, on mobilization, the IDF went to war with some 13,000 civilian vehicles pressed hastily into service, ranging from farm trucks to buses, delivery vans, jeeps, and taxis.[12]

Israel's Air Force: 1953–56

Following the initial clash between Yadin and Remez over the status of the air force, Laskov had managed to smooth out many of the difficulties. During his tenure as commanding officer of the IAF the basic concept of a single-type force was accepted and the personnel situation stabilized. At the end of 1953 he was succeeded by Dan Tolkowsky, a pilot officer, who remained in office until 1958. Building on foundations already laid, Tolkowsky achieved a considerable degree of autonomy for the air force, a compromise between the complete independence demanded by Remez and the subordinate corps status advocated by Yadin. The IAF maintained its own operational headquarters, air staff, and, except for basic training, its own instructional system. Its major problem was access to up-to-date equipment to replace the mix of ageing and obsolescent planes in its inventory and to make the transition to a jet force.

Jets were expensive and difficult to obtain. Only a few countries produced such aircraft and even when Israel could come up with the money, political considerations interfered with sales. As early as 1950 there were intimations that the French Ouragan fighter, a first generation jet, might be available. Actual acquisition, however, was delayed by the French Foreign Ministry. Even after Israel and France signed a purchase agreement in June 1952, involving the sale of three Nord-2500 transporters and 25 Ouragans, the jets did not reach the IAF until October 1954. Meanwhile, Israel had succeeded in obtaining small quantities of jets from Britain and Belgium. In 1953 the British sold Israel three Meteor T-7 jet trainers and three more were bought from Belgium. The next year a total of 24 Meteor M-8s were acquired. But the Meteors were inferior to the Mig-15s and used primarily as trainers. Only 15 remained operational in 1956.

Israel continued to negotiate for more sophisticated jets, especially for a multi-purpose fighter-bomber. The French military offered Mystère fighters in early 1955, but deliveries were delayed. This time it was not merely the result of French diplomatic waffling. There was a dispute within the IAF. Fighter pilots like Weizman argued that the Mystère II, basically a pure fighter, should be bought because it was available, while Tolkowsky held out for the far more advanced Mystère IV which had some bombing capabilities. The first eight Mystère IVs arrived in Israel in April–May 1956. Airmen rejoiced, but Levi Eshkol, the finance minister, present with other dignitaries to welcome the new planes, was less impressed. He considered them a poor buy: '$36,000 and only one seat', he complained.[13]

The Mystères, together with the Ouragan 6s and the remaining Meteors, provided a jet force of some 60 planes by October 1956, the balance of Israeli fighters consisting of Mustangs and a few Mosquitoes. Israel remained outnumbered in the air and both Tolkowsky and Weizman accepted this as a fact of life. Quality had to make up the difference. Pilot qualifications were stressed. Selection and training criteria were set high, and Weizman, heading the fighter command, insisted that only pilots signing on for extended tours of duty would be allowed to fly the new jets. Short-termers would pilot the remaining propeller-driven fighters and utility aircraft.[14]

At the same time, the IAF realized that the all-important question was not how many planes were in the inventory, but how many were operational. Maintenance and turn-around time became major preoccupations. With manpower short, the IAF had a much smaller ground crew-to-plane ratio than other air forces – about 25 to 1 – and efficiency in maintenance, repair, refuelling, and rearming were considered vital. As the opening of its first major campaign approached, the IAF felt confident that it could carry out its assigned mission, though Ben Gurion remained apprehensive about the threat to Israel's cities posed by the new Egyptian jet bombers.

Towards Operation 'Kadesh'

Ever since the large-scale transfer of Soviet arms to Egypt, coupled with the closing of the Straits of Tiran, Israel had considered that the situation was becoming intolerable. As early as November 1955, Dayan was contemplating an operation to break the blockade and to guarantee Israel's access to the Red Sea by capturing the coastal strip at Sharm el Sheik. Dayan believed that such an operation would be far easier if launched before Egypt had assimilated the new Soviet equipment, but Ben Gurion refused to authorize such action. The prime minister agreed that Nasser's major objective in procuring such a formidable arms supply, exceeding in volume the cumulative total of previous arms transfers to all the Middle Eastern countries, was the destruction of Israel. At the same time, however, he recognized that the contest between the United States and the Soviet Union for influence in the Arab world, complicated by last-ditch British attempts to hold on to her shrinking influence in the region, had placed Israel in an isolated position and in accordance with his doctrine, formulated in 1949, Israel should take the initiative only when assured of major power support.

In the event, France came to be that power. Leading members of her defence establishment had long been sympathetic to the Jewish state, though these feelings were not shared by the Foreign Ministry, which had opposed Israel's admission to the UN and had not established full diplomatic relations until September 1952. After 1954, however, France was at odds with the Arabs over control of the north Sahara states and fighting a bitter insurrection in Algeria. The Egyptian refusal to desist from assisting the Algerian rebellion finally turned the scales. There was an increased supply of French armaments and some exchange of intelligence between Paris and Tel Aviv. By the summer of 1956, France felt pushed beyond endurance by Egyptian policy and plans to co-operate with Israel to obtain redress of the several and quite different grievances by force emerged in seminal form. During the summer of 1956, finally, the French diplomats approached the British with proposals for joint action.

On 27 July 1956 Nasser seized the Suez Canal. This constituted the point of no return for France and even moved the British to consider the use of force. French military supplies reached Israel in increasing quantity, while Paris tried to arrange for joint Anglo–French and Israeli operations. The French government, still dominated by leaders whose thinking had been shaped in the wartime resistance, established intimate relations with Israel, but the partnership with Britain was difficult and beset with mutual misgivings. Just as negotiations got underway, the Kalkilya raid brought Israel and Britain into an open confrontation. Jordan appealed to Iraq to send troops under a defence treaty of 1947, while Israel warned that entry of Iraqi troops would constitute a *casus belli*. In turn, the British declared that they would then be obliged to come to the aid of their Jordanian ally. On 15 October 1956, however, the Iraqis decided not to dispatch troops and the crisis passed. Ben Gurion was furious about the possible predicament in which Israel would find herself allied with

France in an attack on Egypt, while England was allied with Jordan and Iraq in a war against Israel. This danger passed, though Anglo–Israeli relations remained strained.

To salvage the prospects of joint action, the French called for a top secret meeting at Sèvres on 22 October. Ben Gurion, accompanied by Dayan and Shimon Peres left for France amid great secrecy. At first the meeting was bilateral between Israel and France, joined later by British Foreign Secretary Selwyn Lloyd who, according to Dayan, 'expressed distaste – for the place, the company, and the topic'. In view of the British record and attitude, and also worried about the Egyptian air threat, Ben Gurion insisted on French air and sea cover for Israel's major urban centres and a formal British commitment. Moreover Dayan declined to divulge details of his operational plans. The main British concern, Dayan wrote later, was to get a 'real act of war' not a raid, so that British intervention could be justified. When the conference appeared headed for collapse, Dayan disclosed his intentions. The IDF would provide the necessary pretext for Anglo–French action by dropping paratroops close enough to the Suez Canal to pose a realistic threat, though he cautioned that there would be no major operations until British and French forces actually had been committed. If this did not happen within 48 hours after the initial Israeli drop, set for afternoon of 29 October, then the paratroops would be withdrawn and the action represented as another reprisal raid. This satisfied the British and agreement on principles was reached. There also was talk about post-campaign diplomatic co-operation, though in view of the past record of the French and British diplomats the Israelis expected little. On 26 October Israel began to mobilize.[15]

Operation 'Kadesh'

The Israeli war plan had been elaborated by Dayan and Colonel Meir Amit, Laskov's successor as the head of the General Staff Branch. Its execution was entrusted to Major-General Assaf Simhoni of the Southern Command. There were three major objectives: (1) the destruction of the *fedayeen* bases in the Gaza Strip and along the Sinai frontier; (2) elimination of Egyptian offensive potential by the demolition of her advanced bases and logistics infrastructure in the Sinai; and (3) the opening of the Gulf of Aqaba to Israeli shipping. Because of the intense pressure expected both from the United States and Russia, it was considered absolutely vital that the scope of the operation be concealed as long as possible and that the objectives be attained within the shortest possible time. These considerations induced Dayan to prohibit, much to the disappointment of the airmen, the IAF from opening the campaign with a classic strike against the Egyptian air force on the ground and also led him to order that armour should be employed only after the second day when, according to the Sèvres agreement, Anglo–French operations had begun. As he pointed out, the most difficult problem was not how to defeat the enemy, but how to achieve this within the constraints imposed by the international political situation.

Patterned on Liddell Hart's principles, the plan envisaged swift penetrations and manoeuvres against the rear of the enemy. During the opening phase the paratroop drop would serve both as a diversion and as the trigger for Anglo–French action, while other units would seize starting positions just across the frontier. Then, if the operation continued, the advance would isolate the main Egyptian defence complex in the triangle. Frontal attacks, Dayan ordered, were to be avoided if possible and units were to proceed ignoring orthodox tactical preoccupations with the security of their flanks or communications. There was no need, Dayan wrote, 'to fear that Egyptian units who will be by-passed will launch a counter-attack or cut our supply lines'.[16] In fact, he expected that once isolated, the Egyptian defences would collapse and the final objectives be reached with a minimum of fighting during the last stage.

Dayan's predictions were based on the fact that the Egyptian deployment had become unbalanced. Expecting an Anglo–French reaction to the seizure of the canal, the Egyptian high command had returned one armoured brigade and two infantry positions from their forward positions and lacked capability to respond offensively. Still, in October 1956 forward Egyptian forces amounted to six reinforced infantry brigades with attached armour and artillery located in the triangle, two reinforced battalions at Sharm el Sheik, and some garrison and patrol units in the central region.[17] The nine Israeli brigades allocated to the assault fell far short of the two-to-one superiority of the attacker over the defender called for by conventional military doctrine and Dayan had difficulty convincing French officers that the attack could be accomplished against such numerical odds. Dayan, however, hoped that superior leadership, training and morale, coupled with mobility would compensate for numbers.

Israeli forces detailed for Operation 'Kadesh' included one armoured brigade, the 7th with two tank battalions, two mechanized (armoured) brigades, the 27th and the 37th, one paratroop brigade, the 202nd, and the six infantry brigades, the 1st, 4th, 9th, 10th, 11th, and 12th. Except for the 7th and the 202nd, all were reserve formations, reinforced with attached artillery, engineer, NAHAL, and local territorial defence units.[18] In accordance with established Israeli command practices, brigade commanders were given wide latitude in attaining their objectives. On the two northern axes, Rafah–El Arish–Kantara and from Nitzana to Abu Ageila and then on towards Ismailia, provisional divisional task forces headquarters, *ugdot* in Hebrew, were established. The northern task force was composed of the 1st and the 27th brigades commanded by Laskov; the second was constituted of the 10th and the 37th brigades, directly under Simhoni. Also in this region, instructed not to enter combat until the second phase of operations, was the 7th Brigade. The remaining brigades had independent assignments. After its initial drop, the 202nd was to exploit towards the western shore of the peninsula; the 4th was to take the important road junction at Kusseima on the first day, opening a passage into Sinai south of the Um Katef position, while the 9th was to make its way down the roadless eastern shore to Sharm el Sheik. Finally, the 11th and 12th brigades, supported by a battalion combat team of the 37th, were to attack the Gaza Strip after it had been cut off from the triangle.

The attack was to be covered by the IAF, whose mission was to establish control over the battle area, interdict hostile movement, and provide close ground support. With two French squadrons, 36 Mystères and 36 F-84F Sabrejets stationed at Haifa and Lod respectively, the IAF could concentrate on the battle area, putting some 100 jets and 50 piston-engined planes into the air.[19] At the same time, a French squadron, including the cruiser *Georges-Leyges,* took up station off the Israeli coast. Their task was to prevent sorties by Egypt's superior navy, four destroyers against two Israeli, and it also provided some ship-to-shore fire support during the battle for Rafah.

To maintain security Dayan delayed mobilization for most units until the last possible moment. Initial mobilization, begun on 26 October, was by messenger and only on the 28th did the system move into the radio call-up phase. The short time allowed for preparation created difficulties for the reserve brigades. Vehicles, hastily collected, were not always well maintained or properly equipped; certain items never reached units from mobilization stores, and senior officers, transferred from staff and instructional duties to combat assignments, did not always have time to familiarize themselves with their men. Dayan, however, considered these problems minor when compared with the need to maintain surprise.

Actual operations took only 100 hours and all major fighting was over by 1 November. Although brief, the campaign can be divided into three distinct phases. The opening phase, 29–30 October; the breakthrough phase, 31 October to 1 November; and the exploitation phase, 2–5 November. Action began in the afternoon of 29 October when four IAF Mustangs cut telephone lines throughout the Sinai, followed at 16.20 hours by the drop of one weak paratroop battalion, 395 men, at Parker's Memorial just east of the Mitla Pass. While the battalion dug in, the remaining units of the brigade, mounted on half-tracks and supported by an AMX-13 squadron, moved 190 miles across the central Sinai towards Mitla, overrunning defended positions at Kuntilla, Thamad, and Nakhl, and linked up with the parachuted battalion late the next day. Also during the night of 29–30 October the 4th Brigade captured

Kusseima and by the morning of 30 October the Israeli forces were in a position to outflank the Egyptian defence complex in the triangle.

On the morning of the 30th Simhoni discovered that the Deika Pass leading to the rear of the Abu Ageila defences was open, permitting the 7th Armoured to fall on this key position from the rear. He decided that a tactical opportunity of such magnitude had precedence over the politically motivated instructions not to engage armour until the 31st and ordered the tanks forward. At first Dayan, moving around the battle area by light plane, command car, and jeep, wanted to countermand the order, but realizing that it was too late to halt the 7th, already engaged against the outer rim of the Egyptian defences, he told its commander, Ben Ari, to continue the action with one combat team and send his other two west along the road towards Ismailia. Late in the evening, the 10th and 37th brigades advanced against Um Katef, but their attacks stalled and, when resumed the next day, failed to break into the defences. The commander of the 37th, personally leading a mechanized battalion forward, was killed, while the commander of the 10th was relieved on the spot. The attacks, Dayan concluded, had been poorly planned and pushed without adequate resolve.

Returning to GHQ late on the 30th, Dayan had been informed that the Anglo–French air strikes scheduled to start at dawn on the 31st had been postponed. Although Ben Gurion was worried, Dayan convinced him that the IDF could continue the campaign even if the French and British failed to honour their commitments. During the 30th and 31st, the IAF had gained air superiority over Sinai, downing a number of hostile jets, while in the decisive battle at Abu Ageila the 7th Armoured battalion combat team took a number of fortified positions. Meanwhile, on the 31st, after fighting some sharp engagements against Egyptian armour, two of its three battalion combat teams reached the Jebel Libni area where they prepared to ambush an Egyptian armoured column reportedly advancing from the canal. That column, however, was intercepted and stopped by air attacks between Bir Gafgafa and Bir Hamma, leaving the Ismailia road open. Earlier that day the northern task force breached the Rafah approaches and on 1 November the 27th reached El Arish and maintained its advance towards Kantara. Fighting continued around Um Katef where the Egyptians, though cut off, put up a stout defence.

Other major fighting on the 31st included an unauthorized advance by Sharon and elements of the 202nd through the Mitla Pass, a fiercely contested action. Although Dayan was miffed and several senior staff officers urged him to crack down on Sharon, he decided, perhaps remembering his own exploits, that while there had been disobedience, this was critical only 'when a unit fails to fulfill its battle task not when it goes beyond the bounds of duty and does more than is demanded of it'.[20]

On the evening of 30 October Britain and France had issued their ultimatum calling on both Egypt and Israel to withdraw to a distance of 10 miles from the canal and permit a temporary Anglo–French occupation. As agreed beforehand, Israel accepted while Egypt rejected the demand. Late on the 31st, after many delays, the Anglo–French air assault, designed to neutralize the Egyptian air force, commenced and continued the next day. Under orders to withdraw west, Egyptian resistance in the Um Katef region disintegrated on 1 November. Decision in the Sinai had been achieved and Dayan now issued orders for taking the Gaza Strip and for the advance on Sharm el Sheik. Finally that day an Egyptian destroyer, the *Ibrahim el Anwal*, attempting to shell Haifa, was intercepted by what appears to have been a joint French–Israeli force and captured.

During the next 72 hours, 2–5 November, Israeli spearheads reached the 10-mile limit on all roads leading to the canal and halted their advance. On 2 November a paratroop detachment was dropped on the last remaining Egyptian airfield at Tor on the western shore of the peninsula and on the following day a battalion of the 202nd moved overland to Ras Suder and the Abu Rudeis oil field, while the parachute detachment moved on to Sharm el Sheik. Meanwhile the 9th Brigade, 1,200 men and 200 vehicles, supplied over the beaches by two landing craft, reached the Ras Nasrani defences on 4 November and, following a spectacular air attack, speedily overcame the last Egyptian resistance. On 5 November it was all over. The IDF had conquered the Sinai and destroyed the Egyptian forces there at a cost of 172 killed and some 700 wounded, losing four prisoners and taking 5,581, and capturing great quantities of war materiel.[21] Despite the set-backs suffered by the 10th and 27th it had been a most spectacular victory, fought by an army of hastily mobilized reservists.

Reflections on the Sinai Campaign and its Aftermath

Dayan had good reason to be satisfied with the performance of the Army he had forged. The decisive battles already had been fought before the Anglo–French air attacks commenced and the entire operation had been completed before the first British and French landings on 5 November. Before Operation 'Kadesh', Dayan had misgivings about how well conscripts and reservists would fight against an enemy with heavy firepower and strongly entrenched positions. In the event, except for the 10th and 27th brigades, all had done well and even the two shaken formations had recovered. Overall, the informal discipline and the insistence on the primacy of combat had paid off. A veteran English observer confessed that he did not know how it worked. 'All my own experience in the British and American Armies had taught me that first-class discipline in battle depends on good discipline in barracks. Israel's Army seems to refute that lesson.'[22] The price, of course, had been high. Over 50 per cent of all Israeli casualties were officers.

There had also been shortcomings. The decision to enter combat without preparation and following a hasty mobilization had created problems. During the 'silent' mobilization phase many reservists had failed to respond, though once the radio call-up was used units rapidly filled up and in some cases were over establishment. The lack of preparation also was manifested in poor maintenance, a high rate of vehicle breakdowns, and the shortage of certain equipment. Command and control had been too loose. With Dayan insisting on being in the field and with communication equipment either blacked out or failing, there had been some confusion. Finally, artillery had failed to keep up with the rapid movement and fighter-bombers had served as 'flying artillery'. Bravery and individual initiative, so highly prized by Dayan, had righted all, though against an enemy less rigid and less tied to static defences there might have been trouble.

There had also been shortcomings. The decision to enter combat without and light armour had failed to dent enemy strongholds that continued to resist even when cut off, and the tanks of the 7th Armoured had made the decisive breaches. It had been Israeli doctrine, an American expert wrote, 'that tanks should not be used in direct assault' but, he continued, 'war's necessity decreed otherwise. And so the book came to be rewritten.'[23] Dayan conceded that the armour officers had been right and from now on armour, together with the air force, received the highest priority in Israeli military thinking.

Increased emphasis on air and armour was also the result of certain political and strategic considerations. The Sinai Campaign had been fought under special, and most likely non-recurring conditions. Effective Egyptian opposition was compromised by the Anglo–French threat and later by the Anglo–French air activities, and Egypt received no help from the other Arab states. In any future war, however, Israeli military thinkers had to take into account that Israel would no longer enjoy the luxury of fighting on only one front, and very likely would have to do so unaided. In addition, Israel lacked a natural defence frontier capable of blocking an efficient attack and space to retreat. Finally, the international situation made it appear likely that great power intervention would stop any Israeli military undertaking within a short time.

All these considerations led in one direction – a rapid and decisive campaign, leaving both strategic and tactical initiative in Israeli hands and achieving its goal with maximum speed. Only thus could the military power of a potential enemy be broken on one front before the enemy on a second front could pierce Israeli defences. And all this required emphasis on two principal weapons – the tank and the aeroplane.

At the same time, however, the final outcome of the Sinai Campaign demonstrated that there were severe limitations on Israel's ability to achieve decisive advantages. Israel had been victorious in 1948–9 and again in 1956, but twice she failed in the true purpose of any war: to force the enemy into submission and put an end to the war itself. Therefore the Israeli military doctrine of a *Blitzkrieg* was not a means to achieve an ultimate military decision, it used the strategic and tactical offensive for defensive purposes. Ultimately, peace and security for Israel would have to be found by diplomatic means. And diplomatically the Sinai war failed to achieve its objectives.

The aims of the Anglo–French invasion of Egypt, coupled with the Israeli Sinai campaign, were frustrated when Washington and Moscow agreed to impose a cease-fire on the British and French, followed by Russian threats of open intervention. At the same time the United States put enormous economic pressures on Israel. On 9 November 1956, already, Ben Gurion was compelled to declare Israel's intention to withdraw, though he still hoped to retain a presence in the Gaza Strip. Anglo–French forces evacuated the Canal Zone on 22 December, while the Israeli pace was slower. The Army retreated slowly, destroying military roads and air fields as it left. Assailed from many sides, Ben Gurion told the Knesset early in 1957 that Israel had not gone to war for conquest but for salvation from what had been perceived as a mortal danger. Israel's main objectives, he asserted, had been achieved. Still, it was clear that Israel's policy-makers had been harshly reminded that their freedom of action was severely circumscribed and behind Ben Gurion's statements there was his realistic appreciation that Israel could not afford a confrontation with one, let alone both super powers.

All this, however, did not make the withdrawal more palatable to the soldiers. As in 1949 they complied with the orders of the government, though the mood was bitter. Weizman recorded that Dayan was angry when on 16 March 1957 he left El Arish, riding on the last half-track.[24] Yet, all had not been in vain. Israel had defeated Egyptian forces that in many cases had fought bravely and well, and inflicted a severe set-back to its offensive potential. Moreover, before Israel withdrew its forces to the armistice demarcation lines, it obtained a number of assurances: that Israel's right of peaceful passage through the Suez Canal and the Straits of Tiran would be respected; that Egypt would prevent guerrilla attacks on Israel; and that peace would be made in due course. The placement of a United Nations Emergency Force on the Egyptian side of the border and at Sharm el Sheik was to provide further security and it was also agreed that if Egypt should demand the removal of these forces, the UN Secretary General would undertake negotiations to prevent this occurrence.

These international understandings were embodied in a series of memoranda, statements, and letters at the UN and in the several capitals and in addition Great Britain, France, and the United States guaranteed the international status of and the free access through the Straits of Tiran. Israel's basic claims against Egypt were upheld and buttressed by international agreements and understandings, though between 1957 and 1967 every term was eventually violated. More important than all these undertakings, however, was the fact that Operation 'Kadesh', executed with courage and resolution, had gained new respect for the Israeli Army and its ability to preserve the homeland.

1 *Above* British troops imposing martial law in Tel Aviv, March 1947

2 *Left* Haganah troops capture Castel during fighting on the road to Jerusalem, March 1948

3 *Above* The burnt-out home-made armoured vehicles of the ill-fated Hadassah Hospital convoy, 13 April 1948

4 *Above* Israeli troops in action in the Negev south of Beersheba, October 1948. Note the improved home-made armoured cars in the background

5 *Above* The new army in training. Israeli recruits during basic training, carrying Czech rifles and wearing British-style equipment. The period is about 1952

6 *Left* Two members of the CHEN in basic training. No longer used for combat duty, women nevertheless received basic field and weapons training. Again, the period is the early 1950s

7 *Below* Israeli reserves waiting to advance in Sinai. Note the bolt-action rifles and British equipment. The date is 30 October 1956

8 *Above* Israeli tank-infantry team in action near Um Katel, 1 November 1956. The tank is an M4 Sherman

9 *Below* Israeli infantry, carrying Czech bolt-action rifles and Sten guns, in action during Operation 'Kadesh', October-November 1956

10 *Above* Generals Assaf Simhoni and Moshe Ðayan address troops shortly before the official conclusion of the Sinai Campaign, 1956. General Simhoni was killed in an aircraft accident during the last hours of the war

11 *Below* War booty. Israeli tankers on top of a captured British Archer self-propelled gun, November 1956

12 *Above* March 1957. Under heavy pressure from the United States, Israeli forces evacuate the El Arish area and the Gaza Strip

13 *Left* Israeli soldiers retain their individual dress. A reservist on duty in the late 1950s, still carrying a bolt-action rifle

14 *Above* Women soldiers on parade carrying Uzi submachine guns. Increasingly women were being withdrawn from fighting formations and shifted to support units

15 *Below* Paratroopers during a night reprisal raid into Jordanian-held territory. Note the predominance of automatic weapons and the mortar bombs carried

16 *Above* In the 1960s Israel began to acquire modern armour. This picture shows M48 Pattons and Israeli Centurions in action during the Sinai campaign of June 1967

17 *Below* Perhaps the oldest armoured vehicle still on active service, the Israeli M3 half-track. Repeatedly modernized, the M3 saw extensive service in 1948, 1956, 1967 and 1973, and in many smaller operations.

18 *Left* General Israel Tal, commander of the Armoured Corps 1964-69, developed new doctrines and training standards. He is shown here during the 1967 campaign on the Southern Front

19 *Below* On 7 June 1967 Israeli paratroopers captured the Old City of Jerusalem. Here they are shown on the Temple Mount overlooking the old Jewish Quarter and the Wailing Wall

20 *Above* The War of Attrition led to the establishment of a defense line along the Suez Canal. Here a section of young regulars are shown in front of an unhardened outpost. All are now equipped with automatic weapons

21 *Left* On 10 September 1969 an Israeli armoured force raided Egyptian coastal installations along the Gulf of Suez. This picture shows captured Soviet T-54/55 tanks used during this operation being unloaded from an Israeli LCT

22 *Above* On 26 December 1969 Israeli strike forces captured Shadwan Island in the Gulf of Suez, then dismantled and flew away an entire Soviet P-12 radar installation. This picture shows an Israeli helicopter hauling up one of the crates containing the dismantled equipment

23 *Below* After 1969 the IDF began to receive substantial supplies of war material from the United States. Here mechanized infantry mounted on a US M113 APC are shown passing through a village during a limited protective operation in Southern Lebanon in the early 1970s

24 *Above* Israel always captured equipment. Here gunners demonstrate the loading of a truck-mounted Katyusha 240mm rocket launcher. Large numbers of these weapons were used during the 1973 war

25 *Left* During the first desperate days of October 1973 individual tankers provided the margin holding back the Syrian armoured onslaught on the Golan

26 *Left* An Israeli reservist on the Golan in 1973. All attempts to introduce smartness have not succeeded in making him cut his hair. Note that he still carries a bolt-action rifle

27 *Below* From 1974 on Arab guerrillas resumed their operations from Lebanon, answered by air and ground reprisal raids. This picture shows two Israeli paratroopers inside Arab fortifications

28 *Left* in 1975 the IDF Artillery Corps received the Lance missile system, an inertially-guided surface-to-surface weapon capable of delivering a 45 kilogram warhead over a range of approximately 60 miles

29 *Below* Following the success of its missile boats in the Yom Kippur War, the Israeli Navy built a larger class of boats with an 850-tons displacement. Shown here is the *Keshet*

30 *Top* and **31** *Bottom* Although many commentators argued that the Yom Kippur War had shown that the tank had become obsolete, the IDF did not agree; it developed its own new Main Battle Tank, the heavily-armoured *Merkava,* or *Chariot.* Shown here is the *Merkava* 1 with a 105mm main gun

32 *Above* The increase in the size of the IDF after 1973 prompted a reconsideration of the role of women. Although they are still not used in fighting units, women are now employed in a wide range of jobs. In 1978 it was announced that women would be employed as instructors in the Armoured Corps School.

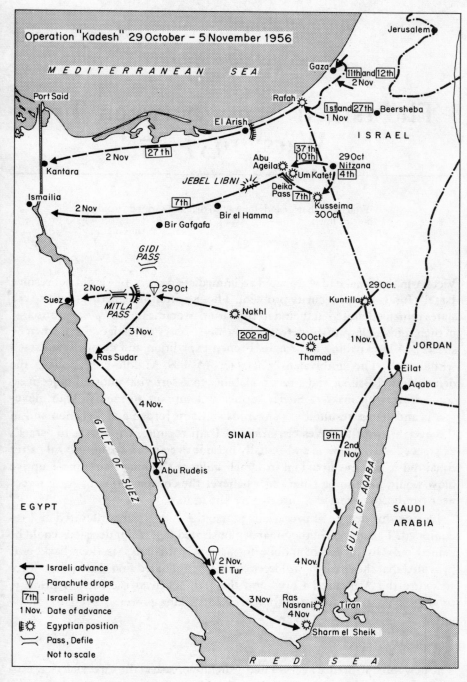

Operation "Kadesh" 29 October – 5 November 1956

MEDITERRANEAN SEA

Jerusalem

Gaza — 11th and 12th / 2 Nov

Port Said

Rafah — 1st and 27th / 1 Nov — Beersheba

El Arish

ISRAEL

Kantara — 2 Nov / 27th

37th / 10th — 29 Oct / Nitzana

Abu Ageila — Um Katef / 4th

JEBEL LIBNI — Deika Pass / 7th

Ismailia — 2 Nov / 7th — Bir el Hamma — Kusseima / 30 Oct

Bir Gafgafa

GIDI PASS

Suez — 2 Nov. / MITLA PASS — 29 Oct — Nakhl — Kuntilla / 29 Oct.

202nd — 30 Oct / Thamad — 1 Nov — JORDAN

3 Nov. — Ras Sudar — Eilat / Aqaba

4 Nov.

SINAI — 9th / 2nd Nov

GULF OF SUEZ

Abu Rudeis

EGYPT — SAUDI ARABIA

GULF OF AQABA

2 Nov. / El Tur

3 Nov — Ras Nasrani / 4 Nov — Tiran / 4 Nov.

Sharm el Sheik

Legend:
- → Israeli advance
- ⛱ Parachute drops
- 7th Israeli Brigade
- 1 Nov. Date of advance
- ☼ Egyptian position
- ⊱ Pass, Defile
- Not to scale

RED SEA

5

The Israeli Army between Two Wars: 1957–67

'Who traineth my hands for war, so that mine arms do bend a bow of brass.'

Psalms 18: 19

Victory in the Sinai had eliminated an immediate danger, but it did not resolve Israel's fundamental security problem. Though often at loggerheads, the Arab states remained united in their determination to eradicate the 'western abscess' in their midst. Despite the defeat of his army, Nasser's prestige soared when he succeeded in expelling the Anglo–French expedition and compelling Israeli withdrawal. The ambivalent character of US Middle-East policy, the demonstrated British and French inability to assert vital political objectives, contrasting with massive Soviet supply and support to radical Arab movements and states, resulted in dangerous shifts in Jordan and Lebanon and in the overthrow of the Western-oriented Iraqi regime. The threat to Israel's existence remained grave and actually became even more alarming. Only after Sinai did it become an axiom in Israeli military thinking that a pre-emptive blow would have to be launched whenever the concentration of Arab forces near her border created a threatening situation.

During this decade of precarious peace, the IDF was restructured and re-equipped. The lessons of the Sinai demonstrated that major decisions could be gained only by means of mobile formations with tanks as their backbone, provided that the enemy's air forces could be eliminated first. In this new force structure the Armoured Corps and the IAF received the highest priority, producing an army with greatly increased striking power.

The Israeli Soldier

The new force structure necessitated a slight increase in the career service, especially in the air force, but the IDF retained its basic character – a large reserve force with an active duty contingent of conscripts and a small nucleus of career soldiers, an army, Chief of Staff Yitzhak Rabin proclaimed in July 1967, which 'came from the people and returns to the people'. To some this pattern of a nation in arms recalled Prussia, another small state having to maximize its resources against more powerful hostile neighbours, but the Prussian system had militarized society while the Israeli system civilized the Army. Foreign observers continued to marvel at the absence of parade-ground discipline and military ceremonial, and noticed at the same time that the part-time soldiers often showed greater proficiency than regulars in many advanced countries. A former British brigadier wrote that every Israeli soldier 'knew the main elements of his job which he carried out with dispatch, rigorous self-discipline and amazing efficiency'. The Israelis, he asserted, were 'the toughest, most reliable, most aggressive, most indefatigable' fighters in the world.[1]

Perhaps this was an overstatement, written in the euphoria following the Six Day War. Then too, the Israeli citizen army, though spectacular in action, had parallels elsewhere. The Israeli pattern was close to the Swiss citizen army, Yadin's original model, which also practised a simple utilitarian style and had traits similar to the Australian troops in both world wars. General Sir John Monash, a Jewish reserve officer and one of the outstanding commanders of World War I, observed that his troops rejected 'obsequious homage to superiors', but rendered unquestioning obedience in battle 'because their intellect told them that this was necessary'. It was the same in Israel. Realizing that attempts to enforce formal military discipline would only create resentments among the bulk of the reservists, and these in practice constituted the Army, no effort was made to more than the absolute necessary minimum of outward conformity. Instead, the Army relied on the corporate spirit as the reserve units became veteran formations, as good as and sometimes better than active units. While reserve duty was, and remains, a heavy burden, there were compensations. During the annual tours of duty relations between workers and managers, students and teachers were transformed when they met in uniform, and men of various backgrounds met and came to understand one another.[2]

This common experience was especially important as the state was rapidly changing after 1956 into an industrialized and urban society and the traditional image of the highly motivated, politically conscious fighter of kibbutz and collective farm background no longer fitted the overwhelming number of conscripts and reservists. No longer embattled farmers, officers and men came from the many occupations of a modern society, many of them less than physically fit, and all of them highly individualistic. The total Jewish population from which the Army was drawn stood at about 2,500,000 throughout the decade, and about half were of Oriental origin with Arabic or French as their first language. The new urban life styles and the educational and social gap between Western and Oriental Jews caused some fears among old-timers about how well the new generation would perform when push came to shove, but these apprehensions proved unfounded in 1967 and again in 1973.

For the most part the young soldiers displayed little interest in the Zionist rhetoric of their elders and even simple nationalism was not their main motivation. Allon's injunction, reminiscent of Cromwell, that all Israeli soldiers should 'understand why they were recruited and for what they must fight', just did not hold true.[3] Personal leadership, growing unit cohesion, and determined personal initiative all contributed to the fighting spirit, though the morale and efficiency of the Israelis were not primarily the product of military training and indoctrination. Rightly or wrongly, most Israelis were convinced that the Arabs were bent on destroying their state and that they were fighting with their backs to the wall. For them there could be no retreat because there was no place to retreat to and in every war the individual soldier believed that he was fighting for the life of his family, his home, and his nation. Such men make formidable fighters.

At the same time there existed, and still does, a curious ambivalence towards the enemy. Basically the Israeli soldier regarded himself as a humane, even charitable fighter, a view that might not be accepted by his adversaries. Still, even in combat, it never became the objective to inflict maximum casualties and prisoners were treated with consideration. During the Sinai Campaign Dayan was relieved to find captives well treated and that 'possible revenge takes only one form – the prisoners are being fed Israel Army rations.' He admitted that there had been looting, but no wanton killings, rapes, or despoilation. In 1967, too, Israeli units entering Arab towns were sternly warned not to shoot at surrendering or fleeing enemies and to respect civilian life and property.[4]

As always, there was an exception, though it remained just that, and led to stern punishment and preventive measures for the future. The exception was the affair at Kfar Kassem, an Arab village near the Jordanian border, where, on 29 October 1956, 43 peasants returning to their village after curfew, were summarily shot by a Border Police unit. Although most of the unit was Druze, and only temporarily part of the Army, the killings shocked the IDF. A military court sentenced two officers and six men to long prison terms and in confirming the sentences, the Supreme Military Appellate Court ruled that soldiers not only had the right but the duty to disobey manifestly inhumane orders. This decision was widely publicized throughout the Army and incorporated into standing orders.[5]

Conscription continued to be applied to women, though regulations governing service were more liberal in regard to age limits, deferments, and exemptions. Almost 40 per cent of females subject to conscription were exempted. Since 1948, when women had fought in the ranks of the Palmach, stood in the trenches of the settlements, and died in the assaults on Latrun, the role of the Women's Army Corps (CHEN) had changed. Women no longer participated in combat, though they provided an important element in the administrative and communications sections at the brigade level. In 1956, and again in 1967, they moved forward with their units and served in combat areas.

Throughout their service girls, never permitted to serve in groups fewer than 15, remained under the jurisdiction of their branch, and could be disciplined only by female officers. There was little promiscuity – normally it led to an immediate administrative discharge – and also from the early 1960s the Army adopted the policy of stationing girls close to home, enabling them to return to their families at night. The policy was not universally appreciated. Many women soldiers would apply for the job of company clerk, a position providing greater social opportunity and the chance to get away from home. Altogether, women contributed much to the spirit of the Army, providing an important socializing influence and alleviating manpower shortages.

Despite the many safeguards and the provision of religious exemptions, the conscription of women remained a point of contention between the government and ultra-orthodox factions, provoking angry exchanges in the Knesset, public protests and demonstrations. It should be noted, however, that the orthodox were by no means united in their opposition. The orthodox kibbutzim, to be sure, constituting only a tiny minority within the kibbutz movement, itself a minority in the total population, continued to take pride in the service of their girls in the Army.

Officer–enlisted men relations remained close and informal. Within units all ranks commonly addressed their officers by their first or nicknames and, except for general officers, titles were rarely used. Dayan had reconfirmed the ideal of the officer as a heroic combat leader and had succeeded in implanting this concept. Israeli officers at the brigade and battalion levels always led out in front, achieving extraordinary results by this 'follow me' style. Casualty figures showed the price. In every war and in every action officer losses were heavy, amounting to 20 per cent of unit commanders, compared to an international average of around 10 per cent. Technology and the inevitable increase in bureaucracy incidental to the growing size and complexity of the military establishment did produce a number of military managers, but as a group their prestige fell far short of the combat officers and many managers had begun their careers in fighting units.

The Israeli officer was not a 'gentleman' in the old English sense of the word. There were, and still are, no social or educational qualifications and all entry into the officer corps was through the enlisted ranks. Selection and training stressed leadership, bravery, endurance, initiative, and teamwork, basically the values developed by the Palmach. An officer was to serve as a model on and off duty and the code was rigorously applied. Uri Ben Ari, whose 7th Brigade had played a decisive role in the Sinai, was dismissed because he had covered up for a subordinate who had misappropriated a few sacks of sugar. Retention, promotion, and assignments were by merit alone and officers who did not measure up, even if their conduct was passable, found their careers short-lived.

Conscripts or volunteers selected for officer training normally would be commissioned at 20, and if they signed a regular service contract for five years, would reach company command within three years. Battalion commanders ranged between 26 and 31 years of age and even at the very top the IDF was young. During its first two decades, from 1948 to 1967, there were seven chiefs of staff, all but two under 40 when appointed. Other senior ranks showed a similar range. Brigadiers were between 40 and 44, colonels 35 to 40, and lieutenant-colonels were 30 to 35 years of age. Bearing greater responsibilities and taking heavier risks had considerable appeal to members of the kibbutz movement, now a distinct ideological elite comprising only 4 per cent of the population. Kibbutz members provided a disproportionately high number of officers, especially in combat units, and suffered 25 per cent of all officer losses. If kibbutzim were over-represented in the officer corps, Israelis of Oriental background remained under-represented in the 1960s and even then there were few senior officers from the Sephardic community. The situation, though worrisome to many, did not evoke much resentment. The feeling that in matters of national security one could not afford to take chances, combined with the realization that merit alone determined selection and promotion, did much to defuse a potentially explosive issue.

Another reason for the small number of Sephardic senior officers was the small number and the homogeneous nature of the general officer ranks. Compared to the United States, and adjusted for the respective size of the two military establishments, Israel's generals numbered only one-third the number of their American counterparts – and the same was true in the field grades. Four-fifths of the Israeli officer corps consisted of captains and lieutenants. Until after the 1967 war, *rav aluf*, equivalent to major-general, was the highest rank, held only by the chief of staff; the Northern, Central, and Southern Commands were headed by brigadier-generals, while brigades were normally commanded by colonels. Many senior officers served in dual roles and heads of branches, corps, as well as senior service school instructors had mobilization assignments to combat formations.

Most senior officers, that is officers above the rank of lieutenant-colonel, had served together for a long time, beginning in the Haganah and the Palmach, some in the British Army, and continued through the War of Independence, the retaliatory raids, and into Sinai. This made for considerable intimacy. The strengths and weaknesses of each were well known to his peers. On the positive side this permitted informality and give and take among commanders; on the negative side it could, and did, lead to friction and the formation of cliques. Yet the negative effects were neutralized by the rapid turn-over at the senior levels. Dayan already had institutionalized the concept that officers should regard their active service as a 'first career' only. All senior officers, he insisted, should retire at 40 and pensions were set to permit early retirement, while a generous leave policy enabled them to obtain degrees before discharge. Although retirement at 40 was never fully implemented, the concept of a 'second career' became firmly embedded. Turnover was rapid enough so that by 1967 men who had been junior officers during the Sinai Campaign had advanced to senior rank.

Many high-ranking officers with academic credentials and proven managerial talents found prominent positions in the fast-developing Israeli industrial complex, others entered government service, and a few, like Dayan, remained active in politics. Age limits did not apply to reserve service and many of the senior officers, recalled to active duty in emergencies, distinguished themselves in 1967. Finally, the introduction of increasingly high technology into the IDF led to the retention of specialist officers well above the statutory age limit.[6]

During their active service career and reserve, officers attended a variety of schools. The most important, a requirement for promotion, was the Command and Staff School (POUM), established in 1954. Competition here was stiff. Only about 20 per cent of those eligible were selected to attend and had to agree to extend their service for five years following graduation. There was no differentiation among courses between career and reserve officers; all courses were open to both. Beyond the Command and Staff School there existed for some time a National Defence College which, structured along the lines of the US Army War College, enrolled both military and civilian students. Lavon, already, had advocated such a college, but the idea had been resisted. It opened in 1963 and operated for four years. When it closed it had graduated 102 students, though only 39 officers among them. After 1973 the need to integrate political, economic, and sociological considerations with military thinking once again became important and in the autumn of 1977 a new National Defence Academy opened.

Ground and Naval Forces: 1957–67

Between the end of the Sinai Campaign and the Six Day War the Israeli Army grew in size and striking power. By 1967, the fully mobilized Army mustered over 250,000 effectives, some 11 to 12 per cent of the population. It was organized in 21 to 32 field brigades, the order of battle remaining a closely guarded secret to this day. Field forces were reputed to consist of 9 armoured, 3 mechanized, 3 paratroop, and 6 to 16 infantry brigades, equipped with about 1,000 tanks.[7] The IAF first-line strength consisted of some 200 jet planes, supported by a small number of second-line machines. Strategically this force was geared more than ever towards a short war. The experience of 1956 indicated that if there was to be any kind of decisive victory, it had to be done before great power intervention nullified battlefield achievements.

This basic assumption determined the Army's new emphasis on armour and air forces, already recognized as all important by Dayan during the Sinai Campaign. His successor, Chaim Laskov, was singularly well suited to supervise the transition of the Army into an armour and air centred force. Perhaps Israel's pre-eminent military theorist, he had been an effective commander of the IAF and the Armoured Corps. Now he was concerned to develop an organizational structure permitting exploitation of the fluidity of the modern battle, combining the strength of large armoured formations with tactical flexibility for subordinate commanders. He elaborated the divisional task force organizations, *ugdot*, provisionally used in 1956, which, in contrast with the conventional divisions, provided a more flexible framework accommodating various combinations of armoured, mechanized, paratroop, and infantry brigades. Basically the *ugda* commander merely directed the general direction of the battle, while subordinate commanders were free to pursue and exploit immediate tactical objectives. To provide the required logistical support, Laskov introduced the US Army 'constant flow' concept, which moved supplies forward in a constant stream without waiting for specific requisitions.

Unfortunately Laskov was not able to complete his work. His three-year term in office was cut short in 1960 when he became embroiled in a jurisdictional wrangle with Deputy Defence Minister Peres, who enjoyed Ben Gurion's full backing. Laskov was succeeded by Zvi Zur, an able administrator, who completely supervised the introduction of major new weapons systems into the IDF. The last chief of staff during this period was Yitzhak Rabin, the first Palmach veteran to hold the highest military post. From 1963 on, with the security situation becoming ever more alarming, he completed the organization of the new military structure and prepared the plans implemented during the Six Day War. Rabin's tenure coincided with an important shift in the post of defence minister. In 1963, following a revival of the debate regarding the 1954 covert operations fiasco, leading to a split in the ruling Labour coalition, Ben Gurion resigned and was succeeded by Levi Eshkol, who continued the tradition of combining the portfolios of prime minister and minister of defence. Unlike Ben Gurion, Eshkol lacked confidence in military affairs and depended on Rabin for advice on Israel's military needs. Although he had not given up his concern with economy, he provided the means to purchase the new and expensive weapons systems required and kept in close touch with developments. His greatest failing was lack of charisma and personal leadership which Ben Gurion had used so effectively during his prolonged tenure. While Eshkol was hardly admired by the IDF's high command, the principle of civilian dominance over the military had become so firmly established that even in the crisis preceding the June war there never arose the threat of a military revolt.[8]

The most important development in the ground forces was the expansion of the Armoured Corps and its transformation into the decisive arm. Between 1957 and 1967 the corps had three commanding officers – Generals Chaim Bar Lev (1957–61), David Eleazar (1961–64), and Israel Tal (1964–69). All three acted as corps commanders as well as branch chiefs and exercised wide authority including doctrine, training, design, and procurement. All three also shared the belief that armour alone could win a decision. Individually they made different contributions: Bar Lev developed the organization necessary to deploy massive tank formations; Eleazar devised new doctrine and acquired much needed new equipment; Tal perfected the doctrine and raised maintenance and gunnery standards. By the mid-1960s the Armoured Corps had become a powerful and largely self-contained striking force with organic infantry and support elements.

Re-equipment was the most basic requirement for the new role assigned to armour. During the Sinai Campaign armour had relied heavily on manoeuvre, had made only a few daylight assaults and engaged other tanks only on a few occasions. Even so, there was solid evidence to show the need for harder hitting and better protected vehicles than the light tanks available from France. As a first step it was decided to further modify the already upgunned Shermans. Additional Shermans were acquired abroad and together with some 40 captured Egyptian vehicles were modified in Ordnance Corps workshops to M-51 standard. By 1962, however, the need for a heavier gun to counter the growing number of Soviet T-54/55s in the Arab arsenals became evident and Bar Lev ordered ordnance and armour specialists to start a crash programme to rearm the Shermans with 105mm cannon. At first this proved difficult. The French and British 105mm cannon available produced a recoil that cracked the obsolete Sherman hulls and damaged optical and electronic equipment. After much experimentation the Shermans were re-engineered to absorb more recoil while ordnance experts came up with a combination of French and British designs for a powerful 105mm cannon capable of firing rounds that penetrated all existing armour. The new battle tank, officially designated as the M-51HV, colloquially known as the Israeli Sherman–Isherman, was retrofitted with a 460hp Cummings diesel engine, capable of moving the 39-ton vehicle – 9 tons more than the original M-4 – at 27mph for a 150-mile range. Relatively expensive and complicated, the conversion was not completed by 1967. Older Sherman models remained in service and were used as support vehicles for the mechanized and infantry brigades.

Among the reasons behind the development of the M-51HV had been the desire to become, at least partially, independent of foreign sources, even though in the 1960s Israel for the first time was able to buy modern equipment in reasonable quantities. Continuing and ever closer Soviet connections with Egypt, Syria, and Iraq worried the Western powers and while the United States was not prepared as yet to provide major weapons directly to Israel, it used its good offices to have Britain supply tanks and other major equipment. In 1959 the Armoured Corps acquired its first heavy tanks – British 50-ton Centurions, both Mark III and V, armed with a high-velocity 20-pounder gun. Israeli workshops modified these heavily armoured machines for desert conditions and eventually retrofitted them with the British L7 105mm gun, which was stabilized both in elevation and azimuth and could be fired while the vehicle was moving. By 1967 about 250 Centurions, some still with their original cannon, were available.

Another new source of supply was West Germany. Already in 1952 West Germany had agreed to make reparation payments to individuals and to the Jewish state and, despite violent protests by left- and right-wing extremists, German–Israeli contacts continued. In 1957, Dayan made an official visit to Germany and the following year Peres, the deputy defence minister, met with Franz Josef Strauss, West Germany's defence minister. Finally, in March 1960, Ben Gurion conferred with Chancellor Adenauer in New York. The upshot of the various meetings was that between 1960 and 1964, when deliveries stopped because of media leaks, the *Bundeswehr*, then in the process of updating its equipment, furnished the IDF with 200 Patton M-48 tanks. The Pattons were modified in Israel by replacing the original 90mm gun with the British 105mm gun and by exchanging their petrol for diesel engines, bringing them up to the standard of the new US M-60A1 tank, as yet unavailable to Israel. And when German deliveries stopped after 1964, the United States completed the promised shipment by making direct deliveries.

Finally, Israel maintained its close relationship with France, though this became increasingly commercial in character and all purchases were paid at market prices. The new French AMX-30, a fast, medium tank, was rejected by Tal, who preferred the slower but more heavily protected Centurions. Just before the 1967 war, however, Israel purchased a small number of French AML-90, a 4×4 armoured car mounting a 90mm cannon. France also continued to supply most of the self-propelled artillery supporting the Armoured Corps, including French M-50 and US 105mm howitzers, as well as

155mm French M-50 gun-howitzers, mounted on radically modified Sherman M-4 chassis, the heaviest gun in Israel's arsenal into the 1970s. Additional armour support was provided by locally manufactured 81 and 120mm mortars mounted on half-tracks and SS-10 and 11 anti-tank guided missiles.[9]

These large-scale acquisitions of new fighting materiel produced major changes in doctrine and required increased technological proficiency. In 1956 the size of the Sinai and the Egyptian deployment in self-contained but isolated hedgehog positions had enabled Israeli armour to penetrate to the rear of the enemy and this had contributed to his collapse. By the early 1960s, however, the Egyptian Army had grown in size and had been re-equipped with Soviet materiel and restructured in accordance with Soviet tactics. It now was deployed in the critical areas of the Sinai in several fortified lines flanked by natural obstacles. Behind these lines there were armour concentrations. This conformed to Soviet doctrines of the 'sword and shield', the defences being the shield and the armour being the sword. Blocking the major axes of advance, these defences could no longer be bypassed and armoured head-on assaults as well as major clashes with enemy armour became unavoidable. To deal with this new situation, General Tal established a committee headed by Colonel Avraham (Bren) Adan to reassess tactical methods.

After considerable study and experimentation there was agreement that the Armoured Corps had to reorient itself towards massive daylight assaults on a brigade or even divisional scale, exploiting psychological shock, maximum mobility, and disrupting the enemy's defences simultaneously at many points. These new tactics required tanks able to advance against enemy fire and this was why Tal preferred the slower but more heavily armoured Centurion over lighter and more mobile vehicles. To produce break-ins at many points, armour, firepower, and men had to be concentrated in one sector, even if this meant temporarily weakening others. Finally, it was proposed to conduct the armoured battles as a 'continuous operation', with combat sustained for up to three days at a stretch. Morale was considered decisive here, the assumption being that one side was bound to break under the strain and the side with the stronger will would prevail.

To sustain continuous action also demanded a high standard of vehicle reliability. By the early 1960s, however, the acquisition of new materiel had outstripped the Armoured Corps' maintenance capabilities. There were a great number of breakdowns and equipment malfunctions, especially with the Centurions, which troops blamed on the machines. Tal was convinced that they were wrong and that slack maintenance standards were at fault. He realized that modern tanks were complex vehicles and that the average conscript or reservist did not have the time to master the entire mechanical, hydraulic, electric and optical systems involved. The problem, moreover, was complicated by the fact that not counting half-tracks, the corps' inventory consisted of a mix of vehicles – ten different makes and configurations of tanks in 1967. It would have been desirable to standardize equipment, but that would have meant discarding fighting vehicles still useful. Tal found a solution. Previously tank maintenance personnel had not specialized but had worked on all vehicular systems. When he took over the corps in September 1962 he decided to compartmentalize maintenance, perfecting each tanker's skill in one particular area. Moreover, maintenance and adjustments were to be carried out by the book, according to strictly defined and rigidly adhered to procedures. Arguing that both operational and maintenance discipline required external conformity, Tal rejected the casual disciplinary approach prevailing in the Army. Regulations for the Armoured Corps, published in final form in 1965, stressed military courtesies and appearance, though at the same time they also established fair standards for grievances, leave policies, and other privileges. Although Tal's approach set his corps apart from the rest of the Army he was able to convince his men that it was necessary and achieved a high level of compliance. Under Tal tank reliability and combat readiness improved drastically, while constant training enabled his gunners to score an astonishing number of first-round hits. Altogether the performance of the IDF armour in the Six Day War was unexpectedly high and almost entirely the result of the high standards of maintenance and training.[10]

The development of armour, making it the pre-eminent fighting element in the IDF, outstripped the growth of infantry. For that matter, the Israeli Army did not have a single type of infantry, but three distinct types with differing functions and doctrine (if the defence units of the border settlements were counted there were four types). The first consisted of the mechanized infantry battalions, mounted on half-tracks and assigned to the armoured and mechanized brigades. These actually were part of the Armoured Corps and were trained and deployed under its control. Normally armoured brigades comprised two tank battalions and one battalion of mechanized infantry, while the ratio was reversed in the mechanized brigades. Mechanized infantry fought on the move, delivering fire from its vehicle-mounted heavy machine-guns. Of course, it could also fight on foot, though Tal's plans, envisaging the employment of massed battalions of Centurions and Pattons – a scheme which ran counter to the generally accepted doctrine of combined arms – assigned only a subordinate role to the infantry. Tal believed that heavy armour, provided it had effective air cover, could fight on in its own, and that the obsolescent half-tracks and the self-propelled artillery did not have enough cross-country mobility or protection to be of much effect in the fluid tank mêlée he had planned.

Standard infantry brigades had been streamlined and partially mechanized and motorized, though there were only very few armoured personnel carriers, trucks, and jeeps. Mobilized Israeli infantry brigades continued to have to rely on requisitioned vehicles. Except for the overstrength Jerusalem Brigade, infantry brigades were organized in three battalions. Self-loading rifles were available for all first-line units, supplemented by a liberal allocation of light and medium mortars and rocket launchers.

Paratroops, administratively responsible to the chief infantry and paratroop officers, in practice continued as an independent elite force, all-volunteer with special physical, mental, and moral qualifications. After 1956 the 202nd Brigade had been broken up to provide cadres for three independent paratroop brigades. Each of these units maintained two active duty battalions. There was an overall strength of 12 reserve battalions. While retaining their airborne and commando capabilities, the paratroopers also were trained to fight mounted on armoured personnel carriers, though their units had no integral heavy transport. Because of their varied assignment, the exact establishment and equipment of each battalion tended to differ.

Normally a paratrooper battalion was organized into three rifle companies, a support company, and a headquarters unit. The support company had 81mm mortars and at least one medium machine-gun platoon. In addition each brigade had a strong scout company with jeeps mounting recoilless rifles. The Uzi submachine-gun remained the main personal weapon of the paratroopers, supplemented by self-loading rifles, belt-fed machine-guns, 3·5-inch rocket launchers, and light mortars. Demonstrating individualism, paratroopers often reverted to the practices of 1948 and armed themselves with captured Russian, Czech, or Chinese weapons, the Russian AK-47 and its Chinese copy being especially prized.

Paratrooper tactics were offensive, stressing rapid movement, surprise, psychological shock, and fire power. Night fighting was favoured, though continuous round-the-clock combat was anticipated. If at all possible, the paratroopers would motor on, or through, the objective. If resistance was light, the mounted troopers would fire their machine-guns about 250 yards ahead, while rifles and submachine-guns fired to the side, and a few men in each vehicle threw grenades behind the vehicle as it rolled through the objective. If the attack was made on foot, the paratroopers, in wedge formation, would rapidly close with the objective, firing their weapons on the run. Officers and senior noncommissioned officers would lead at the point, and if they were killed or wounded would be replaced at once. While costly, this tactic was thought to provide maximum strength at the impact point. During night attacks, fire-support groups placed between the wedges, would keep up continual fire with all available weapons. Overall, the paratroopers maintained a high reputation as shock troops and justified this reputation during the fighting in June 1967.[11]

Artillery did not catch up with the rapid development of other IDF combat arms. IDF artillery encompassed all field artillery – guns, mortars, rockets, as well as anti-aircraft artillery. It was organized in battalions and trained as a support weapon. The main problem was shortage of fast-moving, mobile pieces of sufficient hitting power. The bulk of the artillery still consisted of towed pieces, supplemented by some batteries of light self-propelled 105mm gun-howitzers and some French 155mm pieces on a radically modified Sherman chassis. All officers commanding self-propelled batteries were graduates of the Armour School and Colonel Ben Amitai, chief artillery officer had worked out close-support tactics. Still, the development of Israel artillery forces posed serious equipment and manpower problems. With finances strained, most of the money went to the Armoured Corps and the IAF and there also was a shortage of men with the required education and technical training to handle the more modern and sophisticated weapons, fire-control and acquisition systems.

Similar problems faced the remaining supporting services and branches, engineers, signals, ordnance, and supply. The Israeli Army always had been fond of special devices and Major David Laskov of the Corps of Engineers devised several super-heavy spigot mortars for demolishing heavy enemy fortifications. For the most part, however, support services had to rely on civilian equipment and facilities. On the one hand, this created problems of assembling the required vehicles, bulldozers, and other equipment, and often the machinery was not in good condition; on the other hand, reliance on civilian facilities reduced the teeth-to-tail ratio. In 1967 the IDF fielded rather more than 50 per cent of its mobilized strength in combat units, a ratio comparing favourably with the 20-to-80 ratio common in major Western armies.

Finally, the Israeli Navy also lagged behind the other fighting branches and remained a coastal defence force equipped with obsolete and unsuitable ships. Overall, its size declined as the original corvettes and frigates were phased out and the only major additions were two British S-class submarines, 400-ton boats built in 1941, which came into Israeli service in 1959. In the early 1960s, the newly established Israel Shipyards at Haifa produced the first landing craft, but plans for a gunboat and missile-craft navy, already on the drawing boards, had to be held in abeyance. The main fighting units of the navy were two Z-class destroyers obtained from Britain in 1955 and the Egyptian destroyer captured in 1956. The navy maintained shore installations at Haifa, Tel Aviv and Eilat.

The IAF: 1957–67

Even before 1956 Israel had recognized the importance of airpower, but budgetary restrictions and the difficulties in acquiring suitable aircraft had prevented the IAF from reaching its full potential. Although its operations had been severely constrained in 1956, Dayan had noted in his campaign diary that the air force 'had a decisive impact on the campaign'. From then on, it received the highest priority, even ahead of the Armoured Corps, in the military establishment. Even so, by 1967 it still was outnumbered more than four times by the air forces of its immediate adversaries and when it destroyed the combined air forces of Egypt, Syria, Jordan, and Iraq within a few hours in June 1967, enabling the Israeli ground forces to gain victory in six days, it wrote for itself a chapter without parallel in the annals of air war.

The main architect of this achievement, turning the IAF 'from a bird into an eagle', was Ezer Weizman, one of Israel's pioneer pilots, an explosive and on occasion flamboyant air officer, who commanded the force from 1958 to 1966. On assuming command in July 1958, Weizman realized that the IAF faced two major problems. First there was the small size of the country, which placed its population centres and airfields within minutes flying time of hostile air bases and in several instances within the range of enemy artillery. The second problem was obtaining assured supplies of first-rate combat aircraft, together with pilots and ground staff of superior quality to offset the Arab quantitative advantage.

The solution for the first problem, according to Weizman, was an active forward defence. In case war became inevitable, the IAF had to gain immediate air superiority by a first strike against enemy air installations, destroying his planes on their runways and in their hangars. Only in this fashion could the country be protected and an air umbrella provided for the deploying ground forces. The proper place to defend Israel, Weizman asserted, was in the skies over Cairo. To execute such a strike required highly skilled pilots, a high rate of operational readiness, and careful planning. Here Israel's small size and central location provided an advantage. Although in theory the various Arab enemies had plans to co-ordinate their forces, in practice this proved difficult and even impossible in view of their shifting political relationships. In contrast, the IAF was able to use its bases omnidirectionally and could, in a matter of minutes, concentrate over any sector.

The second major problem – an assured supply of first-rate combat planes – was just as difficult and depended on the willingness of outside powers to sell modern aircraft and armaments. From 1956 to the eve of the 1967 war, France remained this supplier, even though by 1959 the French Foreign Ministry reverted to its previous policy and repeatedly tried to block transactions. For the time being, however, relations between the armed forces of the two countries remained close and the French chiefs of staff, prepared if necessary to go direct to General de Gaulle, the head of state, were able to override diplomatic objections. French–Israeli co-operation extended beyond the sale of planes and armaments into the exchange of information and a limited amount of joint research and development. This was not necessarily based on sentiment. The French aircraft industry needed customers and Israel paid the full market price. Even then, certain Israeli officers warned of the danger of relying on only one country, though with United States – the only other potential source – still unwilling to sell combat planes, the IAF had no other option. Moreover, the French aircraft industry offered a suitable mix of expensive and relatively cheap planes. Weizman planned to use the expensive high-performance machines as air-superiority fighters while slower and less costly aircraft would serve in ground support and attack roles.[12]

In July 1957 the Israel Aircraft Industries (IAI), a government-owned enterprise founded in 1953, and Air Fouga, a French company, signed a licensing agreement for the production of the Fouga Magister CM-170, a twin-jet trainer. The Magister permitted the IAF to conduct its own jet training and also, modified to carry 2 machine-guns, 16 unguided air-to-ground rockets, 1 napalm package or a 100lb bomb, could be used as a close-support plane. Production began by the end of the year. Also that year France agreed to sell Israel 24 Vautour light tactical bombers and when Russia supplied Egypt with advanced Mig-17 and 19 aircraft, the French provided 24 Super Mystère B-2s, the first supersonic planes in service with the IAF, and delivered in 1959. Negotiations also began for sale of the Mirage IIIC, a Mach 2 fighter, though on the suggestions of General de Gaulle, who had begun to cool on direct relations between the French and the Israeli military establishments, the sale was consummated directly with the manufacturer. The Mirage, originally designed to carry Matra air-to-air missiles only, was modified to incorporate two 30mm cannon, cheaper and more effective, according to Israeli fighter pilots, than the missiles. The 72 Mirages, delivered from 1963 onward, were an adequate counter to the Mig-21s and SU-7s supplied to Egypt, but they also were expensive, troublesome to maintain, and even when modified carried only a very small bomb load. In 1964, therefore, the IAF placed orders for 50 Mirage Vs, a simplified ground-attack version of the Mirage III, with twice the ordnance-carrying capacity and much increased range. Although paid for, these were never delivered. When war broke out in 1967, France imposed an arms embargo on Israel, though French military and defence officials, ashamed at what they regarded as the craven betrayal of an ally, managed to 'loan' 20 Mystère IIIs to the IAF and also circumvented the embargo to send spare parts and some other materiel to the IAF.[13]

By the time of the abrupt French reversal, there had been a change in the position of the United States. As early as 1961 President Kennedy had indicated willingness to sell a substantial quantity of Hawk ground-to-air missiles. Although this was a major political breakthrough, the first time that the United States had been prepared to provide Israel with a major weapons system, Weizman, holding to the doctrine that the IAF should act offensively, opposed the acquisition of large numbers of these expensive weapons. Both Ben Gurion and Zur were prepared to entrust air defence to these missiles, but on Weizman's insistence acquisition was restricted to one battalion, deployed near Haifa, Tel Aviv, and Beersheba. In the event, deliveries were slower than expected and few batteries were operational by June 1967.

Realizing that relations with France were becoming precarious, the Israeli government sought to buy aircraft in the United States. In late 1965, Prime Minister Levi Eshkol, who also held the defence portfolio, arranged for an Israeli delegation to visit America and convince a sceptical Pentagon of Israel's need. The new Phantom F-4 was considered the most desirable weapon, but realizing that chances to acquire it were small, Weizman, designated to head the mission, decided to concentrate on buying 60 A-4 Skyhawks, relatively inexpensive though powerful ground-attack planes. Before his departure, Weizman was carefully briefed by Eshkol how to make his case, neither showing weakness nor looking too strong. The correct stance, Eshkol told him, was to present himself as *'Shimshon der nebbichdicker'*, a Yiddish phrase inadequately translated as 'a pitiful Samson'. Weizman found the Americans courteous, though he also felt exposed to a curiosity that was not entirely friendly. Finally, he wrote in his memoirs, that while 'willing to undress as far as my bellybutton', he would not take off his pants.[14] In the end, an agreement on the sale of Skyhawks was reached but none arrived before 1967.

During the June 1967 war the jet combat force of the IAF was entirely composed of French machines. By contrast the first IAF helicopter squadron, becoming operational in 1960, consisted of 24 medium-lift S-58 helicopters, American-built but furnished secondhand by West Germany. In addition the IAF had four Super Frelon and four light Alouette helicopters of French origin. Although some of these machines were equipped with SS-10 and 11 anti-tank missiles, Israel then had no helicopter combat doctrine. The main tasks for helicopters were troop lift, casualty evacuation, and most important, rescuing pilots downed in hostile territory. The reason why Israel's air commanders considered this all important was both a reflection of the old Palmach tradition never to abandon a man to the enemy, coupled with the realization that pilots would be even more daring if convinced that everything possible would be done to bring them back.

Both Weizman and his hand-picked successor, Colonel Mordechai (Motti) Hod, believed that the human factor ultimately was more important than technology. With probably the lowest people-to-plane ratio in the world, 25 to 1, counting all base personnel, the IAF had achieved an extremely high combat-readiness rate and a fast turn-about capability, but it was the excellence of its pilots that ultimately counted. Future IAF pilots were selected from young men who had just completed their secondary education. All pilot candidates were volunteers who signed up for five and a half years of active duty. All candidates were exhaustively screened and then had to go through the regular paratrooper course, the object being to provide them with survival and evasion skills and also to ensure that no money was wasted flight training unsuitable men. Only in their second year did the candidates begin actual flight training, with the emphasis entirely on flying skill. No attempt was made to teach academic subjects; the IAF ran a flying school rather than an air academy. Performance during flight training determined ultimate assignments. Only the best became fighter pilots, a small elite, with a surprising number from collective settlements, living in closely knit communities on air bases and maintaining a high degree of operational readiness.

Weizman continued Tolkowsky's policies, seeking greater status and privileges for the air force. In 1959, when the air staff moved from Ramleh to the GHQ compound outside Tel Aviv, he insisted on maintaining a separate enclosure within the compound, guarded by his own air police. The issue, and it became a point of controversy, was not important by itself, but Weizman lost no opportunity to assert the IAF's new role as the main strike force of the Army. Meanwhile, however, he had hoped to become chief of staff, but had to settle for the post of head of the General Staff Branch. Even so, it was a step forward, being the first time an airman had held this position.[15]

From War to War

While the IDF increased its size and striking power, the Arabs, liberally supplied both by the Soviet Union and the West, actually set the pace of the Middle East arms race. Egypt got the IL-28 bomber in 1955; it was over two years later that France provided Israel with a squadron of comparable Vautour bombers. Again, Egypt received Mig-17s in 1957; Israel obtained the equivalent Super Mystères in 1959 and only after the Egyptians deployed the Mig-21 did Israel order the Mirage. Egypt received ground-to-air missiles, the SA-2, in 1960; Israel did not receive the Hawk missile for more than two years after that. The list could be continued, but the main point was that Israel's armament always was one step behind that of its most powerful potential adversary. Moreover, where a strained Israeli economy had to pay for most of the equipment at the going market rate, between 1955 and 1967 Egypt received an estimated $1 billion worth of Soviet arms at bargain prices and in exchange for cotton and with cheap-money credits.

In 1956, the Soviet Union had concluded an arms agreement with Syria and, following the revolution of 1958, it concluded similar arrangements with Iraq.

Jordan remained the only Arab country armed by the West. In 1967 the Arab arms inventory exceeded the Israeli several times over. Egypt alone had 1,200 tanks; Syria 450, and Jordan about 200. In the air, Egypt had over 500 combat planes, Syria about 100, and Jordan 36. Moreover, these 'confrontation' states could count on support and resupply from other Arab states. Iraq would provide armoured forces and several Mig squadrons; Algeria sent a brigade and three squadrons of Migs, while Saudi Arabia and Kuweit each dispatched a brigade. Altogether the combined order of battle of Egypt, Jordan, Syria, and Iraq, Israel's most likely opponents, was over 500,000 men, 2,000 plus tanks and nearly 1,000 combat aircraft.[16]

There also had been qualitative changes in the equipment delivered by the Soviet Union to its Arab clients. Before the 1956 war the Soviets had supplied World War II era tanks, T–34s, in large numbers. After 1963, however, they began to provide modern T–54/55s, faster and with a longer cruising range than the British Centurions and the American M–48s acquired by the Israelis, and much superior to the upgraded obsolete Shermans still in Israel's armoured brigades. The ultimate value of the great mass of Arab armour would be determined, of course, by their ability to use them, together with their large artillery and their new aircraft, to neutralize and destroy Israel's tank–aircraft combination. To this end the Soviet Union provided its newest interceptors, the Mig–21. There were over 200 of them, a number which substantially exceeded the 72 Mirage IIIs and 20 Super Mystères in Israeli hands. Together with the 27 SAM–2 sites deployed in Egypt, these were to protect major air fields and deny Israel control of the air space over any future combat area. Soviet supply of such large numbers of advanced weapons permitted the Arabs to contemplate another conflict with Israel with considerable confidence.

Newly acquired strength and systematic propaganda calling for Israel's eradication led to a series of confrontations culminating in the Six Day War. The surrounding Arab states never wavered from their claim that they were in a state of war with Israel. They continued their economic warfare and the Suez Canal remained closed to all Israeli shipping. However, the 3,400-man United Nations Emergency Force camped in the Sinai desert, in the Gaza Strip, and at Sharm el Sheik kept passage to Eilat open and at the same time prevented guerrilla raids. Moreover, for all his belligerent rhetoric, Nasser was facing severe economic problems and after 1963 became involved in supporting a left-wing faction in a civil war in Yemen that within a short time absorbed more than 50,000 of his best troops.

Things, however, did not remain quiet along the Syrian and Jordanian armistice lines. From 1961 on, Syria actively supported guerrilla groups staging their raids into Israel from Jordanian-held territory and with the rise of the Ba'ath party to power in 1963, and the military take-over of the government in 1966, the Syrian border became the scene of most bitter friction between Israel and the Arabs. Syrian gunners resumed their shelling and mortaring of villages below the Golan Heights while a new guerrilla group, *El Fatah*, founded in 1959, made its first major appearance in 1965. That year Israel counted 35 raids, the following year there were 41, and during the first four months of 1967 there were 37 raids and other incidents. Israeli complaints to the Security Council were futile. Tension escalated when in February 1966, Nasser, frustrated in his Yemen war and with economic difficulties at home, made a bitter speech lashing out at Israel and the United States.

Responding to the provocations, Israel took a tough line. In July 1966, Israeli guns and planes stopped a Syrian attempt to divert the waters of the Jordan and on 13 November the IDF staged a major daylight raid against a guerrilla base at Samu in Jordanian-held territory. The raid was deliberately planned on a large scale, employing light armour, mechanized infantry, and aircraft circling overhead. Chief of Staff Rabin hoped that this massive deployment would overawe the guerrillas and allow the operation to be bloodless. Unfortunately a motorized battalion of Jordanian regulars rushing to the aid of the guerrillas ran into the Israeli road block and lost 18 men. World public opinion as well as the Security Council condemned Israel, but in view of the council's failure to condemn the Syrians she was not impressed. An even more serious incident exploded on 7 April 1967 when Israeli artillery answered Syrian fire against a tractor ploughing land in the demilitarized zone south of the Golan. When Syrian Migs appeared, Israeli fighters scrambled and in the ensuing battle all six Syrian planes were shot down. During these two incidents the Egyptians had not moved to support their allies and Nasser was criticized by the Syrians for hiding behind the UN force and he now moved to bolster his shaken claim to leadership of the divided Arab world.

In late April the Russians informed him that they had discovered signs of an imminent major Israeli operation against Syria and in early May the Syrians sent Nasser an alarming report of Israeli troop concentrations on their border. The Israeli government offered to allow the Soviet ambassador to conduct an on-the-spot inspection, but this was refused. The Soviets were apparently determined to provoke Nasser into rash action, though possibly merely a show of brinksmanship. On 14 May, Nasser sent armoured forces into the Sinai, doubling Egyptian strength there to 95,000 men with some 900 tanks. On 16 May, Cairo's official radio, the *Voice of the Arabs*, proclaimed that 'Egypt is now prepared for total war that will put an end to Israel'. The same day, Nasser demanded the withdrawal of all United Nations troops and to everybody's surprise, Secretary General U Thant meekly complied, though cautioning Nasser against rash moves. But by now events seemed to move beyond Nasser's control. In the streets mobs demonstrated for war and the extermination of Israel. Going one step further, and reaching the point of no return, Nasser on 22 May declared the Straits of Tiran closed to all Israeli shipping, a blockade which by historic precedent constituted an act of war. Jordan and Syria, too, were mobilizing and once again the Israeli government was faced with the agonizing choice of striking first or passively awaiting a potential fatal attack by vastly superior forces.

Israel mobilized its reserve forces in several waves, beginning with the call up of two brigades and key personnel for several more on 17 May. For the moment, however, Eshkol was determined to resolve the crisis by diplomatic means. In any case, the Egyptian concentration in the Sinai alone would not have been enough for the cabinet, representing a torn and feuding Labour Party coalition, to go to war and from his Negev retreat, Ben Gurion, the much respected elder statesman, warned against Israel going it alone. The situation changed with the blockade of the Straits of Tiran. Freedom of the straits had been guaranteed by various international undertakings, but when Israel appealed to the powers she found the pledges worthless, though all advised Israel not to act on her own. France, Britain, and the United States were not willing to do anything more. As President Johnson, deeply preoccupied by Vietnam, told Foreign Minister Abba Eban: 'You are by yourselves.'

To Israel's commanders the odds in a war looked far from hopeless, but as the Arab forces deployed the public mood in Israel became apprehensive. The nation had experienced a long succession of broken promises and now its ally, France, and even the United States had abandoned them. Only the IDF remained as the last and best hope. Gradually more men and women were called up, though the last reservists were not called until 5 June. The long wait made Eshkol appear weak and indecisive, though the delay gave the Army time to ready its equipment and do final rehearsals. In 1956, Dayan had been incensed at the poor maintenance and in 1973 again there would be vehicles and equipment in poor shape. In 1967, however, the reserve Army had three weeks to complete mobilization. 'Never', Rabin commented ten years later, 'had Israel's Army been more ready and more prepared for war.'[17]

This was true, though it did little to help the public's mood. Eshkol's policy reminded many of the discredited diaspora approach of calling for help and it had failed. Alarm deepened when King Hussein of Jordan, long Nasser's enemy, openly joined the alliance against Israel and on 30 May placed his forces under Egyptian command. On 1 June, Ahmed Shukeiry, the head of the Palestine Liberation Organization, *El Fatah*'s political branch, proclaimed that those native-born Jews who might survive the coming war would be allowed to remain in the country, but, he added, 'it is my impression that few of them will survive.'

At this point popular pressure, including mounting discontent in the Army, representing in a very real sense an important sector of the electorate, forced a reluctant Eshkol to form a government of national unity, including Menahem Begin, and to relinquish the Ministry of Defence to Dayan, hero of the 1956 victory.[18] Several weeks before, the retired Dayan had requested and received authorization to review military plans and tour troop concentrations. On assuming the defence portfolio he decided that the IDF would execute the larger of the two operational plans prepared. Instead of merely seizing the Gaza Strip and the Rafah approaches and holding them as bargaining counters for an Egyptian withdrawal and the opening of the Straits of Tiran, he insisted that the main objective was the destruction of the Egyptian Army in the Sinai. At the same time, Dayan took a cautious stand towards the other Arab states. Against Syria he was prepared to stand on the defensive and he hoped that Jordan would stay out of the war. Even so, he made certain last-minute preparations in case of a Jordanian move, including stationing the 10th Armoured (Harel) Brigade, a Sherman-equipped reserve formation, at the foot of the Jerusalem corridor.

Further delay, however, was judged to be dangerous. It was not so much a question of whether Israel could afford to remain mobilized longer; during the War of Independence a much weaker state had sustained mobilization and hostilities for over a year. The real question was that with every day the enemy became more formidable as Iraqi, Saudi, Moroccan, and other Arab contingents arrived. On 4 June, Dayan put the issue to an emergency session of the cabinet. He requested authority for the Army to decide the timing, dimension, and method of countering the Arab armies, now deploying in an offensive posture. Of 18 ministers present all but two agreed. Dayan called Rabin and informed him that the revised operational plan should be implemented the next day with zero hour set at 7.45 in the morning.[19]

6

The Six Day War: 1967

'And he waged war against his enemies all around.'
1 Samuel 14: 47

In June 1967, for the third time in two decades, the Israeli Army went to war against an enemy stronger in numbers and weapons. Six amazing days later the campaign ended. In the south the victorious IDF had reached the banks of the Suez Canal; in the east, Jerusalem had been reunited and the Jordanian bulge eliminated. In the north, the Golan Heights had been stormed and Israeli forces were at the gates of Damascus. They had won not because the Arabs fought badly – Egyptians, Syrians, and Jordanians fought well enough – but because the Israelis fought better and showed that outdated equipment in determined and skilled hands could be superior to newer models. By any standard, the victory was a remarkable achievement.

Though victory had been clear cut, peace remained elusive and there was but little celebrating the discomfiture of the enemy. The most fervent outpouring of sentiment came at the Western Wall, the last remnant of the ancient Temple, Judaism's holiest place, to which the Jordanians had barred access since they had seized Jerusalem's Old City in 1948. At the Wall, Chief Army Rabbi Goren blew his *shofar*, steel-helmeted paratroopers, non-observant for the most part, reverently touched the weathered stones and Moshe Dayan wrote out a prayer and placed it in a crack. It read: 'May peace be upon all Israel.'

The Air War

The foundation of Israel's victory was laid by the IAF, which during a few hours on 5 June 1967 destroyed the air potential of its enemies. There never had been any doubt in the minds of the Israeli air staff that their major function would be a pre-emptive strike. 'For over five years', Weizman wrote, 'I had been talking of this operation, explaining it, hatching it, dreaming of it.' His successor, Brigadier-General Hod had brought the plans up to date, though when war came, the IAF was in a transition period. Orders had been placed for 50 Mirage Vs and 60 A-4 Skyhawks, planes with much greater ordnance-carrying capacity than the machines in the actual inventory. Had they been available, the first blow would have been even heavier. Even so, the IAF gained an astonishing and probably decisive success, based on precise timing, hard training, accurate shooting, and excellent intelligence, including a remarkable psychological assessment of the enemy.

The capacity of the Israelis to get the most out of their men and planes took their adversaries by surprise. When at 7.10 in the morning Hod gave orders for the first sections to taxi down the runways, the IAF disposed of only 196 operational strike planes, about half the number commonly estimated. By 7.30 the force was airborne and shortly before 8.00, flying low and from the north to avoid radar detection, it hit nine major Egyptian bases, four in the Sinai, three near the Suez Canal, and two in the Cairo area. The attacks were timed to give each pilot three passes at his allocated target then he returned to base, refuelled and rearmed and returned to the attack. Operating in sections of four, and arriving over the target at intervals of less than 10 minutes, the strike continued for nearly three hours. All targets were hit from as low as possible to avoid misses and detect decoys. Accuracy was so remarkable that foreign commentators looked for a secret weapon, some kind of air-to-ground homing missile. It did not exist. Special rocket-assisted 'Dibber' bombs were used to break up concrete runways, but the main damage was done by close cannon and machine-gun fire, delivered at the range of about 100 yards. During the initial strike surprise was achieved everywhere; planes were caught on the ground and within minutes were burning and exploding. In accordance with instructions, Israeli pilots gave first attention to the supersonic fighters, then to bombers, and only then to transport planes. When the first phase of the attack was over, shortly after 10.30, a jubilant Weizman concluded that the war had been won.[1]

During the morning hours there was hostile action from Syria, which had been expected, and also from Jordan, a development Israel had hoped to avoid. The IAF reacted first against Syrian and Iraqi air bases, destroying 52 Syrian and nine Iraqi planes. Jordan, however, was given a chance, though Jordanian artillery had been firing since 8.30 in the morning. After several messages to King Hussein remained without effect and as Jordanian ground forces swung into action, the IDF struck back. By noon her air force had finished with the Egyptian air fields and pounced on Jordan's two main bases, putting 27 Jordanian aircraft out of action by mid-afternoon. Thereafter, the IAF returned to Egypt, hitting its radar installations as well as eight additional bases, including Cairo International and the field at Luxor several hundred miles up the Nile. When the day ended, the IAF had destroyed 286 Egyptian planes, 52 Syrians, 27 Jordanians, 9 Iraqi, and claimed some 30 more probables. Since midday, moreover, first-line fighters had been redirected to ground-support missions, aiding the Fouga Magisters which had carried the load until then. Israeli air losses amounted to 19 planes, proportionately to the number of aircraft and sorties, a higher rate of losses than those suffered in October 1973.

Air supremacy had been achieved by taking some very real risks. Israel gambled on the first strike, committing practically all of its first-line combat aircraft. Only one fighter squadron was retained to provide air cover for the country. If the surprise had failed and if the enemy had managed to intercept the heavily loaded aircraft there might have been serious losses. But gambling on surprise, the habits of the Egyptian air force which called for a stand-down after a dawn alert, and on the superb training and dedication of its pilots and ground staff, the IAF accomplished its mission. Effective command of the air allowed the IDF ground forces freedom of movement, lifted the nagging fear of major air attack from Israel's cities, and allowed the IAF to provide effective ground support, strafing, bombing, and napalming of enemy positions, armour concentrations, and supply lines. The deadly accuracy of the Israeli attack was all the more striking when compared with the haphazard way in which the few Arab planes which succeeded in reaching Israeli airspace dropped their bombs. The Iraqis attacked Natanya, dropping several bombs in the suburbs, but hit no military targets. And in air-to-air combat the story was much the same. During the war the Arabs lost 452 planes, Israel 46. Of these, all but three were lost to ground fire while the IAF downed 42 enemy planes in the air.[2]

The War Against Egypt

Israel lacked sufficient strength for an offensive on all fronts concurrently. The Southern Command, where seven Egyptian divisions and 1,100 plus tanks and self-propelled guns stood poised to attack, was considered the most decisive and received priority in the strategic deployment. Israeli forces adopted a defensive posture against Syria, and because no one expected Jordan to enter the war, or at worse only in a token fashion, the Central Command consisted only of a few reserve brigades and territorial defence units.

Command on this front was entrusted to Brigadier-General Yeshayahu Gavish, who directed three divisional task forces, *ugdot,* as well as several independent combat groups, a mixed infantry–armour brigade facing the Gaza Strip, an armoured brigade in the Kuntilla sector, and the 55th Paratroop Brigade held in reserve. In addition a naval task force and some paratroops were designated to take Sharm el Sheik. As in 1956, geography imposed the main lines of the attack. The three divisional task forces were to operate in the northern part of the Sinai, the 40 miles between Rafah and Abu Ageila and break through the Egyptian front by a combination of frontal assault and envelopment. Once this was accomplished, they were to advance rapidly towards the Canal, supported on their left flank by the independent armour brigade moving through Kuntilla to Nakhl.

The Israelis never published their order of battle for this war and few unit designations or exact figures are available. Collation of available data, however, indicates that the three *ugdot* varied in strength and composition, reflecting the diverse nature of the IDF's equipment and the mission assigned to each force. General Tal's powerful northern task force consisted of two armoured brigades, including the 7th with Centurions and Pattons, a half-track-mounted paratroop brigade supported by a battalion of Pattons under Colonel Raful Eytan, as well as artillery, reconnaissance, supply, service and headquarters element. The central task force, headed by Avraham Yoffe, a 54-year-old reservist, was almost entirely armoured, consisting of two brigades equipped with Centurions, but lacked artillery. Finally, the southern *ugda*, headed by Sharon, was a mixed force. It included one armoured brigade, Shermans as well as Centurions, two paratroop battalions, an infantry brigade, six battalions of artillery, a combat engineer battalion, and the usual divisional service and supply troops.[3]

Pitted against the three Israeli *ugdot* and their small supporting brigades were no less than seven Egyptian divisions deployed in a series of fortified zones laid out according to Soviet doctrine. The first defence line was based on the fortifications of the Rafah–El Arish–Um Katef triangle, with strong forward positions in the Gaza Strip and at Kuntilla junction. The Gaza Strip was defended by the 20th (Palestinian) Division; the Rafah–El Arish positions were assigned to the 7th Infantry Division; the critical Um Katef defence complex was manned by the 2nd Infantry Division. A second line, giving depth to the forward positions, went south from El Arish through the Jebel Libni towards Nakhl, and was held by the 3rd Infantry Division, with its flanks secured by the 6th Infantry Division, spread from Kuntilla to Nakhl. Each of these five divisions had three infantry brigades, and each infantry brigade was supported by a battalion of T-34 tanks or Su-100 self-propelled guns and a battalion of AT-1 SNAPPER anti-tank guided missiles.

It appears that these defensive elements were to engage and hold the Israelis, permitting the two major Egyptian armoured elements, the 4th Armoured Division and the so-called Shazli Force, to counter-attack. The 4th Armoured, pride of the Egyptian Army and equipped with the newest Soviet tanks, was deployed in the Bir Gafgafa area, while Shazli Force – four tank battalions, a

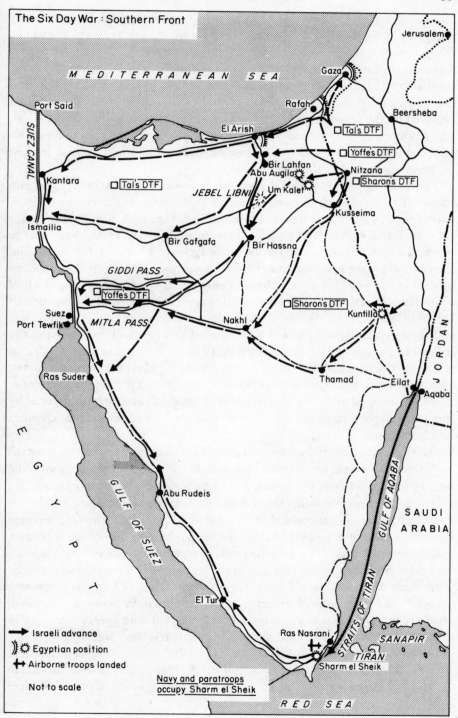

The Six Day War : Southern Front

MEDITERRANEAN SEA

Jerusalem

Gaza

Port Said

Rafah

Beersheba

SUEZ CANAL

El Arish

Tal's DTF

Kantara

Bir Lahfan

Yoffe's DTF

Tal's DTF

Abu Augila

Nitzana

JEBEL LIBNI

Um Kalet

Sharon's DTF

Ismailia

Kusseima

Bir Gafgafa

Bir Hassna

GIDDI PASS

Sharon's DTF

Kuntilla

Yoffe's DTF

Suez
Port Tewfik

MITLA PASS

Nakhl

Eilat

JORDAN

Ras Suder

Thamad

Aqaba

GULF OF AQABA

GULF OF SUEZ

E G Y P T

SAUDI ARABIA

Abu Rudeis

El Tur

STRAITS OF TIRAN

→ Israeli advance

)☼(Egyptian position

✛ Airborne troops landed

Not to scale

Ras Nasrani

SANAPIR

TIRAN

Sharm el Sheik

Navy and paratroops
occupy Sharm el Sheik

RED SEA

motorized infantry brigade, one commando battalion, and three artillery regiments – was stationed between the 3rd and the 6th Infantry Divisions. Altogether the Egyptian forces were, both in manpower and in firepower, superior to the Israelis, but their deployment had been executed among confusion, marches and counter-marches, which had lowered morale and interrupted communications. There existed a wide gap between the situation depicted on the maps of the High Command and that prevailing in the Sinai, and it was an open question whether they could counter Israeli moves with adequate speed. As it turned out, most Egyptian units would remain in their hedge-hogs, repeating the 1956 mistakes.

The basic Israeli operational plan called for initial breakthroughs in two sectors. Tal was to crash through the Rafah approaches, outflank and isolate the Gaza Strip, and continue west to El Arish. Simultaneously Sharon was to take the Um Katef defensive complex. In the second phase, Yoffe's *ugda* was to make its way over ground impassable by the Egyptians north of Abu Ageila and then swing into the north-central Sinai to engage the major Egyptian armoured formations. It would be assisted by elements of Tal's *ugda*, which would wheel south from El Arish into the Bir Gafgafa area. During this phase an attempt would be made to seal the Mitla and Giddi passes against an Egyptian retreat and the Egyptian armour would be destroyed in a vast tank battle east of the passes. In the final phase all units would press on to the Canal, while a naval task force and paratroopers would secure Sharm el Sheik, the west coast of the Sinai Peninsula. Finally, the Gaza Strip, already cut off during the first phase, would be mopped up by the independent armour–infantry brigade assisted by infantry detached from the main battle once the Um Katef defence complex had been taken.

Israeli tactics were to be based on principles already enunciated before the 1956 sinai Campaign. Dayan then had ordered that 'the enemy will be given no time to reorganize after the assault and there will be no pause in fighting. We shall organize separate forces for each of the main objectives, and it will be the task of each force to get there in one continuous battle.'[4] In 1956 the separate forces had been of brigade strength, now the larger *ugda* framework was used, but the principles had remained the same. Commanders retained wide latitude in their immediate dispositions and in the exploitation of tactical advantages. The three divisional task forces, Dayan wrote, 'showed superior fighting capacity' and 'professional expertise, close co-operation between armoured, artillery, infantry, and engineering forces', coupled with 'great flexibility in deployment to meet the rapid changes in the battle situation'.[5]

On receipt of the code words *Sadin Adom* (Red Sheet), Gavish attacked at 8.15 in the morning of 5 June. In the north, Tal struck against the Rafah approaches at the junction of the 20th and 7th Divisions. Colonel Shmuel

(Gorodish) Gonen's 7th Armoured broke through the Egyptian lines to the north of Rafah, then swerved through the town towards El Arish, overrunning a series of fortified positions. El Arish fell around midnight and by morning Gonen was some 35 miles west of the town. The 55th Paratroop Brigade, held in reserve for an air drop into El Arish was never needed and could be diverted to fight the Jordanians in Jerusalem. Meanwhile Tal's other armoured brigade, supported by Eytan's paratroopers and tanks, engaged the main Egyptian force in the Rafah perimeter and, after five hours of bitter fighting, enemy resistance caved in. Towards nightfall the second armoured brigade was withdrawn to join the 7th Brigade slated to fall on the 4th Armoured Division in the Bir Gafgafa area. Eytan's force continued fighting in the Gaza Strip, encountering strong resistance from heavily fortified positions that had to be taken and retaken in a day of hard combat. By mid-morning of the next day, Israeli infantry–armour had taken Gaza and now came down to relieve the paratroopers. Tal now regrouped his forces. The two armoured brigades moved south, while a newly formed combat team, mainly reconnaissance elements, was sent to continue along the coastal road towards Kantara. Hastily mounted on captured vehicles, Eytan's paratroopers were sent to join them.

The battle of Rafah, together with Sharon's night conquest of Um Katef, broke the back of the Egyptian forward line and made armoured advances and the destruction of the Egyptian tank forces possible. Even so, after the war critics charged that Tal, overrating the power of his heavy tanks, had not given enough attention to co-operation with his infantry. The charge can only be partially sustained. The 7th Armoured, in fact, was committed to a frontal assault, though in view of the almost continuous belt of fortifications facing him, Tal had very little choice. He also was aware that much depended on the initial victory which would establish the psychological and moral climate and he had instructions from Rabin to achieve a decision at the earliest possible moment, before great power intervention would complicate matters. Moreover, his mechanized infantry, still mounted on obsolete M-3 half-tracks, was unable to keep up with the battlefield pace of his heavy armour, though after the first assault, the 'at all costs' approach was modified to permit outflanking manoeuvres. Finally it may be argued that Tal's decision to attack at a strong point in the Egyptian defences in itself constituted an element of surprise.[6]

By contrast, Sharon fought a model combined-arms team battle, using armour, artillery, motorized infantry, and vertical envelopment against the very large and heavily fortified Egyptian position around Um Katef. Shielding the central crossing point leading to the Giddi and Mitla passes, the position was defended by extensive minefields, barbed wire, tank obstacles, some 70 field guns and 22 SU-100 self-propelled guns. It was manned by a reinforced infantry brigade, supported by 66 medium T-34 tanks. During the night of 5–6

June, Sharon's *ugda* took this stronghold with tanks smashing the outer perimeter, infantry and engineers crossing the ditches, while paratroopers, helicopter-lifted to the rear of the defences, silenced most artillery positions. Then, as dawn broke, the tanks moved forward to fight enemy armour and put down the last resistance, though fighting continued to flare up throughout the remainder of 6 June.

Even before Sharon had mounted his night attack, Yoffe's division had moved through the sand dunes, north of Abu Ageila, considered 'impassable' by the Egyptians and took up positions in the Jebel Libni area with orders to intercept any remnants of the 7th Division and to halt any counter-attack to recover El Arish. By evening of 5 June, Yoffe's Centurions, deployed near Bir Lahfen, were ready to meet any counter-attack.

The fall of the Um Katef position opened the road to the centre of the Sinai. Leaving the continuing mop-up to his infantry, Sharon reassembled his armour and moved south west towards the Nakhl area. Meanwhile the Egyptian High Command had ordered two armoured counter-attacks. The first was to recapture El Arish, but was halted by one of Yoffe's brigades waiting hull-down at Bir Lahfen, while his second brigade, struggling up a track from Abu Ageila, caught it in the flank. The Soviet-built T-54/55s put up a stout battle for several hours, when the intervention of the IAF decided the issue. The IAF also aborted the second counter-attack which never even got going and stalled west of Abu Ageila. For all practical purposes, two Egyptian armoured brigades were lost. In Cairo, the High Command, losing confidence, now ordered all commanders to extricate their forces as best they could, even though the 6th Division, the 3rd Division, and Shazli Force also, had not yet entered combat.

On the morning of 6 June also, Tal's armoured brigade, coming down from El Arish made contact with Yoffe in the Jebel Libni area. The remaining Egyptian forces were still very substantial; they were disrupted and could be trapped if the roads leading to the Suez Canal through the Mitla Pass and Bir Gafgafa were blocked. The Israeli advance continued throughout the afternoon, encountering only sporadic resistance on the way to Mitla, which was reached on the evening of 7 June by Yoffe's leading brigade. Fighting continued everywhere. The heaviest battles that day – a confusing series of armoured clashes – developed in the Bir Gafgafa area, where Tal's armour battled elements of the 4th Armoured Division. By the end of the third day of fighting, Tal's forces had badly mauled the Egyptian armour, not without taking heavy losses when an Egyptian counter-attack surprised a battalion of light AMX-13s. At the Mitla, however, though only a few tanks of the brigade remained operational, the road to Suez was barred and hundreds of tanks, trucks, and other vehicles tried to make their way through the narrow defile, facing the fire of the Centurions and the pounding by the IAF. It was an appalling carnage, with burnt-out vehicles blocking the road and others piling up in the debris. By this time Israeli troops had fought for almost 60 hours non-stop, but the elation of victory compensated for physical fatigue. That day also, without encountering any resistance, a small Israeli force had been landed at Sharm el Sheik.

The next day, 8 June, Egyptian resistance in the Sinai collapsed and retreat turned into rout. Sharon's armour reached Nakhl, where it clashed with the armoured elements of the 6th Division, almost totally destroying them, while at the Mitla Yoffe's exhausted men finally were relieved when his second brigade arrived. On the coastal road, Tal's reconnaissance elements were separated from the Suez Canal only by a stretch of marshy terrain, while major elements took Kantara and a vast stretch of the east bank. During the night, Yoffe's second brigade also moved a battalion combat team across the Mitla Pass and arrived opposite the town of Suez. In the interior of the Sinai thousands of Egyptian soldiers had abandoned their vehicles and weapons and roamed the desert with only one thought – to escape west. The Israelis made little effort to take prisoners and allowed them to cross the canal as best they could. Thousands, however, perished in the desert. They left behind 800 tanks and self-propelled guns, many destroyed or damaged, but scores in running order, and also vast quantities of other war materiel, including an operational SA-2 missile battery.

The War Against Jordan

Although King Hussein had become entangled in warlike commitments to Egypt, there were hopes that he would limit his participation to rhetoric, or military demonstrations. Israel was eager to avoid hostilities with Jordan. As Dayan explained, war with Jordan posed an immediate threat to major military installations and civilian population centres that would have to be countered swiftly, and all available first-line troops already were committed to the Egyptian front. For that matter, Dayan also favoured restraint against Syria. He realized that conflict with Syria was unavoidable, but since, as he put it, 'there was no objective in Syria vital our interests', he gave orders to adopt a defensive posture only.[7] On the morning of 5 June, therefore, the Israeli government sent several messages to King Hussein urging him to abstain from war.

It was a futile hope. With his army under the command of an Egyptian general and with two Egyptian commando battalions airlifted into the Latrun area on the eve of the war, Hussein no longer had much of an option. Moreover, with *jihad*, the holy war against the infidel proclaimed from Cairo, and Syria,

Iraq, Kuweit, Algeria, Yemen, Morocco, and the Sudan entering the conflict, Hussein could not afford to stand aside. Some states, to be sure, were more cautious than others. Saudi Arabia moved troops to the Jordan frontier, but remained in its own territory. And in Lebanon, despite presidential orders, the chief of staff prudently refused to commit his forces. The only Lebanese action was the appearance of two fighters over the northern Galilee, with one plane promptly shot down. Hussein, however, decided to enter the war on a large scale. Perhaps he was persuaded by a telephone conversation with Nasser, who assured him that scores of Israeli planes had been downed and that Egypt was about to take the offensive to crush the Israelis. Around 11 in the morning, Jordanian planes attempted to bomb Israeli targets and shortly before noon, Jordanian batteries opened fire in Jerusalem. This soon spread along the entire length of the armistice line. Shells fell on the outskirts of Tel Aviv; heavy 155mm barrages were directed at IAF bases near Lod and at Ramat David, and Jordanian infantry occupied the UN Headquarters at the former government house in Jerusalem, a vantage point overlooking the entire city.

Israeli GHQ was forced to improvise a swift and decisive response. By midday, the IAF was directed to neutralize the small Jordanian air force and plans were made to counter the Jordanian threat by a rapid offensive. In view of the paucity of forces available, this was a gamble, but it had to be taken. The Jordanians deployed seven infantry brigades in well-entrenched lines, with two Patton-equipped armoured brigades in reserve near the Jordan Valley, and an Iraqi division reported moving up in support. Against this array, Major-General Uzi Narkiss, heading Central Command, had only a few units. In Jerusalem, where only yards separated Jewish and Arab positions, there was Colonel Eliezer Amitai's 16th Infantry Brigade, a reserve unit reinforced with five territorial defence battalions and one company of 18 Sherman M-51 tanks. Dug in along the Jerusalem corridor and along the armistice line were territorial defence formations, NAHAL settlements, and units of the Border Police. The only readily available mobile force was the 10th (Harel) Armoured Brigade – in fact no more than a mechanized unit with only a single tank battalion, four companies of Shermans and one of Centurions, commanded by Colonel Uri Ben Ari. Even so, GHQ decided that only an immediate counter-attack could stabilize the situation. To provide additional striking power, it was decided to send the 55th Paratroop Brigade, Colonel Mordechai (Motta) Gur commanding, held in reserve for an air drop on El Arish, to Jerusalem. In addition, one reserve infantry brigade, then assembling in Tel Aviv, was directed against the Latrun salient and General David Eleazar of the Northern Command was directed to detach two armoured brigades and attack the Jordanian bulge from the north. Altogether, counting static territorial defence units, the IDF deployed two armoured, one mechanized, and the equivalent of eight infantry brigades against Jordan.

Though the campaign was hastily improvised, its execution revealed the very high standards of tactical flexibility attained by the IDF. From a strictly military point the advance of the two-brigade armoured *ugda* commanded by Brigadier-General Peled was decisive, but the focus of the struggle, at least emotionally and politically, was in Jerusalem. Except for the static defence units already deployed along the armistice line, the mobile elements and the paratroopers received their new assignments shortly after 1 pm; Gur's paratroop brigade in its entirety was not committed to Jerusalem until three hours later. Meanwhile the 16th Brigade fought a defensive action and managed to prevent Jordanian penetrations into Jewish areas. The position of the small Israeli garrison on Mount Scopus, however, seemed to become critical.

The first penetration of Jordanian territory was made by the left-wing brigade of Peled's two-pronged attack. It crossed into Jordanian territory at around 5, but spent much of the night and the following day battling stiff Jordanian resistance in and around Jenin. Meanwhile his second brigade had taken a round-about approach and, after overcoming some resistance, reached Nablus from the east, a direction that the Jordanians had not expected, on the morning of the third day, 7 June. A third prong of what was in effect a concentric advance into Samaria, the area of the so-called West Bank north of Jerusalem, was provided by Ben Ari's brigade, which moved up from the coastal area to a few miles west of the city, and then turned north to ascend the hills in the direction of Ramallah, reaching the plateau about 7 the next morning, Also during the night a reinforced reserve infantry brigade from Tel Aviv stormed Latrun, defended by a Jordanian garrison stiffened by the Egyptian commandos. During 6 June, these armoured and mechanized forces repeatedly were counter-attacked by Jordanian armour, though heavy air strikes and accurate tank gunnery threw back or halted these attacks, inflicted serious losses, and led to a collapse of Jordanian morale.

During the night of 5–6 June, Gur's paratroopers arrived in Jerusalem and immediately began a frontal attack to relieve the Mount Scopus garrison. Inadequately briefed, lacking detailed maps, and with little artillery support, they cut through barbed wire and made their way across minefields, and stormed successive Jordanian lines in bitter night fighting. It was an unco-ordinated attack led by junior officers, sergeants, and even privates and the struggle for the central Jordanian positions on Ammunition Hill was the toughest action of the entire campaign. Fighting raged from trench to trench, bunker to bunker, until the position finally was secured at about 6 am on 6 June. With daylight the IAF was able to intervene with telling effect, and after regrouping his troops, Gur went on to take the Mount of Olives position, aided by some tanks detached from the 10th Brigade. Simultaneously the Jerusalem Brigade, made some advances and by evening the Old City was virtually surrounded. Even so, the government hesitated. Dayan, always attuned to political speculations, worried about adverse American reaction and permission to seize the Old City was not granted until early on the morning of 7 June.

Fighting for the Old City presented special problems. Air strikes were ruled out by political and religious considerations, while tanks could not penetrate into the narrow streets. Infantry would have to carry the main burden. As in 1948, the massive 30-feet high granite walls surrounding the Old City, defended by riflemen, machine-gunners, and bazooka teams were a formidable obstacle, and time was pressing. At the United Nations, the Soviet Union, beginning to realize the dimensions of the Arab defeat, was beginning to call for an immediate cease-fire, though, for a few hours longer, the Arabs still were not prepared to concede. Shortly before 10 am on 7 June a half-track carrying Gur crushed through the Lion's gate into the Old City, with paratroopers following behind. They encountered only scattered resistance; most of the Jordanian garrison had filtered out during the night. The Temple Mount and the Mosque of Omar were secured and soon thereafter the blue and white flag with the Star of David was hoisted over the Western Wall. For the first time in nearly 1,900 years, the holiest place of the Jews once again was in the control.[8]

That morning Ben Ari's mechanized and armoured forces fanned out towards the Jordan, overtaking the broken remnants of the Jordanian Army making their way across the river. On the other side of the Jordan lay the charred hulks of the Iraqi armour which had been caught by the IAF and bombed to pieces. Although the road to Amman was open, Ben Ari had strict orders not to cross into Jordan and halted his tanks at the Damia and Allenby bridges. Also that day, units of the 16th Brigade occupied Bethlehem, fought a brief skirmish on the outskirts of Hebron, and finally linked up with elements of the Southern Command. The entire West Bank was occupied and the war against Jordan was over.

The War Against Syria

Syria had provoked most of the troubles which finally had led to the war, yet when it came, the Syrian Army ignored Egyptian requests for a second front. During the first day it limited itself to sporadic fire against Jewish settlements and installations and to a few bombing sorties in northern Israel, resulting in the subsequent destruction of her air force by the IAF. That evening the Syrian command apparently abandoned any thought of an offensive and instead took up a defensive deployment.[9]

The Syrian defensive positions were extremely strong and well-sited. They stretched for 20 miles from Kibbutz Tel Dan in the north to Lake Kinneret in the south and on the Syrian side the Golan Heights presented a steep escarpment rising 1,000 feet above the plains below. Along the crest there were three successive, deeply entrenched and concreted infantry lines, liberally provided with anti-tank weapons, while some 270 guns, including long-range 160mm guns, were positioned behind the crest, and some 200 anti-aircraft guns provided a dense shield. The forward positions were manned by three infantry brigades, each supported by a battalion of T-34s or SU-100s, while a five mechanized-infantry and three armoured-brigade 'shock force' was held some miles back. Tactically the position, laid out by Soviet advisers on the 'shield and sword' principle was strong indeed, though weapons and vehicles were poorly maintained and standards reputedly did not please the Russian mentors.

On the second day of the war, 6 June, the Syrians, covering their action by a heavy barrage, made a battalion-strength attack, supported by some 30 T-34s against Tel Dan. The attack promptly was repulsed by the local kibbutz defence units, assisted by an IAF strike. During the next two days, 7–8 June, the Syrians again limited themselves to sporadic, and occasionally heavy, shelling of Jewish settlements, inflicting substantial damage, though no casualties. By this time, the campaign against Jordan was over. Peled's *ugda* had returned to North Command control and the 55th Brigade was being redeployed to this front. There now was heavy political pressure on the Israeli government to seize the opportunity to settle accounts with the Syrians. Primarily for political reasons, above all because of a desire not to antagonize the Soviet Union with whom the Syrians had close ties, the cabinet hesitated. On the morning of 9 June, however, it changed its mind. Fighting in the Sinai had ended; the Russians showed no indication that they were prepared to offer anything but verbal support to the Syrians, and the United Nations was ready to enforce a cease-fire. It seemed important to demonstrate to the Syrians that even their defences, Russian equipment and advisers could not shield them from retaliation. Early on 9 June, Dayan ordered General Eleazar to seize the Golan Plateau, drive off the Syrian tanks, and destroy the guns.[10]

Fighting on the Syrian front lasted only 27 hours. General Eleazar's plan was a bold frontal attack delivered simultaneously against several points in the Syrian line, both to mask his main thrust and to prevent the enemy from concentrating against any one point. For his main effort Eleazar deliberately chose the northern sector, the steepest and most difficult, but also the line of 'least expectations'. Altogether, he disposed of some 20,000 men with 200 tanks, inferior to the Syrians on the ground, though he had the potential of the IAF available. Elements of eight brigades, three armoured, four infantry, and one paratroop were available, though during the crucial initial stage topography and timing permitted only the employment of less than a third.

The main attack in the north was entrusted to the 1st (Golani) Infantry Brigade, supported by two Sherman companies, with the Banias ridge as its objective. Operating on the right flank of the Golani was an armoured brigade, assigned to break through the defences and swing towards Kuneitra, the main administrative and military centre of the Golan. Further south another infantry–armour team, equipped with AMX-13s, was to secure a foothold on the crest, while armour–paratroop elements were to come up south of Lake Kinneret and push towards Kuneitra. The advance was supported by heavy air attacks. The IAF flew more sorties against the fortifications on the narrow Syrian front than against all other fronts combined, losing some 40 aircraft during the first few hours to the concentrated anti-aircraft guns. Many Syrian bunkers withstood bombardment, and in the end napalm had to be used.

Despite maximum air support the attacks proceeded slowly. With gradients of one in eight, tanks had to be preceded by combat engineer bulldozers and advancing in single file presented easy targets. Out of the 35 tanks accompanying the Golani, only two made it up the escarpment, and all of the officers, except for a wounded second lieutenant were killed in this first attack. At nightfall, the attack drew to a halt, but the Israelis had secured a number of footholds on the escarpment and the next day new lodgements were made and new units thrown into the fight. Especially important from the IDF viewpoint was the performance of the Golani, a formation composed mainly of Jews with Oriental backgrounds, many underprivileged and undereducated, who had distinguished themselves in the hand-to-hand fighting and laid to rest any doubts about their combat performance.

That day, 10 June, Syrian morale began to waver and then broke. Officers abandoned their units which fell apart; retreat turned into rout as the Syrians fled towards Damascus, abandoning artillery and armoured vehicles. Kuneitra fell early in the afternoon, and at 6 pm, when the UN sponsored cease-fire went into effect, Israeli spearheads had reached a line some 30 miles from Damascus. Israeli commanders believed that the Syrian capital could be taken within 36 hours. But with Russian threats growing louder, and with United States pressure being felt, Dayan insisted on a pull-back to a line over a dozen miles to the west from its furthest line of advance. This new line, chosen for its defensive potential, they were to hold until October 1973.[11]

The War at Sea

When war erupted, the Israeli Navy was ordered to prevent Egyptian naval operations against the Israeli coast, harass the enemy in his home waters, and provide logistic support for operations in the Sinai. These missions were accomplished though by this time the Egyptian navy was several times larger

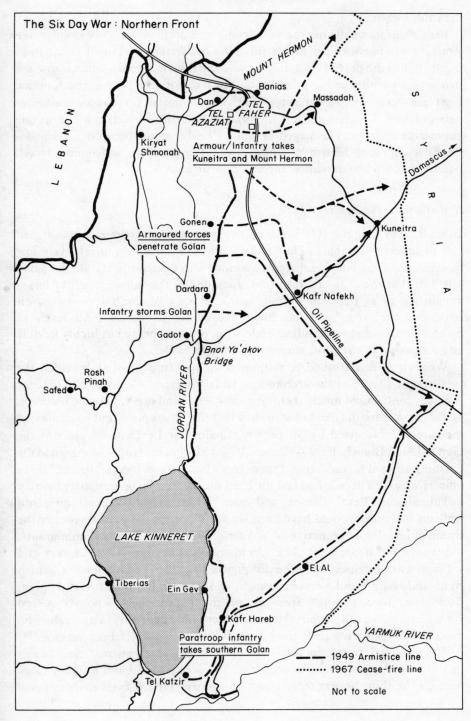

The Six Day War : Northern Front

MOUNT HERMON

Banias

Dan

TEL FAHER

TEL AZAZIAT

Massadah

LEBANON

Kiryat Shmonah

Armour/Infantry takes
Kuneitra and Mount Hermon

DAMASCUS

S Y R I A

Gonen

Kuneitra

Armoured forces
penetrate Golan

Dardara

Kafr Nafekh

Infantry storms Golan

Oil Pipeline

Gadot

Bnot Ya'akov Bridge

JORDAN RIVER

Rosh Pinah

Safed

LAKE KINNERET

Tiberias

Ein Gev

El Al

Kafr Hareb

Paratroop infantry
takes southern Golan

YARMUK RIVER

Tel Katzir

— — — 1949 Armistice line
· · · · · · 1967 Cease-fire line

Not to scale

than the Israeli.

Because of its small size, the naval command decided that only an offensive strategy was likely to be successful. The infiltration of Israeli commando frogmen into the port of Alexandria and a small surface raid against Port Said damaged a number of Egyptian units. More importantly, it put the superior Egyptian Navy on the defensive. The only action at sea was an encounter between Israeli destroyers and Egyptian submarines, which resulted in one submarine apparently damaged or sunk. Finally, motor-torpedo boats based on Eilat captured Sharm el Sheik without opposition, welcoming Israeli paratroopers helicopter-lifted for an airborne assault.

Reflections on the Six Day War

In six days in June the IDF inflicted serious defeats on enemies better armed and in superior numbers. The victory, moreover, was won at relatively low human cost – 679 killed and 2,563 wounded – in contrast to the almost 6,000 killed during the War of Liberation. Included in the toll were officer losses amounting to 23 per cent overall, again evidence of the 'follow me' spirit pervading the Army and one major reason for its success. All levels of command provided outstanding leadership, not only brave but highly flexible and adaptable to the fluid nature of a mobile battle.

Western media, attuned to the notion of supermen, widely heralded the picturesque Dayan as the architect of Israel's victory. Certainly the defence minister contributed much, including confidence and unity. He was, however, not alone. Rabin, the chief of staff, had laid the actual plans and co-ordinated the campaign, assisted by his deputy, Chaim Bar-Lev and his chief of the General Staff Branch, Ezer Weizman. It was Mordechai Hod who designed the crushing air strike. And beyond them was a long row of less publicized young officers who for a decade had laid the basis for the Army's operational planning – Tal, Sharon, Peled, Gonen, and many others. Finally, all planning and brilliant leadership would have been wasted if not for the performance of the common Israeli soldier, native-born *Sabra*, Western and Oriental immigrants, old-timers and newcomers alike. On many occasions individual bravery and willingness to sacrifice made the difference. Brigadier Peter Young, a British commando officer and former commander of the 9th Regiment Arab Legion, paid them high tribute. Speaking of the paratroopers who conquered Jerusalem, but equally applicable to all other units, he wrote: 'The Arabs who can remove them *may* have been born. They have not yet been trained.'[12]

The personal factor, in fact, was more important than materiel. Israeli fighting and support materiel remained non-standardized and in many cases obsolete. Within the armoured *ugdot*, equipment ranged from modern tanks such as the Pattons and the upgunned Centurions to World War II half-tracks, buses and delivery vans. Artillery included up to seven different calibres and four different national origins. Most of the first-line infantry carried automatic and semi-automatic weapons, though some second-line and territorial-defence units still used bolt-action rifles. Air force materiel was up to date, though its pilots relied more on old-fashioned skills, flying and cannon fire, rather than on sophisticated missiles. The only major materiel surprise of the war was the number of Israeli tanks. On the eve of the conflict Israel was credited with about 800 to 900 tanks, an estimate considered accurate because all tanks had to be bought abroad. However, by rebuilding the obsolete Shermans the IDF acquired about 200 additional combat vehicles capable of standing up to the T-54/55s of the Arab armies.

Tactically the IDF managed to use its mobility and flexible command arrangements to gain local superiority at the decisive point, taking risks by denuding certain sectors, and pressing on where exploitation seemed possible. Armoured and mechanized formations played a predominant part in the fighting, for the most part in combined arms teams rather than as pure armoured forces. Far from being a useless encumbrance, infantry repeatedly carried the day – at Um Katef, in Jerusalem, and in the assault on the Golan Heights. In all cases, however, infantry was supported by tanks. Informally, there was a revival of the old distinctions between Palmach, HISH and HIM. The infantry that went forward with the armoured *ugdot* was, except for the Golani, mainly composed of the mechanized battalions that were an organic part of the Armoured Corps, augmented when necessary, by the shock paratroopers, also a separate and distinct branch. For the most part the line infantry brigades and the territorial defence formations were composed of overaged reservists and assigned a static defence role. Even so, when called upon, they revealed a surprisingly active spirit and managed to improvise mobile strike forces.

Some Western observers ascribed much of the Israeli victory to superior intelligence. This was only partly true. There had, in fact, been considerable and ongoing intelligence efforts, including agents, electronic surveillance, and photographic reconnaissance, but there was no single espionage feat that provided the decisive margin. If any single factor had to be singled out, it was the achievement of total air superiority, coupled with excellent tank gunnery. This, at any rate, was the consensus of the Israeli command and in the years after the war the air force and the armoured formations continued to receive the highest priority.

Although her victory was acclaimed in the West, Israel had received no actual support. Arab claims of United States carrier planes' intervention were pure fabrication. France abruptly cancelled arms deliveries and adopted a pro-

Arab stance, while the United States, after persuading Israel to delay action, made a weak effort to persuade Europe's maritime powers to help break the Egyptian blockade by either diplomacy or force. When these efforts met with no response and war broke out, President Johnson offered no assistance, proclaimed a much resented total neutrality, both militarily and diplomatically. Even in the United Nations sessions, where Russia, once Arab defeat became obvious, vociferously denounced Israel's 'fascist-imperialist' aggression and pressed for an immediate cease-fire and withdrawal, the Americans retained a low profile. Perhaps this reflected pre-occupation with Vietnam, oil supplies and concern with the growing Soviet naval presence in the Mediterranean. Nonetheless, contrary to the widely held belief that the United States always was Israel's staunch ally, she continued to follow her traditional policy of trying not to antagonize the Arabs. Even at the height of the fighting, Dayan and the cabinet worried about American reactions – at one point considering halting the advance short of the Suez Canal, at another hesitating before ordering capture of the Old City, calling off any movement into Jordan proper, and delaying action against Syria. For many reasons, American support for Israel always remained limited and circumscribed and never matched the intensity and size of Russian efforts on behalf of her clients.

For the moment, however, all this was overshadowed in the exhilaration and euphoria of victory. As Major-General Rabin proudly stated on the seventh day, 'all this has been done by the IDF alone, with what we have, without anybody or anything.'

7

After the Six Day War: 1967–73

'And the cities which the Philistines had taken from Israel
were restored to Israel from Ekron even unto Gath.'
                                                    1 Samuel 7: 16

Since 1948, Israel had been forced to fight for her very survival. The outcome
of the Six Day War changed her perspectives and raised hopes for a negotiated
settlement. Dayan declared that he was expecting a call from Cairo or Amman
at any moment and there was broad consensus that except for Jerusalem and
minor modifications on the Golan and along the coastal sector, all territories
were to be exchanged in return for peace. And even if the Arabs refused, the
danger of war appeared to have receded into distant future. Sharon, for one,
was sure that his generation had seen its last war. 'The enemy', he stated, 'is not
going to be able to fight for many, many years to come.'

The Israelis were to be disappointed on both counts. On 29 August 1967 an
Arab summit conference in Khartoum decided on a policy of 'no peace with
Israel, no recognition of Israel, no negotiations with Israel'. Israel's destruction remained the ultimate goal, though for the time being the Arab states
decided on a political and military strategy to 'attain immediate limited
military objectives, rather than strive for total aims in the future'. Gradually
the combination of economic warfare, terrorist attacks, and armed confrontation along the Suez Canal would erode Israel's position until, if necessary by
the intervention of the two super powers, she would be forced to give up her
gains and perhaps even collapse under the strain. On 21 October 1967 an
Egyptian *Komar*-class missile boat sank the Israeli destroyer *Eilat* in
international waters off Port Said, an act initiating hostilities that eventually
escalated into the 18-months-long War of Attrition. These developments
changed thinking in Israel. Hopes for an early settlement evaporated and
instead Israel, relying on the assumption that she was in a position of strength,
adopted a policy of waiting the Arabs out. Addressing the graduating class of

the Command and Staff College in 1969, Dayan said that there was no answer to the question 'and what will be the end?' This question, asked by Jews for thousands of years, could be answered only by continued readiness to endure and if necessary to fight. 'We must prepare ourselves, morally and physically', Dayan declared, 'to endure a protracted struggle.'[1]

The New Geostrategic Position

After the Six Day War Israel's strategic concepts changed. The new lines held by the IDF, resting on the Suez Canal, the Golan Heights, and the Jordan were shorter and much more defensible than the long and vulnerable pre-war boundaries. In addition, they provided Israel with strategic depth and appeared to permit abandoning the principle of the 'first strike'. Believing that time was on her side, Israel adopted a posture of 'compellance', holding on to the conquered territories and improving her military capabilities in the expectation that the Arabs would not dare to attack and that if they did, they would suffer heavy losses and strengthen her bargaining position. Maintaining this posture was made easier by the considerable expansion of Israel's economy and by a new, though by no means untroubled, relationship with the United States.[2]

Whether this strategy was the best possible has been debated both inside and outside of Israel and, rather ominously, it was not shared by Israel's former close ally – France. Although, except for the 50 Mirage Vs, all French equipment on order was delivered, French policy after 1967 tilted clearly towards the Arabs and in 1968, France imposed a total arms embargo against Israel. The reasons for this shift were coldly calculated. France saw the eastern Mediterranean coming increasingly under Soviet influence. The United States, already engaged in a major war in South-East Asia, could do little to boost its strength in the area; in fact, its 6th Fleet was weakened to provide units for service in the Pacific. With the prospects of its oil supplies falling under Soviet influence and its southern flank turned by a Soviet fleet, coupled with fears of alienating millions of Moslems to the south, France decided to sever its special relationship with Israel and instead began to court the Arabs, offering arms, technical assistance, and diplomatic support.

United States policy-makers, on the other hand, regarded the situation from almost the opposite direction. For a few short years after 1967, Israel assumed a new role in American calculations, serving to check forces detrimental to American Middle-East interests. A military victory for the radical Arabs, in particular for Nasser, not only would have crippled or destroyed Israel, but also would have endangered the oil-rich countries and eliminated the remaining American positions. In that event the United States would have faced the dilemma of either having to take direct action at a time when the Vietnam War was sapping its national will and absorbing a major part of its military resources, or resign itself to the loss of the Middle East with incalculable consequences for its global position. As it was, Israel's swift victory, achieved without the involvement of American forces, removed these dangers. It weakened Nasser's position and Soviet power, and protected the Saudis with whom Nasser still was engaged in a shooting war in the Yemen. The United States now decided to use Israel's victory to promote its own interests, roll back Soviet advances, and strengthen its friends – Israel as well as the conservative Arab states.

From the outset there were contradictions in this policy. The so-called moderate conservative Arab states, led by Saudi Arabia, were no less hostile to Israel than the most rabid Nasserite, though perhaps an exception must be made for Jordan. Moreover, the rivalry of the two super powers in the area produced intense diplomatic manoeuvring and fluctuations in US policy which sometimes clashed with that of Israel. Still, for the first time, the IDF became the recipient of American arms on a fairly large scale, though it has to be noted that the supply never was entirely assured and with the United States supporting both Israel and the conservative Arabs, substantial deliveries also reached Jordan and Saudi Arabia, while on occasion supplies, especially aircraft, were withheld from Israel in order to pressure her into making concessions deemed desirable by the Americans. In balance, nonetheless, the IDF gained immensely from American support and by 1973 it was largely equipped with American rather than French weaponry, supplemented by the increasingly sophisticated products of a growing domestic arms industry.

Israel's New Society and the Army

After 1967, Israel became less and less the austere utopia envisaged by the early pioneers. There was an upsurge in many fields of civilian life. Industrial development and building boomed; investments, educational facilities and social services grew. Some became rich, for many others there now were growing numbers of managerial, professional, and academic positions that created a substantial bourgeoisie adopting many of the values of an affluent Western consumer society. Although the ruling Labour coalition tried to maintain a comprehensive welfare state, these developments made social stratification more pronounced and widened the gap between the well-to-do and the poor, many of the latter Israelis of Oriental background. Relieved from the immediate threat of destruction, social pressures relaxed. There even arose a small group of middle-class intellectuals and left-wing doctrinaires, who challenged the level of military spending, the morality of holding on to the conquered territories, and indeed, in some extreme cases, the validity of the entire Zionist undertaking. Always present, these pacifist–utopian elements had been submerged by the events of the past, but once Israel had emerged from mortal peril, they surfaced again, though their political impact remained small. Even so, the apparent divisions within Israeli society caused some observers to fear that they might constitute weaknesses in a future emergency.[3] In the end, such apprehensions were proven unfounded in October 1973, though shortcomings during the mobilization and in the combat readiness of a few units indicated laxity in defence preparations. Ezer Weizman, for one, felt that the Army had adopted a nonchalant attitude mirroring the country's complacency.[4]

In some ways, of course, this reflected the passing of a generation. The much hailed 'generation of '48' had grown up in the shadow of persecution and extermination and a time when each weapon was a treasure to be hoarded and cared for. By contrast, after 1967, young Israelis had little experience of persecution, they were used to a plenitude of weapons, they were self-confident, took the existence of the state for granted, and were ready, to a degree, to imitate their peers in the rest of the Western World. Still, the values of a consumer society affected the IDF adversely. From 1969 on the reports of the State Comptroller General, the highly respected Yitzhak Nebenzahl, repeatedly charged the Army with lower performance standards, faulty equipment maintenance, loose inventory control, and even corruption, including the diversion of heavy equipment captured in the Sinai to private contractors.

The corruption issue unleashed a debate in the press. It seemed a long way from the time when Ben Ari had been removed from command for shielding a subordinate accused of taking a few sacks of sugar not for private profit but to improve scanty rations. The corruption debate raised wider questions about the administration of the Army, the effectiveness of the higher command echelons, and ultimately focused on the performance of Defence Minister Dayan. Critics charged that Dayan, described as a political soldier of 'indecisive character' with only 'mediocre intellectual ability' paid too little attention to management and administration and at the same time stifled independent thinking in the general staff and the high command.[5]

These accusations, and others, were written during the black mood following October 1973, but Dayan did assume a predominant role in the making of national defence policy, conceiving his role much as Ben Gurion had done when he had been minister of defence. Dayan, however, was not in an equally strong position. He shared decision-making first with Prime Minister Eshkol, and after his death in 1968, with Golda Meir, who set up an informal inner circle of political–military advisers, including the veteran Galili, Dayan, and assisted on occasion by Deputy Prime Minister Allon and others.[6] Basically this circle was composed of cautious men, who, in the absence of a tangible Arab peace initiative, were in favour of retaining the occupied territories. However, they remained willing – at least this was their stated position – to give up almost all of the territories, except for Jerusalem, not incorporated in the Jewish state but designated as the 'administered territories', in return for peace. For that matter, even as hostilities continued, this policy was supported by senior officers. As late as 1972, a survey indicated that on this critical question, 57 per cent favoured far-reaching concessions, 52 per cent endorsed self-determination for the Palestinians, another 9 per cent approved it with some reservations, and only 26 per cent were opposed.[7]

IDF Ground Forces: Doctrine and Force Structure

Visiting Israel in the 1960s, Liddell Hart expressed concern that the IDF, like all victorious armies, might develop a complacent attitude and come to rely too much on the force structure and doctrines that had served it well in the immediate past. These feelings were echoed by certain groups within the Army and were blindly repeated after 1973 by many observers. The main thrust of the critics was that too much emphasis had been placed on armour and air power, the winning combination of 1967, and that infantry and artillery, as well as night-fighting tactics had been neglected. Major-General Herzog, who had held various staff positions, claimed that by 1973 the IDF ground forces were neither well balanced nor integrated and lacked an effective combined arms doctrine. Others, however, disagreed. Two well-qualified students of the Army asserted that 'seldom has a victorious army undergone such radical transformation so soon after its men and methods had proved so successful in battle.'[8]

Armour and air power did continue to receive highest priority. The Six Day War had greatly increased confidence in the pre-emptive air strike and in the performance and capabilities of air-supported armoured formations. 'Crew served weapons systems [i.e. tanks] carried the assault', General Tal wrote in an analysis of IDF doctrine, 'and brought victory in every theatre of war.'[9] It was natural therefore that the two chiefs of staff following Rabin, Generals Chaim Bar-Lev (1968–71) and David Eleazar (1971–74) were chosen from the Armoured Corps. There had been some speculation that Weizman would become the next chief of staff, but a few days before the outbreak of war he had been superseded by Bar-Lev as deputy chief of staff, retaining the position as head of the Operations Branch. His passing over was generally attributed to his brusque manner and unbending commitment to his own political and military views.

Bar-Lev and Eleazar shared Tal's faith in the decisive role of the tank and aircraft combination as did Dayan. Therefore, in the years after 1967, as Israel's defence spending increased steadily, armour and air continued to receive the lion's share of the budget. In 1972, for instance, the IAF received 50 per cent, armour 30 per cent, while the remainder of the IDF had to share 20 per cent. However, expenditures were not as lop-sided as might appear. After 1967 Israel's defence budget increased enormously and in the last full year before the 1973 war defence spending approached $4 billion, nearly ten times the money spent in the year before the 1967 war.[10] This enormous effort was made to counter the growing might of the Arab states, drawing on the practically unlimited arsenal of the Soviet Union and supported by the steadily increasing oil revenues of the various Arab governments.

Neither Bar-Lev nor Eleazar, nor for that matter other Israeli generals, ever shared the tendency of some commentators to denigrate Arab martial skills and to exaggerate Israel's power. They remained only too well aware that the victory in 1967 had not turned David into a Goliath able to match the far more populous and wealthy opponents, whose military effort was underwritten by the Soviet Union and bolstered by more modest, if still substantial, arms acquisitions in the West. Both chiefs of staff realized that the Arabs continued to have a military option, which, with their regular forces deployed, they could exercise rapidly and without mobilization. By contrast, Israel could hope to meet a major assault only if it had sufficient time to mobilize its reserves.

In keeping with the posture determined by the inner circle, the chiefs of staff developed a contingency plan. Its key element was the assumption that the Intelligence Branch would provide at least 48 hours' advance warning. At this point general mobilization was to be ordered. The standing forces would deploy in their advance positions and the air force, always near war strength, would be fully combat ready. When the attack actually came at H-hour, the standing forces and the air force would contain enemy advances, while, with mobilization almost completed, armoured formations would counter-attack at H plus 24 hours. With additional reserve units coming into line, the counter-attack would reach its full potential on the third day, penetrate into the enemy's territory and there destroy his forces in large envelopment battles. The 72 hours' time schedule was based on the assumption that the IDF would only have three days to complete its task before outside pressures compelled a cease-fire.[11]

To carry out these operations, by 1973 the IDF was able to deploy some seven armoured divisions as well as tank-support battalions with the infantry brigades. Normally each division consisted of three armoured brigades with two tank battalions each, a reconnaissance battalion, an artillery regiment with 36 155mm self-propelled howitzers, and small supporting elements. Because experience has shown that the jeep- and half-track-equipped reconnaissance units had suffered heavy casualties, and because the Israelis held that these units should be able to fight as well as scout, these lightly protected vehicles were replaced with 25 tanks. All in all, an armoured division fielded about 200 medium tanks. Mechanized infantry, an integral element of the Armoured Corps, was represented by one battalion in each brigade and each brigade also could call on the supporting fire of its own 120mm mortar battalion.

Basically Israeli armoured divisions were tank heavy, a trend reinforced by the battle-proven belief that more heavily armoured, if slower, vehicles actually had greater effective mobility under fire than lighter and theoretically faster vehicles. Neither the obsolete M-3 half-tracks, nor the new light-weight M-113A1 Armoured Personnel Carriers (APCs), received in limited numbers from the United States, combined adequate protection, cross-country mobility, and firepower. And with funds still limited, Armoured Corps commanders – Tal as well as Avraham (Bren) Adan, his successor after 1969 – preferred to acquire tanks. Half-tracks, and APCs, serving both as personnel and weapons carriers, were considered at best as secondary vehicles, and often as superfluous impediments in an armoured battle. If, as in 1973, limited road facilities required the setting of movement priorities, tanks, considered as the primary weapons system, were brought forward first and engaged without support.

Following the 1967 war there were a number of changes in the Israeli armour equipment inventory. First, the reconnaissance AMX-13 light tanks were eliminated as being inadequate both in armour protection and firepower. Secondly, there were attempts to standardize ammunition, fuel types, and spare parts. The standardization of ammunition was solved by the installation of the British L7 105mm gun in all main battle tanks. This was easily accomplished in both the M-48 and Centurion tanks, but was more difficult in the case of the captured T-54/55 vehicles. Standardization of fuel types and spare parts was accomplished for the Pattons and Centurions by converting all engines to diesel, utilizing commercially available engines. The conversions greatly increased range and reliability. In the case of the T-54/55s, however, engine changes would have required an extensive reconfiguration and because these tanks already were diesel-powered and substantial stocks of spare engines and transmissions had been captured, it was decided to utilize the existing power systems. Finally, in 1972, the IDF received 180 M-60A1 tanks, basically late-model Pattons, which, diesel-engined and armed with the L7 105mm gun, were retained as issued.

All in all, it appears that in 1973 the IDF could field some 2,000 modern or modernized medium tanks, including about 900 Centurions, 450 M-48 Pattons, 180 M-60A1, and about 250 captured T-54/55s, redesignated as the

TI-67. In addition about 250 Sherman M-51HVs also saw limited action during the Yom Kippur War. By comparison, at the outbreak of war, Egypt had 1,850 and Syria 1,500 medium tanks, with Jordan another 250. When the second-line Arab states are taken into account – and many were expected to and in fact did contribute units to the fighting – Arab tank potential stood at an impressive total of 6,000 modern medium tanks.

The apparent trend towards an 'all-tank' fighting doctrine was not universally accepted in the IDF and in 1971–72 there was a debate in which critics, citing 1967 experiences, argued the need for integrated combined-arms teams. In fact, the 'all-tank' concept never became official doctrine. During the large manoeuvres held in February 1972 and in January 1973 in the Sinai, Israeli forces utilized a combination of tanks, artillery, combat engineers, and mechanized and airborne infantry to simulate a breakthrough against a fortified line. At the same time, however, armour commanders remained oriented towards the offensive and over-estimated the capabilities of unsupported armour spearheads, relegating their infantry and mortar battalions to mop-up operations. They also discounted the threat posed by rocket-propelled grenades (RPGs) and anti-tank guided missiles (ATGMs). Primitive versions of these weapons had been encountered in 1967 and more sophisticated versions were employed by the Syrians in a number of local clashes during the so-called 'battle days' between October 1972 and January 1973, but it was believed that massive tank formations could penetrate this curtain of fire and deal with the missile teams at short range. The reserve formations especially of the Armoured Corps remained oriented almost exclusively towards reliance on tanks alone and were not trained to use their mechanized infantry and mortars for suppressive fire. For that matter, by 1972 most of the IDF's French-supplied ATGMs had been placed in storage.

Concentration on armour prevented expansion of the infantry, divided as before into the cadre Golani Brigade, perhaps 15 reserve and territorial defence brigades, and two paratroop shock brigades. Small arms, however, had improved. Bolt-action rifles disappeared from all combat units and were replaced by self-loading and automatic weapons. Beginning in 1970, the IDF introduced the multi-purpose Galil assault rifle, a versatile weapon, weighing only 9lb, capable of short bursts as well as sustained fire, and launching a potent and accurate rifle grenade. Introduced first in the IDF special forces, it replaced both the light machine-gun and the 2-inch mortar at platoon level.

These special forces, usually called 'reconnaissance units' should not be confused with the brigade and divisional reconnaissance elements. They were the descendants of Unit 101, recruited from infantry and paratroop volunteers, occasionally augmented by naval commandos, and entrusted with deep penetration and reprisal missions. Semi-secret, without special insignia and uniforms, they performed a number of spectacular feats during the War of Attrition and in the campaign against the guerrillas. They raided deep into Egypt, attacked PLO headquarters in Beirut and in 1976 they rescued the hostages at Entebbe Airport.

The IDF did not really discover the value of artillery until the Six Day War and the heavy artillery exchanges along the Suez Canal during the War of Attrition. In the Israeli Army the artillery included all guns, mortars, and rockets, except for the anti-aircraft guns and missiles which passed under IAF control in 1970 and were manned by air force troops. In 1967 only one-third of all field artillery pieces had been self-propelled, but by 1973 Israeli artillery was organized in regiments, all entirely equipped with self-propelled 155mm guns, complemented by half-track- and APC-mounted 120 and 160mm mortars.

The standard equipment of the field regiments were the American-made M-109 and the Israeli-made L-33 Soltam howitzers. The L-33, mounted on a diesel-engined Sherman chassis, was provided with a long, 33-calibre barrel, semi-automatic loading, and had a range of up to 17 miles. In addition, Soltam, a Haifa-based firm, also produced a heavy 160mm mortar, again mounted on a converted Sherman chassis, designed to move between rounds and capable of providing indirect fire support for armoured units. The smaller 120mm mortars, also domestically produced, served both with armoured and infantry brigades and were mounted on half-tracks.

The IDF also received long-range weapons and these were organized into independent battalions. They consisted of two US systems, the M-107 175mm self-propelled gun with a range of 25 miles and the M-110 203mm self-propelled howitzer firing a 200lb projectile over a 14-mile range. Artillery also was the beneficiary of much captured material, including Russian long-range, towed 122 and 130mm field guns, as well as 240mm truck-mounted Katyusha bombardment rocket-launchers for which Israel manufactured improved rounds. Older guns, including 105mm self-propelled pieces and 155mm towed guns, in the hands of reserve formations assigned to the three area commands, were in the process of being phased out.

The rapid development of artillery posed a serious manpower problem. Better educated and technically trained men were required to handle the more sophisticated weapons, electronic fire control and target-acquisitions systems and the artillery had to compete for qualified recruits against the air force, the navy, as well as armour and the paratroopers. Still, reflecting the rising educational level of the country, enough qualified gunners were found. By 1973 the IDF artillery, though still outnumbered by a 2·5:1 ratio by the Egyptian and Syrian artillery, was able to come into action at short notice and lay down massive and accurate fire on distant targets. To make up for the inferiority in numbers, Israel continued to rely on aircraft to act as 'flying artillery'.

IAF Force Structure: 1967–73

Before the Six Day War many Israeli leaders had been rather sceptical about the claims made by the IAF; after 1967, the IAF became the country's first line of defence and 'many came to see in the IAF an all purpose weapon which could achieve any and all goals.'[12] To be sure, only a handful of air officers asserted that air power by itself could win wars, though nearly everyone believed in the decisive potential of the aircraft–tank combination. More importantly, in the years of limited hostilities before the Yom Kippur War, the combat-ready air force was given the task of holding the Egyptian, Syrian, and Jordanian armies in check. The IAF was to protect Israel against air attack, provide the cover necessary for orderly mobilization, constitute a flexible strategic reserve, and a quick-response instrument. The tendency to use the air force as an all-purpose weapon was reinforced by the concern over casualties, almost always a primary consideration of the IDF high command. High-performance aircraft, it was held, had the capability of striking hard at a great variety of targets, suffering only relatively low casualties. Therefore, despite the steep cost of sophisticated aircraft, the IDF continued to devote much of its budget – over 50 per cent in 1972 – to the IAF.

In order to carry out its assigned mission, the IAF with 9,000 career, 1,000 conscript, and about 10,000 reserve airmen, had to cope with two major and interrelated problems. The first was the problem of maintaining an assured supply of high-performance aircraft; the second was the problem posed by the interjection of increasingly advanced Soviet missiles, anti-aircraft guns, radar, and fighters into the War of Attrition, which after 1970 were manned by Soviet personnel. In turn, this development induced the United States to be more liberal in supplying Israel with planes and sophisticated electronic counter-measures (ECM), though, anxious to keep down the intensity of the fighting and in order to demonstrate its sincerity to the Arabs, deliveries frequently were suspended or reduced as a means of bringing pressure on Israel to make concessions. To retain a certain freedom of action, the Israelis extended the flying life of their Mirage IIICs by retrofitting them with General Electric J-79 engines. The first Israeli Mirage with a J-79 engine was test flown in October 1970. At the same time, the IAI, using components developed in other countries, proceeded with the production of an Israeli-built fighter and by 1973 at least two squadrons of the Kfir C-I fighter, planes based on a much improved Mirage pattern, were operational.

Immediately after the Six Day War, the IAF jet aircraft inventory – 65 Mirage IIICs, 15 Super Mystères, 35 Mystères, 12 Vautours, 30 Ouragans, and about 80 Magisters – was entirely of French origin and about half of this inventory was obsolete and needed replacement. Israel had ordered 50 Mirage

Vs from France and had planned to purchase another 50 as well as 100 Mirage F-1s, a supersonic fighter then being developed for the French air force. With the French turn-about, Israel had to find other supply sources and turned to the United States. A contract for 48 A-4 Skyhawks already had been signed early in 1967 and the purchase of 25 more was arranged later that year. In December 1968, following a sharp escalation of fighting along the Canal and with an increased Soviet presence in Egypt worrying Washington, an agreement for delivery of 50 F-4E Phantoms, potent fighter-bombers with a speed of Mach 2·4 and a range of 1,500 miles, carrying almost seven tons of ordnance was signed and the first planes reached Israel in September 1969. The Phantoms provided Israel with a true multimission aircraft and permitted it to respond to Nasser's declared War of Attrition with deep penetration raids. In turn, this escalated the Soviet response. New SAM-3 missile batteries, radar-directed anti-aircraft guns, advanced warning radar, and Mig-21-J fighters were deployed in Egypt and manned, at least partially, by Russian personnel.

Forced to cease its deep penetration raids, the IAF continued to fight along the Canal and managed to prevent the establishment of a missile screen on this line. Russian pressure, however, continued and on 30 July 1970, Russian Migs engaged IAF planes. Although five Russian planes were shot down, Israel was unable to engage in an armed confrontation with the Soviet Union and in August accepted an American-backed initiative leading to a cease-fire. When the Egyptians promptly broke this agreement by moving their missile installations back to the Suez Canal, the United States first declared that no violation had taken place and then, confronted with clear-cut evidence, pressed Israel not to reopen hostilities and in return compensated it with additional equipment and planes. By 1973, the IAF had nearly doubled its combat strength, up from 300 to 550 first-line planes, including 127 Phantoms and 170 Skyhawks. Combined with the continued edge in turn-about rates and the percentage of on-line machines, the IAF, though outnumbered four to one by the combined Arab air fleets, could deliver a substantially heavier bomb load.

The Soviet-installed air defence system had seriously eroded the Israeli margin of superiority, but after 1970 on a variety of American and locally made ECM systems, coupled with guided stand-off missiles, radar-homing Shrike and 'Smart' Maverick missiles, made suppression of the Egyptian air defences possible. In July 1972, General Hod, the IAF's commanding officer, asserted that the air force had 'cracked' the Egyptian missile screen and restored, even increased, its air superiority.[13] Air strength was backed up by the introduction of a highly effective infrared homing air-to-air missile, the Shafrir II, designed by the Armament Development Authority of the Ministry of Defence, known as Rafael, which became operational in 1969 and was advertised for sale abroad in 1972. Other weapon developments, though by no means as advanced, included the 300-mile Jericho ground-to-ground missile, never openly acknowledged, and the highly accurate Gabriel ship-to-ship missile unveiled in combat during the Yom Kippur War.

To accommodate the expanded IAF, captured Egyptian fields were improved and new bases built in the Sinai. This doubled the IAF's nine major bases, allowed better dispersal and protection of its planes, and together with a radar surveillance installation placed high on the slopes of Mount Hermon in Syria, provided additional warning time for major population centres. As General Hod told an American journalist, this 'means that I can sleep quietly at least 20 minutes of the night'. Overall, despite the ominous thickening of Arab air defences, the IAF remained supremely confident of its ability to maintain mastery of the air in the event of war.

The New Israeli Navy

While Israel's land frontiers with her Arab neighbours actually were shortened as the result of the Six Day War, her sea frontiers increased fivefold. Moreover, while before the war the likelihood of hostile amphibious operations had been slight, the increased Soviet naval presence in the Mediterranean, coupled with a large increase in Egyptian amphibious capabilities, presented a very real threat. In addition, the long coastline presented the possibilities of commando raids, infiltration of sabotage teams, and naval bombardment of the densely populated coastal sector from Haifa to the south of Tel Aviv. Before 1967, the Israeli Navy (IN) has operated two defensive perimeters. Destroyers and small submarines were to intercept and defeat hostile forces before they approached Israel's coastal waters, while patrol and motor-torpedo boats were to constitute an inshore patrol. The forward defence was augmented by naval commandos to attack enemy craft in their home ports.

The mission had been carried out successfully in 1967, but the requirement for more depth in the defensive perimeter had already become apparent and early that year an order for twelve 220-ton displacement, diesel-powered, high-speed missile craft, based on German designs, had been placed with a Cherbourg shipyard. The sinking of the *Eilat* by an Egyptian Styx missile merely emphasized the already perceived need. Seven of the boats ordered were delivered in 1968, though two of them had to be smuggled out. The remaining five boats involved a complicated deception plan, including their sale to a fictitious Scandinavian oil-exploration company. Despite a total French embargo on arms to Israel, the boats were brought out of Cherbourg and arrived in Haifa on New Year's Eve of 1969.

These *Saar*-class boats, were armed with the Israeli-developed and built

Gabriel missile, a supersonic weapon furnished in two different versions, extremely accurate and defying most ECM systems. Its warhead, about 600lb, was capable of sinking a destroyer. In addition, the *Saar* boats were armed with a rapid-fire twin 40mm Bofors gun, and anti-submarine weapons, and equipped with extensive electronic detection and counter-measures gear. These boats constituted the first IN formation built especially for its requirements and delivered a potent punch.

A second and larger version of missile boats were designed and built in Israel by the Israel Shipyards in Haifa. These were the *Reshef*-class missile boats, larger than the *Saar* and also somewhat slower, but still capable of a respectable 32 knots. With a firepower roughly double that of the *Saar* class, six to eight Gabriel missiles, two Oto Melara 76mm automatic gun turrets, anti-submarine weapons, and light 20mm auxiliary guns, the *Reshef* boats were more seaworthy, and had much longer range and endurance. Construction began in 1970 and several were ready for combat in 1973. The second line of the defence perimeter, the inshore patrol, was composed of a small number of torpedo and patrol boats, including some light gun boats manufactured by an IAI subsidiary. Overall, the IN tended to look towards more, if smaller, craft. The old frigates and the remaining destroyers were phased out and there also was a decline in submarine strength. By 1973 there were only two operational T-class submarines, acquired from Britain after substantial modifications in 1967–68. A third T-class submarine, the *Dakar*, was lost with all hands during transit in 1968 and had not been replaced. One obsolete S-class boat was retained for training. The IN had three small coastal defence submarines on order with Vickers, but these were not delivered until after the Yom Kippur War.

Submariners were considered an elite force; all ratings received parachute training and were required to maintain their proficiency. The second IN elite force were the naval commandos, never more than 500, who had repeatedly distinguished themselves. Naval officers were volunteers signing a career contract and, with the navy's new importance, increasing numbers of enlisted personnel also joined the career service. Although the IN received slightly less than 10 per cent of the IDF budget, remaining the smallest branch, its morale was high and its new material well suited to its mission, defined by Rear-Admiral Benyamin Telem, its commander after 1972, as defending Israel's coastline and sea communications by offensive action.[14]

The IDF Campaign Against Guerrillas and Terrorists

The crushing defeat of the Arab armies gave new importance to the Palestinian *fedayeen* guerrilla and terrorist groups. Incapable of launching a conventional assault against Israel and refusing to negotiate peace, the neighbouring Arab states, now referred to as the 'confrontation states', adopted the intermediate strategy of harbouring and encouraging *fedayeen* activities from their territories. Moreover, these groups also received support from the oil-rich countries and from the Communist World with patrons as far away as Cuba and China. In addition, these groups, curiously interwoven, competing and collaborating, were joined by Third World and Western left-wing and anarchist elements, including the Red Army in Japan and the Baader–Meinhoff gang in West Germany. The objective of the *fedayeen*, of which *El Fatah*, the Palestine Liberation Organization (PLO) became the strongest and most widely recognized group, was not merely to recover the Israeli-administered areas acquired in 1967, but the total destruction of the Jewish state. And since they could not hope to achieve what the Arab armies had failed to do, their central thrust was to prevent any movement, however small, towards an Arab–Israeli understanding. If this violence provoked another conflict that the IDF again would win, the guerrillas were not perturbed. Defeat, they reasoned, would bring about the overthrow of the remaining 'reactionary' Arab regimes, especially that of King Hussein in Jordan, and create a 'revolutionary' situation which alone provided a real basis for ultimate victory.

Immediately, the *fedayeen* pinned their hopes on forming an insurgency infrastructure among the one million Arabs living in compact areas in the administered territories – about 400,000 in the Gaza Strip and 600,000 on the West Bank, and their 350,000 compatriots who were Israeli citizens. But analogies with guerrilla wars of national liberation in Algeria or Vietnam just did not hold. Neither the Arabs of Israel nor those of the West Bank chose to become the sea for the guerrilla fish. No mass insurgency base developed and to the surprise and relief of the Israeli authorities the territories remained quiet even during the early dark days of October 1973.

This did not mean, of course, that the Arabs liked the occupation or that there was no support at all for the *fedayeen*, but the Israelis used a unique approach that, at least temporarily, contained resistance in manageable proportions. The basic policy of the military government on the West Bank was to leave the Arabs alone as much as possible and to encourage them to conduct business with the Arabs east of the Jordan. The Israeli military presence kept a deliberately low profile and all civilian elements of the Jordanian administration were kept intact. It became policy to encourage local economic growth and the free movement of persons and goods both across the Jordan and into Israel proper. No political 'collaboration' was asked for or expected from the local mayors and occasional outbreaks of terrorism were countered on a selective basis. Israeli security services penetrated and destroyed hastily formed guerrilla cells and effectively neutralized any large-scale insurgent activity.

Inevitably, the unexpectedly long occupation generated some criticism of troop behaviour, especially in the Gaza Strip, an area without ties to Jordan and populated by destitute Palestinian refugees, where IDF units, untrained in police duties or riot control, alternately were blamed for not halting incidents of inter-Arab bloodshed or, on the other hand, for being too heavy-handed. Some of the complaints were justified and several officers and men were brought to trial. The Gaza Strip remained a serious internal security problem for Israel until 1971, but if the IDF was unable to pacify it entirely, neither were the *fedayeen* able to convert it into a base for attacks on Jewish areas.

Failure to establish themselves within Israeli-administered territories forced the *fedayeen* to revert to their pre-war tactics of striking across the cease-fire lines. And with neither Egypt nor Syria willing to allow these turbulent and ill-disciplined elements total freedom, they established themselves in the weaker of Israel's neighbours in Jordan and in Lebanon, where they set up heavily armed bases and moved around the country in uniformed contingents, challenging and sometimes usurping the functions of the host governments. From late 1967 on they made short forays to harass Jewish settlements near the borders, striking almost exclusively at civilian targets.

The Israeli response was conditioned by the constraints imposed by the political situation. It was clearly understood that the United States, notwithstanding its 'special relationship' with Israel, something that became more doubtful shortly after President Nixon's election in late 1968, would not tolerate a full-scale ground offensive into Jordan, while the Soviet Union shielded Syria and Egypt. However, air attacks, commando raids, and counter-bombardment were permissible, though they too often drew criticism. Just how damaging these restraints could be was illustrated during the Karameh operation, the largest anti-guerrilla action undertaken by the IDF. Since the autumn of 1967, *fedayeen* based in Jordan had committed numerous hostile acts and on 18 March 1968 they blew up a school bus, killing two children and wounding 27 more. Goaded beyond endurance, the IDF struck back three days later. A brigade-size task force, paratroopers and armour, crossed the Jordan and attacked a guerrilla base centred on the village of Karameh, some 20 miles north of Jericho. Although the assault force easily overcame the *fedayeen*, it suffered heavy fire from Jordanian guns on the adjoining hills. The rules of engagement prevented the Israelis from storming the hills and their tank guns could not silence the dug-in artillery. After destroying a large stock of arms, they withdrew at the cost of 29 killed and some 90 wounded, leaving behind several disabled tanks and half-tracks. Guerrilla losses stood at 232 killed and 132 captured.[15]

El Fatah promptly claimed that it had repulsed an Israeli invasion, while

Premier Eshkol warned on 25 March that Israel would consider continued guerrilla activity as a violation of the cease-fire and would persevere in its long-standing reprisal policy. Barely two weeks after Karameh, helicopter-borne troops crossed the frontier south of the Dead Sea in 'hot pursuit' and destroyed a guerrilla complex near Dahal. Finally, to prove both its capability and will to reach terrorist bases, the IAF mounted a major strike against Salt, a guerrilla centre east of Karameh, on 4 August 1968. After that the *fedayeen* abandoned their bases in the Jordan Valley, though firing across the line and infiltration attempts continued. The IDF fought back with ambushes, pursuit, and electronic detection devices and during the months following about 1,000 *fedayeen* were killed and many more captured. Special paratroop units, often assisted by Bedouin trackers, hunted down the infiltrators and engaged them. Following the paratroopers' creed, senior officers often led the small pursuit groups in person, and a brigade commander, Colonel Arik Regev, eulogized by Dayan as 'first in the assault, a leader in situations of stress, a man of integrity and kindliness', was killed.[16] As the months wore on, the tide slowly turned against the guerrillas, who were driven to more desperate expedients, especially the hijacking of international airlines, a safe undertaking because the reaction of Western powers ranged from indifference to mild protest.

Yet, in the end, this proved too much for King Hussein. He had managed to survive a number of plots aiming to kill or overthrow him and guerrilla leaders were implicated in most of these schemes. The king's patience was severely taxed and ran out in September 1970 when *fedayeen* hijacked three international airliners to Jordan and held their passengers captive in the desert. The event produced an international outcry and made it look as if Hussein no longer was master in his own house. He now ordered his troops to crush the guerrillas and on 13 September, Jordanian forces, using artillery and armour, began a massive assault on the Palestinian camps in and around Amman, killing thousands. When Syria moved to aid the guerrillas and invaded Jordan, the United States ordered its 6th Fleet to stand off the Israeli coast and also asked Israel to prepare for action if the fighting threatened Hussein's rule. IDF concentrations, American preparations, and the unexpected strong Jordanian resistance to their invasion caused the Syrians to withdraw, leaving the guerrillas to their fate. Jordanian soldiers continued to pursue them with great ferocity, so much so that some even crossed the Jordan and surrendered to the Israelis. By January 1971, the guerrilla movement in Jordan had been broken, though its survivors promptly organized a new group, the 'Black September', sworn to eternal hostility against Hussein as well as Israel.

Some of the guerrillas found refuge in Syria, but most went to Lebanon where a second major *fedayeen* base had been established by *El Fatah*. Lebanon, too, was an unwilling host, but could not restrain its unwelcome guests. At first, the PLO used Lebanon primarily as a fund-raising and propaganda centre, though by 1970 it had moved to staging raids into northern Israel and above all to organize attacks on Israeli airliners and offices in Europe. On 28 December 1968 the IDF struck back. Led by the now legendary Eytan, 40 paratroopers descended from their helicopters on Beirut Airport, and while Eytan calmly sat in the airport café drinking a brandy, his men destroyed 13 parked Arab airliners, and departing as they had come.

Although completely without bloodshed, the Beirut Airport action caused an international outcry; by contrast world opinion had been unconcerned when Jewish lives had been lost. Nor for that matter did it deter the *fedayeen*. Virtually unhampered by an increasingly powerless Lebanese government, they established fortified enclaves in and around Beirut and several other cities, and in the south of the country they converted a strip into what the IDF called *Fatahland,* from where they frequently launched Katyusha rockets against Israeli populated areas. Israel answered with counter-fire, and after a particularly heavy attack would mount air strikes against camps identified as guerrilla bases, including two inside Syria. Patrols along the northern frontier were strengthened, and an anti-infiltration fence was built. By February 1972, IDF units crossed the border, patrolled within Lebanon, and on occasion attacked *fedayeen* bases. The tempo of retaliatory operations was stepped up after the massacre of Israeli athletes at the Munich Olympics that year. In February 1973 missile boats, helicopter-borne paratroopers, and naval commandos attacked PLO training camps near Tripoli, and in an even more daring raid, on the night of 9–10 April 1973, Israeli special forces hit PLO headquarters in the very centre of Beirut. Although Yasir Arafat, the leader of the PLO escaped – he was absent from his quarters that night – several of his lieutenants were killed.

Finally, there was the cease-fire line with Syria, which remained quiet. Although Syria was the most vociferous of the 'confrontation' states, it kept its guerrillas on a tight leash. Only a few forays were mounted from Syrian territory, answered by deep penetration raids by IDF special forces. In addition, there were occasional gun duels between regular forces, including one major incident in June 1970 in which the Syrians lost 30 tanks to no Israeli losses.

The War of Attrition and the Bar-Lev Line

Although guerrilla and terrorist attacks, especially those directed against Israeli targets outside the IDF's perimeter, were painful, and the demonstrated refusal of European governments to take effective measures against the terrorists revealed a frightening decline of will, these incidents by themselves did not constitute a major strategic threat. Matters, however, were different along the cease-fire line with Egypt. Here conventional forces faced each other and less than a month after the June war, they were engaged in hostilities. By March 1969, bolstered by Russian aid, Nasser felt strong enough to declare the War of Attrition, actually the fourth of the Arab–Israeli conflicts, which continued until August 1970. Israel was forced to commit a major portion of her air power, and its successes led to the direct involvement of Soviet troops.

The first shooting occurred early in July 1967, but resulted in no major repercussions. Israeli troops along the Canal dug no hard fortifications and this state of affairs continued even after the sinking of the *Eilat* on 21 October was answered with the shelling of the oil refineries at Suez three days later. A new situation developed when, between 8 September and 22 October 1968, Egyptian artillery and commando raids inflicted heavy casualties on IDF troops. The Cairo press proudly gave front-page publicity to these incidents and also published a report by Lieutenant-General Odd Bull of the UN forces that put the blame squarely on Egypt. The Israeli response came on 31 October when airborne raiders eluded Egyptian air defences and destroyed two Nile bridges and an electric transmission station at Naj Hammadi – 125 miles inside Egypt and only 150 miles north of the Aswan Dam. The message of these raids was that Israeli reprisals would not be confined to the Canal area, where the IDF was outmanned and outgunned, but would hit vital objectives deep within Egypt.

The Naj Hammadi operation silenced further Egyptian shelling along the Suez Canal until March 1969. During the four months' interval, the Israeli command authorized construction of a chain of small reinforced concrete strongpoints to provide cover for troops along the waterline – the so-called Bar-Lev Line. The project was controversial from the start. General Adan, who designed the original plans, regarded these posts merely as look-outs, each containing a platoon of infantry with a detachment of tanks, two or three at the most, attached, with mobile forces patrolling the 7-mile intervals between the positions. Gavish agreed that the line could not serve as a shield for the Sinai, but insisted that the positions be given more fighting capability. There should be new access roads and along the high bank of the Canal firing ramps for tanks were constructed. Finally, a switch road, some miles back from the Canal was to allow artillery to move rapidly. Altogether, these installations were supposed to deny crossing points at major road junctions for a few hours and enable reserves to move up. Gavish, of course, realized that the entire length of the Canal could not be held, but he wanted to make the line more than a mere chain of observation posts.

The new concept was a compromise between the advocates of a fighting line along the Canal, who wanted to make maximum use of the waterway as an anti-tank obstacle, and those who advocated a withdrawal from the waterline towards the Giddi and Mitla passes. At General Headquarters both Ariel Sharon and Tal argued that the fortifications and their support installations, roads, water pipelines, and communications were expensive and that the small strongholds, lacking adequate firepower and not mutually supporting, were useless. At the most there should be a few observation posts and roving mobile patrols, while the major defence effort would be carried by armour elements stationed some miles back from the canal ready to smash any Egyptian crossing. Another opponent of the Bar-Lev Line was Major-General Matiyahu Peled, a veteran combat officer and chief of the Supply Branch in 1967, who argued that any defence line was useless. The much stronger Syrian defences on the Golan had been breached and the concept of static defence was harmful to the army's mobility, sapped its offensive spirit, and wasted money.

But except for Peled, who by then had retired from the Army, the opposition did not press its case strongly. There always was the fear that a mere trip-wire observation line could not prevent the Egyptians from establishing footholds on the Israeli side, and that international pressure would prevent the IDF from eliminating these bridgeheads. The result, Gavish for one argued, would be a considerable loss of face, causing great damage to the deterrent stature of the IDF. Even Dayan, who initially had doubted the military and political wisdom of sitting on the edge of the Canal, came to accept the concept, while Rabin, in an interview ten years after the Six Day War, declared that there was 'not a single person in the defence establishment who suggested that we retreat from Suez'. There had been, he admitted, discussion regarding the exact forms of the deployment, but everyone had supported the 'concept of the Suez Canal being used as an important obstacle in our system of defence'.[17]

In any case, the Israelis kept only a few thousand men along the water. At first these were drawn from elite units of the standing Army, but as time went on the line was manned by reservists. Eventually, about half of the posts were closed down and in October 1973 the rest were lightly manned by troops from the Jerusalem Brigade. All this did not prevent foreign observers from painting a rather fanciful picture of the line. In late 1972, for instance, Colonel Imre Szanto of the Hungarian People's Army reported that Israeli fortifications in the Sinai consisted of a first line of up to 40 strongpoints along the Canal, supported by reserves and blocking positions some 10 to 15 miles to the rear, backed up by another line of 40 strongholds about 30 miles east of the Canal and a fourth line, the 'Golda Meir Line', stretching from a point 23 miles west of El Arish to the Mitla Pass. He contended that the first three lines were held by four mechanized and one armoured divisions, while 13 additional divisions could be assembled behind the Golda Meir Line within 12 to 14 hours.[18]

This picture, perhaps inspired by political considerations, was wrong. On the other hand, it was a more accurate description of the Egyptian dispositions.

By March 1969 they had built several continuous lines of fortifications along the Canal, deployed several hundred heavy guns and howitzers, and shielded their complex by a network of SAM-2 missiles and anti-aircraft guns. The Egyptian plan was to inflict unacceptable casualties on the IDF by a continuing series of heavy artillery barrages supplemented by commando raids. On 21 March 1969, Nasser officially repudiated the cease-fire and on 23 June he declared a formal War of Attrition.

As early as 8 March the Egyptians had unleashed a very heavy barrage, but the strongholds proved their protective value and there was only one fatality. On the other hand, an Egyptian commando raid near Port Tewfik on 12 June caused serious losses to an armour unit caught off guard. The Israelis, at this point hopelessly outgunned in heavy artillery and prevented from major cross-Canal operations by the unwritten but nonetheless real shield provided by the Soviet Union, decided to match the Egyptian firepower by using the IAF as flying artillery. On 28 July IDF paratroopers and naval commandos captured the rock fortress of Green Island, the southern hinge of the Egyptian air-defence network, destroying its radar and anti-aircraft installations. Eleven hours later the IAF came into action, bombing and strafing missile and gun positions, troop concentrations and road convoys all along the Canal. Once again, total air superiority was achieved, even in the face of a heavy anti-aircraft defence network and air commanders repeatedly urged that conditions were suitable for a major crossing to destroy considerable portions of the enemy line. For political reasons, however, the government refused to permit such an action and Weizman, already stifled in his advancement, now left the service.[19]

If major ground operations seemed precluded by fear of international, specifically Soviet reaction, the government did permit destabilizing ground raids. On 10 September, IDF landing craft carried five captured Egyptian tanks and two armoured personnel carriers across the Gulf of Suez. For nine hours this column moved north along a 30-mile stretch of coastal road towards Suez, shooting up installations and vehicles in its path before re-embarking with no losses and bringing with it a captured T-62 tank. An Egyptian attempt to retaliate with a major air strike against Israeli positions the next day ended with 11 planes shot down to no Israeli losses. An even more spectacular raid took place on 26 December. By this time the Soviets had installed a new P-12 radar, designed to detect low-flying planes, at Ras Garib, some 250 miles south of Suez. Bar-Lev authorized an operation to capture this installation. Paratroopers carried on motor-torpedo boats stormed the complex while technicians dismantled the radar and carried it back to Israel, where the new apparatus was examined and later turned over to US intelligence agencies.

Having received strong hints from Washington that, while the United States was opposed to raids into Jordan and Lebanon, no such objections existed in the case of Egypt, the IAF began a series of deep penetration raids into the heart of the country. On 7 January 1970 the new Phantoms went into action for the first time, hitting targets in the very suburbs of Egypt. Nasser appealed for aid from Moscow and received new SAM-3 missiles, even more modern radar and radar-directed anti-aircraft batteries. All in all, estimates are that the Russians deployed 1,000 guns, 6,000 missile-launchers, and several dozen radar installations, covering Alexandria, Cairo, and the Aswan Dam. To man these batteries, the Russians brought in some 15,000 of their own troops and in April deployed three squadrons of their newest jets – Mig-21Js, piloted by experienced Russian airmen. On 18 April, Russian pilots encountered IAF Phantoms near Cairo and though the IAF was prepared to fight, caution prevailed and the deep penetration raids that nearly had toppled Nasser were called off.

Encouraged, the Russians now moved east and on 30 July there was a battle between Russian-manned Migs and IAF Phantoms and Mirages. Five Russian planes were promptly shot down; the rest fled. While highly gratifying to the IAF, the war had assumed new dimensions and, mindful of Ben Gurion's doctrine that the IDF should never be engaged against a super power, Israel now accepted a US-sponsored cease-fire that went into effect on 7 August 1970. Although the agreement called for a standstill, it was immediately and massively violated the next day when the Soviets and Egyptians moved some 40 to 50 missile batteries into the Canal Zone. Israel called on the United States to pressure the Russians into pulling back the missiles, but, after first denying that any violations had taken place, the Americans refused to take any action. The most the US would do was to supply a small increment in aircraft and in ECM technology.

The August 1970 cease-fire ending the War of Attrition was regarded with mixed feelings in Israel. Some interpreted it as a victory for the strategic concept of placing emphasis on a fortified defence system manned by a limited number of troops providing the necessary time for the reserves to be mobilized; others, however, considered it a defeat.[20] The massive violations of its standstill provisions meant that the IDF now faced the heaviest concentration of anti-aircraft guns and missiles in the world, shielding an ever-growing build-up of Egyptian troops, armour, and equipment that would make any cross-Canal operation merely an exercise in logistics. Moreover, the missiles ranged some 10 miles into the Sinai and deprived the IDF of its now customary air superiority. For the first time IDF planners had to plan to fight without air cover. However, the planners believed that future hostilities would consist of another round in the War of Attrition and made their preparations to meet the challenge on this assumption.

At considerable expense the 30-odd strongholds on the waterline were improved to withstand the heaviest bombardment; six additional strongpoints were built 4 to 6 miles inland, while the new long-range guns received from the United States were deployed to provide fire support. Further inland, military installations were moved underground and additional communications, water and fuel lines as well as roads were built. All this did not change the basic functions of the Bar-Lev Line, though it tended to blur the distinctions between an observation and a fighting line. It was still designed to permit small Israeli forces to remain along the Canal in order to observe and obstruct minor crossing attempts. Any major crossings were to be contained by the tanks of an active armour division, about 300 in all, deployed in company-strength detachments some miles behind the forward line. When major hostilities threatened, the tanks were to move to their pre-arranged firing positions and hold back the enemy until the reserves arrived for the decisive counter-stroke. Meanwhile the IAF, with new ECM gear and stand-off missiles including the American-supplied Shrike and Mavericks, believed that it would be able to suppress the Egyptian air-defence system without unacceptable losses.

The concept had some serious shortcomings. For one, the Bar-Lev strongholds still did not have adequate firepower to stand off an attack and secondly it was by no means clear that 300 tanks, distributed along a 100-mile front, could develop adequate firepower to stop a determined attack against an enemy who could absorb heavy casualties. For that matter the newly created command of the 'Armoured Forces' in the Sinai was by no means convinced that it was wise to rush tanks forward as soon as the alert was sounded because inevitably many vehicles would be lost in the pre-attack bombardment. On the whole, there seems to have been a feeling among Israeli armour commanders that it would be far better to let the enemy cross the Canal and then destroy him in a conventional enveloping attack in the Sinai. For that reason, General Sharon, heading the Southern Command since 1969, closed down a number of strongholds and allowed manpower in the remaining positions to sink to a new low.

The shortcomings of the Bar-Lev Line – and it did serve both as an observation and in some cases a delaying position in October 1973 – were not the most important flaw in Israel's strategic posture. The major flaw, potential only to be sure, was the shortage of manpower. Israel's strength rested on its total mobilized reserves, while the armies of its adversaries were composed almost entirely of standing forces. All Israeli strategic planning depended on receiving adequate advance notice of enemy intentions and if at any point this was not forthcoming or was interpreted incorrectly, the IDF might be caught off balance.

The major problem for Israeli intelligence was not to discover the enemy's capabilities for attack; these existed permanently. The real problem was to discover his intent and to a large degree this rested on political circumstances. And these looked rather more favourable. In September 1970 Nasser had died and his successor, Anwar Sadat, appeared at first ready to seek a limited solution through negotiation conducted with the United States acting as an intermediary. When these bogged down, he announced that 1971 was to be the 'year of decision', meaning that unless his goals were met Egypt would re-open hostilities. But 1971 passed without agreement and without war. Instead, in mid-1972, Sadat suddenly expelled most, though by no means all, of his Soviet military 'advisers', revealing a rift between Egypt and the Soviet Union that appeared to deprive Sadat of his immediate war option. It still is not clear whether this expulsion, and it was by no means complete, was merely a deception manouvre to throw Israel off guard or a determined bid to gain the support of the United States. In any case, it succeeded.

During the late spring of 1973 Israeli intelligence observed increased Egyptian activity on the west bank of the Canal and there also were signs that Syria was stirring. Early in May, certain junior members of the Intelligence Branch asserted that war was an imminent possibility. Their chief, Major-General Eliyahu Zeira, disagreed, but, weighing all the evidence, Eleazar recommended precautionary measures, including a partial activation of the reserves, to the government. The alarm proved to be false, though on 21 May Dayan told senior members of the general staff that 'a renewal of war in the second half of the summer must be taken into account.' Indeed, throughout the summer there were further indications that war was likely. Egyptian formations were massing on the waterline and new Soviet missiles, the SAM-6s, were distributed to the armoured divisions, indicating perhaps that there was an intent to push beyond the air umbrella provided by the SAM-2 and SAM-3 batteries. Syria, too, had established a similar air-defence system and beneath its cover, Israeli observers could see the Syrian Army manoeuvring in massive attack formations.

Both Israeli and American intelligence experts, however, continued to make their assessments on the assumption that Egypt and its allies had no real war option and, despite the mounting indications, Zeira refused to be stampeded into calling for mobilization. On 24 September the outposts of the Bar-Lev Line were taken over by reservists called up for their annual tour of duty, and two days later, Rabin, now serving as Israel's ambassador in Washington, but still very much a member of the inner circle of the Meir government, told the *Jerusalem Post* that 'there never was a period in which the security situation seemed as good as now.' His confidence was shared by Secretary of State Kissinger, caught up in the new and dramatic improvement of US–Soviet relations, and by American Middle-East experts.[21] It was not shared, however, by all IDF commanders or by junior intelligence officers. Their warnings, however, were largely disregarded by their superiors and by a government pre-occupied with domestic concerns.

8

The Yom Kippur War: October 1973

'And for strength to them that turn back the battle at the gate.'
Isaiah 27: 6

Experience has shown that reliable military history can be written only after a considerable lapse of time and this is particularly true of the fifth Arab–Israeli war of 1973, which ended in a stalemate with both sides claiming victory, though only the Arabs could claim a political success. During and after the war many foreign commentators, and for that matter Israelis, vied in criticizing the IDF, forgetting how the war had started and how it ended. Domestic criticism was rooted, in large part, in personal animosities, party politics, and in the frustrations of a 25 years' state of siege; foreign criticism, especially that expressed by supposedly friendly senior Western officers – American, British, and also West German – was almost malicious. Many had encountered Israeli officers for the first time after 1967 and had found them brash, unconventional, and protocol-defying. Most of them had experienced defeat: the Germans had memories of World War II; the British still smarted under the Suez débâcle and other traumas of imperial retreat, while the Americans were sustaining a humiliating defeat at the hands of a third-rate power in Vietnam. All had been irritated by non–conformist and on occasion brash Israeli officers and were only too glad to take the IDF down a peg or two.[1]

Nonetheless, despite initial confusions of the political and military leadership, the Israeli Army fought brilliantly and, despite the advantage of surprise, numerical superiority, and the massive infusion of the most advanced Soviet technology both before and during the fighting, the enemy – Egypt, Syria, Iraq, and Jordan, joined by a Saudi brigade and contingents from Algeria, Libya, Morocco, Kuwait, and Tunisia, and with pilots from Pakistan and North Korea – once again was routed and on the verge of total defeat. Intervention of the super powers prevented the destruction of the Arab field

177

armies and the interposition of the Soviet Union shielded Damascus and Cairo from attack. As in 1949, 1956, and 1967, Israel was unable to translate military success into an effective and viable peace.

To be sure, the war revealed certain shortcomings in the highest command echelons of the IDF. It exposed an overreliance on a doctrine based on the capabilities of unsupported armour, and above all, serious errors in intelligence estimates. But all this cannot obscure the plain fact that, when attacked by a force equal to the entire European establishment of NATO, taken by surprise and unprepared, a small country managed to contain its enemies and within three days assume the offensive, ending the war within gun range of Damascus and within striking range of Cairo. In purely military terms, the IDF revealed in 1973 that the spirit of '48 still was very much alive.

Warning and Decision

Although there were perturbing signs during the second and third quarter of 1973, Israeli political, and to a lesser extent the military leadership, remained confident that the Arabs would not dare to attack. For one they felt that their country's military posture actually was improving because of their conviction that the 'qualitative gap' between Israel and the Arabs was widening. They assumed that as warfare became more sophisticated, Israel's edge over the Arabs would increase because of her more advanced technology. As proof, Israelis cited their successful breakthrough into the production of sophisticated weapons.[2] In addition, their assessment of inter-Arab rivalries, coupled with the apparent decline of the Soviet position in the Middle East, and finally the control of the territories occupied in 1967 and resulted in changing national defence concepts. Prior to 1967 strategy had been conceived exclusively in terms of a pre-emptive strike; now Israel prepared for a defensive posture which would absorb an enemy assault and then proceed to the counter-attack. Early mobilization of the reserves, an extremely expensive proposition, seemed less vital and, above all, Israeli intelligence categorically asserted that it could provide the government with ample advanced warning.

After 1967 the Intelligence Branch of the general staff had become the senior intelligence agency. While its tactical intelligence usually was good, its strategic evaluations left something to be desired. Before the Six Day War it had failed to spot Egyptian concentrations in the Sinai, but after the war it received much credit for pinpointing enemy installations and predicting reactions. Its head, Major-General Aharon Yariv became widely admired, though during his last year in office a number of spectacular PLO raids, including the massacres at Lod Airport and the Munich Olympics, had tarnished the intelligence image. In the autumn of 1972 he was succeeded by

Colonel Eliyahu Zeira, promoted to major-general the following year. Zeira, a member of the Palmach in 1946–48, later a paratroop officer, and a graduate of the staff college, had been Yariv's deputy before serving a tour as military attaché in Washington. His stay in the United States appeared to give him an inflated view of American power and commitment to Israel, and an inclination to rely heavily on sophisticated electronic equipment. Perhaps his greatest shortcoming was a tendency to dismiss any contrary views once his mind was made up. In May 1973 he had maintained that war was unlikely but then had been overruled by Eleazar. As the danger signals increased during September, he stubbornly insisted that the chances for war remained 'very low' and refused to change his assessment even in the face of the new deployments. His optimism may have been reinforced by the assumption that active IDF forces, up to about 100,000 men and women, would be able to contain an attack and allow completion of orderly mobilization.

Zeira's views were not shared by Major-General Yitzhak Hofi, Commanding General Northern Command. Since 13 September, when Israeli Mirages and Syrian Migs had clashed over the Golan, with eight Syrian planes lost to one Israeli, Hofi had maintained a state of increased alert. Normally, the Israeli garrison on the Golan consisted of one infantry brigade, with two battalions manning 14 small infantry fighting positions, as well as the surveillance post located on the highest ridge of Mount Hermon. Backing up the line was a brigade of tanks, the 188th Armoured Brigade, and several batteries of field artillery. By 24 September, Hofi had become convinced that the Syrian concentrations were not engaged in a routine relief of forward units, as Zeira maintained, and when on 26 September, Dayan paid his customary New Year's visit to the troops, he agreed with Hofi's view. Always considering the Syrians as the most belligerent and unpredictable, Dayan now ordered elements of the crack 7th Armoured Brigade, commanded by Colonel Avigdor (Yanush) Ben Gal, up from its base at Beersheba and also sent in some artillery and infantry reinforcements.[3]

Sending the 7th Brigade north was a wise and, as it turned out, fateful decision, Dayan's major contribution to the war. When fighting erupted, the Golan defences under Brigadier-General Eytan consisted of 177 tanks, 44 guns, and about 5,000 infantry. This force was, of course, far from sufficient, but except for the poorly handled surveillance post on Mount Hermon, manned by non-fighting personnel protected only by one understrength platoon of Golani infantry, all tanks, guns, and troops were at their battle stations. Moreover, already in the spring of 1973, Hofi acting on Eytan's advice, had moved the mobilization centres of the brigades designated for the defence of the Golan up to the heights and so was able to form reserves coming into line with a minimum of delay.

Southern Command, however, was far less prepared. On 15 July 1973 Major-General Shmuel Gonen, known as Gorodish in the Army, had replaced Sharon, who had retired from the service. Gonen, an able and brave tanker, who had commanded the 7th Brigade in 1967, found that the state of defences, discipline, and fortifications in his new command left much to be desired. Fourteen of the 33 forts along the Canal had been closed down; the remainder were lightly manned – less than one battalion for the entire line. The Egyptians, moreover, had raised the height of the earth ramparts on their side to over 100 feet, providing them with a clear field of observation and fire reaching to the second Israeli line, the so-called artillery road running 5 to 8 miles back from the waterline. Gonen gave orders to restore the forts, re-open some that had been closed down, and to build new ramparts and observation towers. Little, however, had been accomplished by the end of September.

In any case, major Egyptian attacks were to be met by Major-General Avraham (Albert) Mendler's three-brigade armoured division, 276 tanks, stationed behind the Bar-Lev Line. Normally one brigade was stationed a few miles from the Canal; the other two were held in reserve at the main base at Refidim (Bir Gafgafa). Artillery support for the line was provided by 12 batteries, 48 guns, and, considering the frontage, it necessarily was dispersed. The northern end of the line, where swampy terrain precluded the use of armour, was held by an infantry brigade. The Israeli war plan, code-named *Shovach Yonim* (Dovecote), envisaged that in the event of a major cross-Canal attack the three brigades would rush forward and occupy firing ramps along the front. With air support, on call within minutes from bases in the Sinai, it was expected that they could contain even a major assault until the reserves arrived.[4]

At the time immediately before the war, Israel, provided it had time to mobilize and deploy its forces, was stronger than ever before. While Egypt and Syria together could muster some 500,000 combat troops, 4,500 tanks, 3,400 guns, and about 1,100 combat planes, the IDF could field over 300,000 combat troops, 2,000 tanks, 900 guns and heavy mortars, and 550 planes. The ratio, therefore, was better than 2:1 in manpower, and planes, though the tank ratio, $1\frac{1}{2}$:1 in 1967, had deteriorated to 3:1 by 1973, and artillery strength remained vastly inferior. If other Arab states were drawn in, the ratios would become more unfavourable, perhaps 3:1 overall, and even worse in some categories. Overall ratios, however, would matter little because Israel would not be able to mobilize; what really mattered were the actual numbers of troops deployed during the various phases of the war and here, at least during the first two days, the ratios generally were as high as 5:1 in favour of the attacker.

For the opening stage, during which the Egyptians hoped to seize two bridgeheads in the northern sector, between the towns of Kantara and Ismailia, and one bridgehead opposite the city of Suez, they deployed two armies, actually corps, with seven divisions and two independent brigades, equipped with 1,400 tanks and 1,000 guns. In accordance with Soviet doctrine, a third army was held in reserve as a second echelon. The Syrians also followed Soviet methods. Attacking on a narrow front of less than 40 miles, they formed a first echelon of three mechanized divisions, one tank and two mechanized brigades each, closely supported by a second echelon of two armoured divisions, and backed up by a third echelon of two armoured and two motorized brigades. Well provided with the latest Soviet materiel, the three echelons contained 1,600 tanks, 1,400 APCs, and 1,300 pieces of artillery.

In contrast with 1967, the Arab war plan was well co-ordinated and called for simultaneous attacks across the Canal and the Golan. Air forces would open the assault by low-level attacks against air fields, communications, artillery positions, and targets of opportunity, but the main burden of fighting devolved on the ground forces. Deployment and rear areas were protected by a concentration of static surface-to-air missile batteries, with mobile SAM-6 and man-portable SAM-7 missiles, buttressed by radar-directed four-barrelled ZSU-23-4 guns, which would provide an air cover for the advancing Arab armies. Altogether the number and complementary mix of surface-to-air missiles and anti-aircraft guns made these defences the most concentrated anywhere in the world. Missiles and launchers also played a considerable role on the ground. The Arabs intended to use their mobile anti-aircraft and anti-tank weaponry to counter the Israeli tactics based on the armour–aircraft combination.

Training of Egyptian and Syrian forces after 1967 was undertaken by competent Soviet instructors, who recognized the necessity to restructure the command and control apparatus in both armies and the need for new relations between officers, non-commissioned officers and men. The required changes were made, with tactical training, procedures, and doctrine updated to comply with the new Soviet weapons systems deployed, but the hallmarks of Soviet inflexibility, a tendency to stick to the book regardless of circumstances, remained evident. And this was a weakness which the IDF was able to exploit in the Sinai. Even so, by 1973 the Egyptian and Syrian soldier was better trained, equipped, and led than he had been in 1967.

Egyptian and Syrian forces completed their deployment on 1 October and signs that a major operation was imminent could be seen and heard. Southern Command's chief intelligence officer, however, discounted the signs and Eleazar too concluded that the deployment was merely an exercise. On 3 October a meeting attended by Golda Meir, Dayan, Eleazar, Bar-Lev and Allon, and by Zeira's deputy – the general being sick that day – came to similar conclusions. The developments were worrisome, but the precautions taken, especially the reinforcements sent to the Golan, were judged adequate moves. Eleazar suggested that the Egyptian was a major exercise, while the Syrian deployment was defensive.

Characteristics of Soviet air defence weapons used during the Yom Kippur War

ANTI-AIRCRAFT GUNS

Calibre	Model	Effective vertical range (metres)	Maximum rate of fire (RPM)	Fire control
23mm	ZSU-23-4	3,000/2,500	1,200	Radar or optical
57mm	ZSU-57-2	4,000	240	Optical
57mm	S-60	6,000	120	Radar or optical

SURFACE-TO-AIR GUIDED MISSILES

Missile	Name	Slant range (km)*	Level of protection
SA-2	Guideline	53	High altitude
SA-3	Goa	24	Medium–low altitude
SA-6	Gainful	37	Low–medium altitude
SA-7	Grail	3·5	Low altitude

* *Exact ranges classified*

However, as signs multiplied, early on the morning of 5 October the defence minister and the chief of staff decided to place the standing forces on 'C Alert', the highest short of mobilization. That morning, too, acting on his own, Major-General Benyamin Peled, the IAF commander, decided to activate his squadrons and to begin calling up reservists. It now was the eve of Yom Kippur, the Day of Atonement, and later that morning Mrs Meir summoned an emergency session of her rump cabinet. Once again Zeira and Eleazar insisted that while an attack was possible, the probability of war had to be regarded as 'the lowest of the low'.[5] When the meeting broke up shortly after noon, the prime minister asked the ministers to authorize her and Dayan to mobilize during Yom Kippur if this became necessary. They agreed. Early next morning, about 4.30, Zeira finally received information that persuaded him and Eleazar that Egypt and Syria would launch a co-ordinated attack at 6 pm that day. This was far short of the 'adequate' warning that intelligence repeatedly had promised and more time was lost when Dayan and Eleazar disagreed both on the extent of mobilization and on launching a pre-emptive air strike. 'I rejected the idea of a pre-emptive strike by the Air Force as well as the mobilization of more reserves than were required for immediate defence', Dayan related in his memoirs, because 'I feared that such moves would burden our prospects of securing the full support of the United States.' Shortly after 8 am the defence minister and the chief of staff took their disagreement to the prime minister who decided for Dayan. Eleazar was authorized to call up between 100,000 and 120,000 reservists, a number he promptly and wisely exceeded, but although the IAF already had fully mobilized on its own initiative, Mrs Meir refused to permit an air strike.[6]

Mobilization orders went out about 9.30 am on 6 October. Deputy Chief of Staff Tal, realizing the urgency of the situation, ordered that there should be no delay to assemble brigades. Temporary companies, even platoons, were to be sent out as soon as they were formed. Inevitably, this improvisation caused some confusion, a break-down in unit cohesion, and occasional shortages of certain items of equipment, but it saved time and the reserves arriving in driblets helped to stem the Syrian onslaught on the Golan. Throughout the morning all over Israel men were called out from the synagogues. The radio, normally silent on the Day of Atonement, began broadcasting the call-up codes for units, and everywhere reservists, called out or not, began to make their way to mobilization centres.

Reactions along the front lines varied. On the Golan, units and individuals moved into their fighting positions and the 7th Brigade took up its station in the northern sector. By contrast, there were delays in the Southern Command. Although Gonen received the war warning about 6 am, he continued to hold his two rear brigades near Refidim and also restrained Mendler from advancing his tanks to their firing ramps until shortly before 2 pm. Gonen later explained that he wanted to avoid exposing his tanks to the heavy preliminary barrage expected, though the Agranat Commission of Inquiry, constituted after the war, rejected his explanation. It has been suggested that Gonen, known as an aggressive fighter, feared that an early deployment might induce the Egyptians to call off their attack and deprive him of the opportunity to inflict a decisive defeat. Perhaps so, but this did little to explain the behaviour of the troops along the waterline. Although they should have been alerted to the imminent attack, life here continued at a relaxed Yom Kippur pace with men spending the morning praying, sleeping, reading, or playing. They were, of course, reservists and their behaviour tended to reflect the complacent national mood. When a high state of alert was ordered, its most important impact was that leaves were cancelled and that the men would not be home for the holiday. Beyond that, most junior officers and men discounted the likelihood of war and did not heed an unpopular, and as they saw it, unnecessary order. The Commission of Inquiry later cited the loose pattern of IDF discipline as one of the shortcomings of the Army.[7]

Of course, the 456 men and seven tanks in line, could not have made that much difference and in the event the resistance put up by the various positions varied according to the quality of individual commanders and garrisons. No position was abandoned without orders, many fought literally to the end, some held out for days, and one – position 'Budapest' at the northern end of the line – withstood all assaults until the end of the fighting.

At noon an emergency session of the cabinet met in Tel Aviv and was told that the attack was expected that evening. Bar-Lev inquired if that hour was really suitable and suggested that the attack might come earlier. The meeting still was underway when news arrived that heavy air and artillery attacks had begun on both fronts. It was at this point that the first of Mendler's 90 tanks were moving into their positions along the canal, sustaining losses from Egyptian anti-tank weapons on the earthworks across the water.

After the war, the Commission of Inquiry eventually blamed a number of senior officers, above all Eleazar, Zeira, and Gonen, for the IDF being caught unprepared both strategically and tactically, but absolved the government and Dayan from responsibility. The verdict was not well accepted and seems unjust. There is little doubt that Zeira and several of his senior intelligence officers failed to evaluate available information properly and that they refused to change their opinion even when the indications had become too obvious to be overlooked. Gonen, though he had only recently assumed command, and had tried to improve the state of combat readiness of his forces, also must be held responsible for his failure to give clear orders whether the Bar-Lev Line was to be held, in which case he should have moved his armour forward promptly, or whether, having served its trip-wire function, the line should be evacuated at once. To be sure, this indecision was not his alone. It was shared by the high command, which never could make up its mind what it really expected from the Bar-Lev Line. Although Gonen had asked for reinforcements before October, the chief of staff had not heeded these requests, and Gonen, unlike Hofi, did not make his case forcefully. Once hostilities began, Eleazar acted decisively, but he did bear a share of responsibility for the initial near débâcle.

All this, however, does not exonerate the defence minister or the government. In a parliamentary democracy, and especially in Israel where, ever since Ben Gurion, the defence minister has exercised wide powers over the military establishment, he cannot be excused. For that matter, while Dayan tended to maximize delegation of authority, he never hesitated to use his powers and the commission's verdict that the chief of staff had primary responsibilities for the

Army seemed to reverse *ex post facto* the long-established primacy of the defence minister.

The most controversial question, of course, was the decision not to mobilize and to abstain from a pre-emptive air strike. In retrospect, a pre-emptive air strike was not indicated militarily. Unlike in 1967, the Egyptian and Syrian armies were in fortified positions, their aircraft protected by semi-hardened hangars, and air-defence systems alert. An Israeli strike would not have reduced their attack capabilities but would have compromised American support. On the other hand, though it has been argued that in order to be fully effective, total mobilization would have had to be ordered as early as 4 October, a date when intelligence still maintained that chances for war were practically non-existent, much could have been done by precautionary call-up of a few reserve brigades. On balance, if the soldiers were guilty of neglect, so were the ministers, especially Dayan.

The Holding Phase: 6–7 October 1973

Overall, the war, lasting almost three weeks, can be divided into four major phases. It began with a desperate holding phase, 6–7 October; and continued with only partially successful counter-attacks on 8–10 October. Then came the Israeli offensive against Syria, complemented by the repulse of an Egyptian armoured assault on 11–14 October, constituting the decisive turning point, and finally there was the last stage, a continued Israeli offensive, 15–25 October 1973.

The Egyptian and Syrian attack began with air attacks against Israeli air fields, communications, artillery positions, Hawk batteries, communications, and targets of opportunity. In addition, on the Egyptian front, some 35 helicopters tried to land commandos to disrupt the operation of forward air fields and interfere with the movement of reinforcements. Finally, from positions inside Egypt, a number of Kelt ground-to-ground rockets were fired against Israeli cities. The air attacks caused only minor disruptions and the most damage was done to the self-propelled batteries behind the Canal. Several attackers were downed in the Sinai and over the Golan. Some of the helicopters were intercepted and the Egyptian commandos suffered heavy losses. Although not all were eliminated, they did not constitute a major problem. The *London Sunday Times* Insight team, not noticeably favourable to Israel, concluded that 'in combat they were not very effective.' Within 20 minutes Israeli planes were in action and for the rest of the afternoon and evening, abandoning its original plan of first suppressing the missile screen, the IAF flew in direct support of the hard-pressed ground forces. Success, though, was limited. Enemy fire was intense, visibility poor, and in many places Israelis and Arabs were intermixed in close fighting.

The actual crossing of the Canal had been carried out according to Soviet doctrine. Forward elements of five divisions, 8,000 men, moved across the waterway in rubber boats. Some engaged Israeli strongpoints; others penetrated through the gaps and set up anti-tank zones with their man-portable SAGGER ATGMs and RPG-7s, screening the crossing of the major body. Assisted by engineer units who breached the earthen rampart, and ferried across on motorized rafts, 40,000 men, including support tanks, were across the water by 9 pm, about the time that the engineers completed the first bridge.

During the afternoon, evening, and night of 6–7 October, Mendler's tanks fought a number of small disjointed actions to relieve besieged strongpoints, evacuate garrisons, and regain the waterline. Little was achieved except heavy losses and the next morning Mendler reported that only about 90 tanks remained operative. That morning the IAF, after first delivering a number of strikes against the missile positions, intervened with good effect, but towards 10 am General Peled informed Southern Command that all available aircraft had to be diverted to the Syrian front. Gonen now gave up his attempts to restore the Bar-Lev Line and ordered a withdrawal to the artillery road. The resistance had not been in vain. The Egyptians, contrary to later and diplomatically convenient claims that they always had intended merely to establish a military presence on the Israeli side in order to break the political impasse, actually tried to press forward to their major objectives – the passes leading into the central Sinai. Throughout the afternoon and the night of 7 October their armour and infantry teams repeatedly tried to advance, but were repelled and in the morning, having penetrated up to 10 miles inland and cut the artillery road in several places, they dug in to repel the expected Israeli counter-attack. By noon on 8 October, substantial elements of two Israeli armoured divisions arrived, albeit without most of their mechanized infantry and artillery, and the immediate crisis was over. Adan's division was ordered to deploy east of Kantara while Sharon's division moved into position covering the Sinai passes.

October 7 also constituted the turning point on the Syrian front. Here too the Israeli forces managed to stop the Arab advance before it reached its initial objective – the Jordan river bridges. The Syrian attack began at 1.58 in the afternoon of 6 October with a series of low-level air strikes, followed by a heavy artillery, mortar, and rocket barrage. Moving against the Israeli line were three mechanized divisions, followed by two armoured divisions. The task of the mechanized divisions was to open gaps in the Israeli defences for the armoured divisions to push to the Jordan and into the Galilee beyond. Simultaneously, a small task force was to attack the surveillance post on Mount Hermon.

The Syrian attack came along three major axes, one to the north and two south of Kuneitra. On the Israeli side, the northern sector was held by the 7th

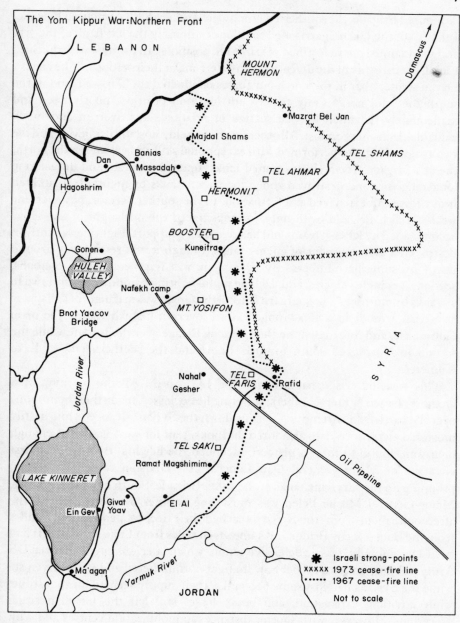

The Yom Kippur War: Northern Front

LEBANON

MOUNT HERMON

Damascus

Mazrat Bel Jan

Majdal Shams

TEL SHAMS

Dan
Banias
Massadah

TEL AHMAR

HERMONIT

Hagoshrim

BOOSTER
Kuneitra

Gonen

HULEH VALLEY

SYRIA

Nafekh camp

MT. YOSIFON

Bnot Yaacov Bridge

Jordan River

Nahal Gesher

TEL FARIS
Rafid

Oil Pipeline

TEL SAKI

LAKE KINNERET

Ramat Magshimim

Givat Yoav
Ein Gev
El Al

Ma'agan

Yarmuk River

JORDAN

✳ Israeli strong-points
xxxxx 1973 cease-fire line
•••••• 1967 cease-fire line

Not to scale

Armoured Brigade, the southern sector by the weaker 188th Armoured Brigade. Infantry of the Golani garrisoned the slopes adjoining the left flank of the 7th, and also manned the 14 fortified volcanic hill positions. In contrast with the Suez Canal, the majority of the defenders were alert and at their stations. 'The fact is', Dayan wrote, 'that in the north our forces conducted the war well, and in the south they did not.'[8] Only the Mount Hermon position, poorly sited and inadequately defended by one section of infantry, was overrun and much valuable electronic gear lost. All other positions held, most until relieved, and the two armour brigades performed with exceptional skill and valour. In the north, the 7th Brigade, 100 well-positioned tanks, opened accurate and devastating long-range fire and destroyed about 300 enemy tanks by nightfall. It suffered heavy losses, but survived as a formation. In the southern sector, however, the weaker 188th Brigade, with only 77 tanks, faced the onslaught of 450 tanks accompanied by RPG-7 teams and heavy artillery support. Fighting valiantly, it destroyed a great number of enemy tanks, though it was relentlessly ground down by superior numbers. By evening it was fragmented into platoons, sections, or single vehicles, and, lacking night-fighting equipment, was down to 15 tanks by morning. The southern flank of the Golan was in danger of collapsing as Syrian armour in a two-pronged attack overran Nafekh Camp, the main Golan base, and threatened the Bnot Yaacov Bridge over the Jordan, while the second prong moved south towards El Al and the southern end of Lake Kinneret.

This was the crisis that diverted the IAF north. All the morning of 7 October, Israeli fighter-bombers, suffering heavy losses, made their bomb runs over the battlefield, attempting to slow down the Syrian advance, while hastily mustered elements of two armoured divisions, sent forward as soon as enough men were found to form a platoon, ascended the heights. By noon, the first elements of Major-General Dan Laner's 21st Division came into action, propping up the surviving tanks of the 188th Brigade. South of Lake Kinneret, Major-General Moshe Peled was mustering another division. Early in the afternoon, about 1 pm, the Syrians reached their deepest penetration, 6 miles from the Bnot Yaacov Bridge and some seven miles from Lake Kinneret. It had been a hard fought, classic defensive action, which later was cited in official US Army publications as a model how 'to fight outnumbered and win'.[9] Even so, while the Syrians had lost some 600 tanks, their supply seemed inexhaustible, while attrition, exhaustion, and heavy losses still left the Israeli position precarious. However, with shorter distances to mobilization centres and with better preparations, fresh troops, perhaps not too well organized, some with equipment missing, and all lacking adequate artillery support, were coming into line. By the afternoon of 7 October, Israeli forces on the Golan began to regroup. General Laner took command of the southern sector; Eytan continued to direct the northern sector. A third armoured division, Peled's, began to arrive during the night.

The Israeli Counter-Attacks: 8–10 October

Although during the course of 7 October the situation seemed to be stabilizing, Israel's high command was troubled and divided. Dayan, a man of changeable moods, was depressed by the failure of the contingency plans and by the heavy losses – 300 tanks and 40 planes – as well as hundreds of casualties and some prisoners. Fearing a collapse, he is reported to have advised the prime minister that Israel might have to activate its last-resort nuclear option. On this point, however, the evidence is not entirely clear.[10] What is clear is that Dayan advocated withdrawal to the high ground east of Refidim and a last-ditch stand on the slopes of the Golan descending to the Jordan. By contrast Eleazar, who expected to have 500 tanks in the south and 300 tanks in the north available the next morning, urged counter-attacks on both fronts. The dispute was submitted to the rump cabinet. Dayan was overruled.[11] Before authorizing the offensive, however, General Bar-Lev was sent to the north and Eleazar was sent to the south to survey the situation and assess prospects. Late that night, both men returned with favourable reports.

About 6 am, Gonen launched a major counter-attack. By this time two additional armoured divisions were available. Mendler's battered force had been reinforced and armoured units, commanded by Major-General Kalman Magen were in the process of coming into line. Gonen's plan of operation was for Adan's division to break through the Egyptians to the waterline near Kantara and then wheel south to roll up the enemy. If the initial stage succeeded, Sharon's division was to attack straight towards the Canal, trapping the major part of the 2nd Egyptian Army. However, this attack failed just as badly as earlier and smaller attacks; one brigade, the 109th, was almost totally wiped out. 'Israel armour attacking', Herzog wrote, 'with the *élan* of cavalry charges, without infantry support, and with inadequate artillery support, made no sense whatsoever in the face of the masses of anti-tank weapons which the Egyptians had concentrated.'[12] Some observers attributed these faulty tactics to the IDF's emphasis on the attack at all costs and its insistence on technical proficiency, pre-occupations that appeared to have deprived armour commanders of adaptability and tactical inventiveness. It was noted that paratroop officers – both Hofi and Eytan were paratroopers – showed far greater flexibility. Although there seems to be some foundation to this judgement, it was rather too sweeping. The classic defence conducted by Ben Gal's 7th Brigade showed that Israeli armour had by no means lost its cunning.

In any case, Adan's attack failed against the Egyptian anti-tank zones and the heavy losses, by then reaching about 400 tanks, caused Southern Command to re-evaluate the situation. Gonen now decided to call off further offensive action – Sharon's division was not even engaged that day – and to stand on the defensive. The entire operation caused much bad blood between Gonen and his divisional commanders. Gonen's handling of the battle had been inept and he found it difficult to impose his authority on his divisional commanders, a difficult enough task for anyone in the case of the irrepressible Sharon. He now was superseded by Bar-Lev, who assumed the title of 'representative of the General Staff'. During the next few days the Israelis limited themselves to holding operations, while the Egyptians consolidated their bridgeheads north of the Great Bitter Lake. Among the various data digested at Southern Command was the discovery by a reconnaissance patrol from Sharon's division that there existed a gap between the Egyptian 2nd and 3rd Armies.

In the north, Peled's fresh division launched a counter-attack on the morning of the 8th, striking along the southern edge of the Golan plateau. On the central sector, Laner's division advanced towards Kuneitra with the 7th Brigade, now reinforced, on his left flank. Syrian resistance was determined, but their missile fire was slackening. The IAF had discovered electronic counter-measures and the Syrians were, temporarily it turned out, low on missiles. Outside Kuneitra, the 7th clashed with Syrian armour and in a close-run encounter turned back its last counter-charge on 9 October and the next day, after almost 72 hours of continuous fighting, the Israelis reached the 1967 'Purple Line' and prepared to drive into the Syrian defences. The Syrians were not routed, but they clearly were defeated, leaving behind on the Golan Heights 867 tanks, many in running order, including some of Russia's new T-62s, thousands of other vehicles and much equipment. That day, Dayan 'stopped worrying whether somewhere along the fronts our forces might prove unable to stop the Arabs'.[13] Instead, the question was whether to continue the advance against Syria or to shift emphasis to the Sinai.

Following a series of conferences between the cabinet and the generals that night, it was decided to press on towards Damascus. This was to be a spoiling operation. Capture of the capital was ruled out by the possibility of Soviet intervention, but it was decided to press forward with close air and artillery support to drive a salient about 12 miles deep on the Kuneitra–Damascus axis. The major objective was to keep the Syrians off balance, discourage Jordan from joining the war with more than a token force, and to meet the three Iraqi divisions moving towards the front in a forward position. About midnight on 10 October, Eleazar ordered Hofi to begin operations before noon the next day.

The ministerial meetings also discussed the problems posed by the unprecedented attrition of material. For the first time, the Soviet Union was supplying arms to its clients in the middle of the fighting, mounting the biggest airlift ever, at first in a clear bid to reinforce an apparent victory and later to stave off defeat. As early as 9 October, transport planes landed in Syria and the next day in Egypt. Russian, Hungarian, and Yugoslav air bases were used. Trains loaded with supplies moved to Black Sea ports and, convoyed by the Red Fleet, ships unloaded heavy war weapons in Syrian harbours. Quantities delivered during the fighting, above all surface-to-air missiles, were shipped in such quantities that some had to be withdrawn from first-line Red Army formations. Although between 9 and 13 October the Syrians were short of certain types of missiles, the following day they again were able to expend them as if they were shot-gun cartridges.

By contrast, Israel found that no European nation would supply her with arms. Britain even embargoed the shipment of tank ammunition already paid for, and all countries, except for Portugal, blocked the shipment of arms from US bases on its territory and forbade US Air Force transports from refuelling. Not that America rushed to Israel's aid. At first it was believed that the IDF could comfortably defeat the attack, later the United States hesitated to endanger détente or endanger its relations with the Arabs by supplying too much aid too soon. A total Israeli victory was considered likely to destabilize the area and be contrary to American interests. Although Israel had requested supplies as early as 7 October, only small quantities of equipment and ammunition were made available and these had to be picked up by unmarked Israeli planes. When the counter-offensive in the south failed and losses mounted, Dayan became more desperate. There even was talk about Mrs Meir leaving the country in the middle of the war to make a personal appeal to President Nixon. By 10 October, though the position had stabilized, the IDF, having counted on a short war, was beginning to feel the pinch in ammunition, aircraft, electronic gear, and ATGMs. Tanks, Dayan observed, were less critical and many vehicles, both Israeli and Soviet, were being salvaged on the battlefield and would be operational again in a few days. The Americans dragged their heels until 12 October, when Kissinger finally recognized the extent of the Russian involvement and the threat to the American position in the area. Major resupply started the next day and on 14 October the first US Air Force C-5 Galaxy flew into Lod Airport. In all, 670 missions airlifted 23,000 tons of equipment, while Phantoms were flown in directly from the operational squadrons of the Mediterranean and Atlantic fleets and Skyhawks came from US bases in Germany. Large supplies also came by sea.

It was an important, perhaps decisive, move by the United States. It illustrated, however, the complex and troubled relationships between Israel and America. Israel depended on the United States for much of her equipment and yet, as Dayan bitterly reflected, 'the United States would really rather support the Arabs.'[14] This statement was unjust, at least in 1973. Still, it was true that for all its magnitude, the American effort never matched the quantities of Russian equipment flowing to the Arabs.

An additional problem was posed by the difficulties of moving supplies from Lod Airport to the fighting fronts, 140 miles away in the Sinai and about 100 miles to the Golan, for the most part over roads that had only limited capacity and with transport consisting mainly of requisitioned vehicles. Aircraft and air equipment, of course, was easier to handle and were taken by Israeli pilots directly to the various air bases and strips. Whatever the difficulties, from mid-October on, American supplies kept coming and reached the Israeli fronts.

Offensive in the North and the Repulse of the Egyptians: 11–14 October

Hofi decided to lead his counter-offensive into Syria from the northernmost sector of his front, with Eytan's division. Not only would the flank of the advance be protected by the slopes of Mount Hermon, it also was the shortest road to Damascus and the threat would force the Syrians to employ their troops defensively. Eytan would be assisted by Laner's division operating on the Kuneitra–Damascus axis, while Peled would guard the flank against an expected Jordanian, Saudi, and Iraqi counter-move. The original break-in was to be made by the 7th Brigade. By the early afternoon of 11 October Eytan and Laner's troops had broken into the Syrian lines, badly mauling a Moroccan brigade in the northern sector. By morning of the 12th, both axes had fought their way through the Syrian defences, though Laner now faced elements of two Iraqi brigades on his southern flank. Also appearing was a Jordanian brigade, sent northward by a reluctant King Hussein, who realized that the war was not going to plan. Laner's units, using the longer range of their 105mm cannon, managed to ambush the Iraqis, destroying some 80 tanks to no Israeli losses, and the next day they also inflicted heavy casualties on the Jordanians. This day, 13 October, the Jordanians were to co-operate with the Iraqis, but there was little tactical co-ordination and the results again were one-sided.

Still, the Iraqis were only mauled, not destroyed, and on the 13th the Syrians, who had been so short of missiles that the day before they actually had committed their air force against the IAF, losing 29 planes in air-to-air combat, once again had ample supplies. Although an Israeli breakthrough on this front, albeit with heavy losses, was probably within reach, the Israeli line now had reached Sasa, a point almost midway between the former cease-fire line and the Syrian capital, bringing its outskirts within extreme artillery range.

For political as well as military reasons, Israel opted to break off offensive operations here on 13 October. A further advance might have forced Jordan to take a more active role in the war and also might have triggered Soviet intervention, which would have forced an end to hostilities with Egyptian forces still entrenched on the east bank of the Canal. Attention shifted to the south. Fighting continued at a much reduced pace in the north, but the only major operation was the recapture of the Mount Hermon position by a combined paratrooper–Golani infantry force on 22 October, only hours before Syria accepted the United Nations cease-fire.

In the north, though the Syrians had not been destroyed, General Hofi had achieved victory against at first overwhelming odds. In all the Syrians lost some 1,150 tanks, the Iraqis about 100, and the Jordanians about 50. On the Israeli side every single tank engaged sustained at least one hit, but only 100 were destroyed permanently, while the IAF had contributed to an extent that cannot be overrated, on occasion in a self-sacrificing manner, to the final outcome. Altogether, the campaign on Golan 'perhaps more than any other, revealed the true quality of the Israeli troops'.[15]

As early as 9 October, Southern Command had made plans to evict the Egyptians from their positions by using Israel's favourite strategy – the approach along the line of least expectations – in this case a crossing of the Suez Canal. On 11 October, while a prefabricated bridge was being moved into the Sinai, Bar–Lev decided that the penetration should be made just north of the Great Bitter Lake. General Sharon's overstrength division, reinforced by a paratrooper brigade, was to make the initial crossing, to be followed by Adan's division and elements from Magen's division.

The operation, however, was delayed. There was concern that, with the bulk of Egyptian armour still west of the Canal (two armoured divisions, two mechanized divisions, and two independent armoured brigades, a total of 900 tanks) such an undertaking might be too risky. The cabinet, including Dayan, also was sceptical about the prospects for the cross-Canal operation and as late as 12 October the issue had not been decided. That day, however, in response to Syrian pleas for assistance, the Egyptians began transferring armour to the west bank, apparently in preparation for a major armoured assault in the direction of the passes. On 13 October, Egyptian armour and infantry teams probed all along the Israeli line. That day also, General Mendler, on his way to attend a commanders' meeting at Sharon's division, was killed by Egyptian shell fire, and was replaced by General Magen. For the first time since 6 October, Egyptian aircraft appeared in force over the Sinai and a series of air battles followed in which the Egyptians suffered heavy losses.

The next day, following a heavy bombardment by 1,000 guns, the Egyptians launched their attack between 6 and 8 am. They attacked on a front of about 15 miles, with Refidim as their main objective. Most of the Egyptian tanks, about 1,000, were concentrated in the centre; the flanks were formed by APCs and assault guns. This time, however, the odds were more favourable to the Israelis. Reinforcements had brought their tank strength up to 700, and their tank guns and the quality of their gunnery were superior. Moreover, the advance moved the Egyptians beyond the protection of their missile network and made them vulnerable to air attack. Throughout the day tanks clashed in the biggest armour engagement since the battle of Kursk in 1943. Repeatedly driven off, the Egyptians kept coming to be destroyed by Israeli tank-cannons, anti-tank missiles, both SS-11s and American TOWs, as well as air-to-ground rockets. By evening the Egyptians were routed, leaving about half their armour on the battlefield. Israeli tank losses stood at six. It had indeed been a good day. Eleazar now issued orders that the canal crossing, Operation 'Gazelle', was to be executed the following night.

The Israeli Offensive into Egypt: 15–25 October

The objective of the cross-Canal operation was to break the stalemate developing along the Egyptian front and to bring the war to an end on favourable terms before the long-delayed intervention of the super powers. Although Egyptian armour had been knocked about badly, there still were over five Egyptian divisions, 100,000 men and 500 tanks, dug in on the eastern front of the Canal and past experience had taught the IDF that the Egyptian Army fought well in defensive positions. Any attempt to dislodge the Egyptians by a frontal assault would prove very costly, if not altogether impossible. Only mobile operations, the type of warfare for which the IDF had trained, would enable Israel to force a quick decision. An operation on the west bank of the Canal would cut off all, or at least part, of the Egyptian forces from their supply bases, make a considerable gap in the missile network, allow the IAF to operate freely, and perhaps bring about the speedy collapse of the Egyptian forces in the Sinai. There never was much speculation about an advance on Cairo. Political considerations alone put this target out of reach.

General Sharon, 'Arik' as he was known to all, was a difficult subordinate, but an inspired combat leader, the embodiment of Dayan's 'follow me' school of leadership. He had distinguished himself as commander of the paratroopers, fought at the Mitla Pass in 1956, led the breakthrough at Um Katef in 1967, and during his tour as Commanding General Southern Command had made plans for a cross-Canal operation as early as 1971. Although the prefabricated bridge was not ready, he insisted on proceeding with the undertaking. On the night of 15–16 October, elements of a paratroop brigade, led by Danny Matt, and the headquarters elements of the entire division, crossed the waterway on rubber rafts and established a bridgehead on the west bank. Meanwhile, engineer troops, unable to position either the prefabricated bridge or a pontoon bridge, improvised ferries and during the day some tanks and APCs were brought over. The surprised Egyptians did not offer much opposition on the west bank.

It was different along the approaches to the Canal on the other side. Adan's forces were to take and hold a corridor to the water's edge and then follow through after the bridges were in place. However, the area known as the Chinese Farm, on the northern edge of the Great Bitter Lake, was strongly held by the Egyptians and Adan's unit was engaged in very bitter and costly fighting from 16 October to about noon on 18 October. Meanwhile, Sharon's forces, receiving some reinforcement, were enlarging their foothold and during the night of 17–18 October the engineers finally completed two bridges. Adan's forces crossed over, while during the night Matt's brigade repelled an attack launched by several Egyptian commando battalions. In the morning of 18 October Adan's division began to drive south along the Canal towards the large air base at Fayid, destroying missile bases in its path. Some hours later, Sharon, having received another of his armoured brigades, began to push north along the Canal in the direction of Ismailia. Also that day, despite very intense Egyptian artillery barrages and air attacks, the engineers threw two additional bridges across the Canal, and following the passage of Sharon's last armoured brigade, Magen's division began to cross on the evening of 19 October, passing through Adan's rear elements and swept west in a broad arc before turning south towards the shore of the Gulf of Suez.

In the event, Sharon's push north, moving through built-up terrain with irrigation ditches and villages, ran into resolute Egyptian resistance. By 22 October he had reached the outskirts of Ismailia and brought the Ismailia–Cairo road under fire, though he had not occupied it. The 2nd Egyptian Army, therefore, was not cut off and in the 'war of the generals' which erupted immediately after the cease-fire, Sharon charged that he had been restrained from advancing earlier – when his forces were still small but Egyptian resistance had not yet coalesced – by the reluctance of certain superior officers, evidently Bar-Lev and Gonen, from gaining a decisive victory. To the south, however, Adan's and Magen's movements were across open terrain, and with the missile network torn apart, the potent Israeli armour–air combination swept all before it. The Suez–Cairo road was cut on 22 October when a hastily imposed UN Security Council cease-fire halted operations. Both Egypt and Israel accepted the resolution, No. 338, but fighting continued as elements of the 3rd Army tried to break out, while the Israelis sought to improve their positions. An attempt to penetrate into the city of Suez proper was repelled with fairly heavy losses. But Adan and Magen had managed to encircle the 3rd Army when on 24 October, with Russia placing seven airborne divisions on alert to prevent a possible Egyptian collapse, the United States pressured Israel into halting all further operations.

During the last phase of the war, the Egyptians showed clear signs of their command and control failing, though, in contrast with 1967, combat units

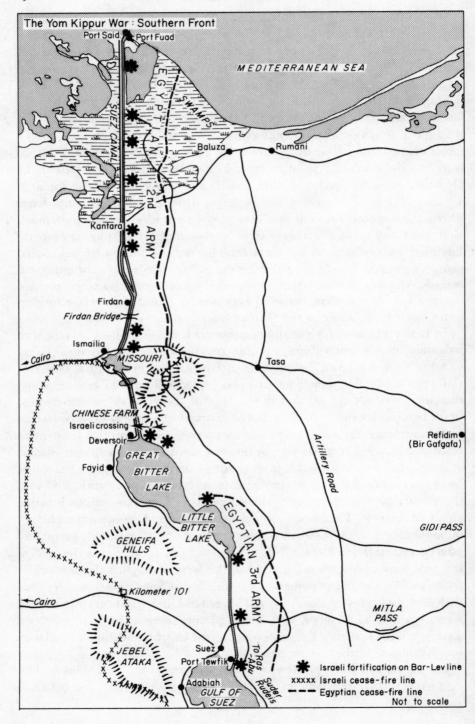

The Yom Kippur War : Southern Front

MEDITERRANEAN SEA

Port Said   Port Fuad

EGYPTIAN

SWAMPS

SUEZ CANAL

Baluza   Rumani

2nd ARMY

Kantara

Firdan

Firdan Bridge

Ismailia

←Cairo   MISSOURI   Tasa

CHINESE FARM

Israeli crossing

Deversoir

Fayid   GREAT BITTER LAKE

LITTLE BITTER LAKE

EGYPTIAN 3rd ARMY

Refidim (Bir Gafgafa)

GENEIFA HILLS

GIDI PASS

←Cairo   Kilometer 101

Artillery Road

MITLA PASS

JEBEL ATAKA

Suez

Port Tewfik

To Ras Abu Rudeis

Sues Rudeis

Adabiah   GULF OF SUEZ

✳ Israeli fortification on Bar-Lev line
xxxxx Israeli cease-fire line
– – – Egyptian cease-fire line
Not to scale

retained their cohesion. The Egyptian command failed to comprehend the importance of the Israeli crossing operation. As late as 18 October, with two Israeli armoured divisions already on the west bank, Sadat continued to believe that this was a mere raid and was convinced only when Soviet Prime Minister Alexei Kosygin, on a visit to Cairo, showed him satellite pictures revealing the full extent of the threat. Only then was Sadat willing to accept Soviet efforts towards an immediate cease-fire in place and also hurled his air force, assisted by some 40 Algerian Mirages, into battle, to destroy the Israeli bridges. Met by the IAF, now freed from the missile threat, the Egyptians sustained heavy losses, but kept coming back with considerable élan though little success. Once again, in air-to-air battles, with as many as 50 planes engaged at one time, the IAF showed its mastery of aerial combat.

The final cease-fire, accompanied by an ominous confrontation of the two super powers as the Russian alert had been countered by an American Stage 3 alert, including nuclear forces, found the Israelis occupying some 600 square miles west of the Canal, encircling the 3rd Army and holding about 8,000 Egyptian prisoners. The Egyptians held an area 5–7 miles deep along the entire east bank of the Canal, except where the corridor passed north of the Great Bitter Lake. They also had taken some 250 Israeli prisoners. In the north, when the cease-fire went into effect, the IDF had occupied 160 square miles behind the Purple Line and held 268 Syrian prisoners, as against an estimated 250 Israeli prisoners in Syrian hands. In terms of materiel, Egypt and Syria lost about 2,000 tanks, while Israel lost about 800, though with the IDF controlling the battlefields, many were salvaged and returned to operations. In the air, the Arabs lost about 500 planes, two-thirds of them Egyptian, mainly in air-to-air encounters. Israel lost about 114 planes, all but 20 to anti-aircraft defences.[16] Arab personnel losses were severe, estimated at well over 15,000 dead and wounded for Egypt and Syria. Israel suffered a total of 2,812 killed and 7,500 wounded, including 606 officers – 80 majors, 25 colonels, and one major-general.

Considerations on the Air and Naval War

The air war provided a number of unexpected problems for the IAF. Considered among experts as being perhaps the world's finest air force, especially in pilot proficiency and ground support, it repeatedly had defeated Egyptian and Syrian attempts to establish an effective air-defence system and had maintained unquestioned supremacy over Arab pilots in air-to-air combat. With this previous experience, the IAF was surprised by the density and effectiveness of the Soviet-supplied air-defence system and, with its relatively old ECM equipment, was unable to jam the acquisition and tracking systems of the SAM-6 and the ZSU-23-4 and 57-2 anti-aircraft systems. Even so, a number of hastily drawn conclusions proclaimed during and soon after the conflict were not substantiated. It was then asserted that the Israeli aircraft losses to SAMs heralded the arrival of an era when tactical aircraft no longer could survive over the battlefield. The IAF did sustain heavy losses in the early stages of the war, but in large part these were due to its all-out effort against the Syrian advance on 6 and 7 October. On the crucial 7 October, the IAF flew hundreds of sorties, sometimes with a turn-around time of only 7 minutes. It absorbed heavy losses against an integrated and fully intact missile system, a screen so heavy that sheer numbers negated most types of evasion tactics. The number of missiles launched during the first three days is supposed to have equalled the total NATO inventory. But against these losses, the IAF has to be credited with a major part in halting the Syrian surprise attack.

To the IAF's credit, it also learned quickly. During the first three days it lost more than 70 planes, mainly to anti-aircraft defences, but downed 144; then during the next 7 days it downed over 120 and lost 25, and during the last 9 days, when the Arabs were forced to commit their air forces, the IAF downed 193 and lost 15 planes.

The heaviest losses were suffered in attacks against static air defences, missile batteries firing salvos rather than single missiles, coupled with radar-directed guns. However, despite the mobility of the SAM-6, SAM-7, and the ZSU anti-aircraft guns, they did not provide adequate protection on the move and once outside the range of their static air-defence envelopes, Arab columns sustained heavy damage. Still, the IAF losses highlighted the need for both passive and offensive means to enable aircraft to offer close support. These include improved ECM equipment, high survivability of attack aircraft and stand-off guided weapons. When such equipment and weapons finally were obtained from the United States, Israeli success in using them was all the more remarkable because of their relative inexperience with them. Together with the excellent air-combat performance, maintaining a 20:1 kill ratio, this indicated an extremely high level of performance by IAF pilots and ground crews.

Throughout the war, the IAF maintained air superiority over Israel and the battlefronts and this deprived the Arabs of the possibility of exploiting their tactical surprise and achieving a strategic success. Lines of communications, population centres, and mobilization areas were free from Arab air attack. For its part, the IAF launched a series of strategic raids against Syrian air fields, oil installations, bridges, and power plants, doing considerable damage, though there is no evidence that this impaired military or civilian morale. On the other hand, the IAF abstained from any strategic strikes against Egypt, possibly deterred by the presence of two battalions of Soviet SCUD ground-to-ground missiles. It also inflicted heavy losses on the Egyptian offensive on 14–15

October, and once Israeli ground forces had made a crack in the canal defences, it was able to exploit this opening. By 22 October about one-third of Egypt's SAM launchers were destroyed or captured.

By all odds the greatest surprise was the showing of the IN, commanded by the newly-appointed Rear-Admiral Benyamin Telem. Heavily outclassed in 1967, it had managed to protect the coastline, made some frogmen raids into Egyptian ports, and seized control of Sharm el Sheik. After the Six Day War, it had been re-equipped with missile boats and these vessels emerged with flying colours. Fighting the first-ever naval actions exclusively with ship-to-ship guided missiles against superior numbers of Soviet-built *Osa* and *Komar* boats of the opposing navies, they inflicted heavy casualties without suffering a loss, and achieved unchallenged control over the contiguous waters of the eastern Mediterranean.

At the outbreak of war the IDF main strike force consisted of 14 vessels, 12 *Saar* and 2 larger *Reshef*-class boats, ranged against an Egyptian force of 12 *Osa*-type missile boats, a number of older *Komar*-class boats, 3 destroyers, 10 submarines, 6 new and about 20 older torpedo boats. The Syrian navy also had grown and consisted of 3 *Osa* and 6 *Komar* boats, 11 torpedo boats and 2 minesweepers. The Soviet-built missile boats were armed with Styx missiles, theoretically outranging the Israeli-built Gabriel, though lacking accuracy and homing capability against small vessels. Moreover, the IN had developed highly sophisticated evasive tactics and ECM gear.

Admiral Telem, despite the relaxed atmosphere at high command, was convinced that war was imminent and by 1 October had placed his force on a state of high alert and by 5 am on the morning of 6 October his entire force was deployed both against the Syrian and the Egyptian navies. On the night of 6–7 October, the northern task force encountered a Syrian flotilla of three missile boats and within 20 minutes sank the enemy without suffering any casualties. The same night the southern task force chased some rocket-launcher-equipped Egyptian torpedo boats into Port Said and during the night of 8–9 October, six Israeli missile boats, approaching the Egyptian coast near Damiette, encountered four enemy missile boats and sank three. Gradually, Arab vessels were driven from the sea, a force of Egyptian submarines deployed south of Crete had to be withdrawn, and the IN, despite heavy shore fire, was able to attack Egyptian and Syrian ports and coastal installations in the Mediterranean. In addition, naval commandos penetrated Egyptian harbours, on one occasion sinking a tank-landing craft, a missile and a torpedo boat inside Port Said.

In the Red Sea, the IN was unable to break a blockade of the Straits of Bab el Mandeb, but it was able to do considerable damage to the Egyptians in the Gulf of Suez, interfering with their attempts to land commandos in the Sinai, disrupting and blockading Egyptian ports.

Of course, the naval battles did not have a decisive influence on the main course of events, though, including the first exclusive ship-to-ship missile engagements, they foreshadowed future developments. The Israeli-designed and partly home-built missile boats proved effective, able to hold their own not only against the Soviet Styx missiles, but also able to operate under the intense fire of Soviet-made 130mm radar-controlled coastal batteries. Except in the range of their missiles, the Israeli boats were superior to those of their opponents in every other aspect – speed and handling, electronic gear, gunnery, crew training and command. The IN was the only major service branch to escape criticism in the 1973 war.[17]

Some Assessments and the Diplomatic Aftermath

During and after the war many commentators exulted the 'new' fighting prowess of the Arabs and declared that they finally had taken the measure of the Israelis. On sober reflection, however, things were not as they appeared. The Arabs revealed political–strategic supremacy in the planning and the preparation of the war and revealed considerable improvement in skill, training, and the handling of advanced technology. But the Arab soldier always had displayed good fighting qualities, especially when competently led, and veterans of 1948, a diminishing band, remembered that Israeli units often had suffered heavily in attacks against Arab positions. The mobile warfare of 1956 and 1967 had obscured this point. This time the Arab level of leadership was higher, though once again there was little capability for improvisation. After 14 October the Egyptians displayed a stubborn fighting spirit, though command and control became hopelessly confused; the Syrians, always tough, broke on 12 October, though they managed to avoid a total collapse. The Jordanians fought well, while the Iraqis did not measure up. Once mobilization was completed, Israeli fighting superiority at every level – soldier to soldier, tank to tank, plane to plane, ship to ship, and commander to commander – reasserted itself. Once the mainstay of the army and the envy of foreign generals, Israel's infantry went to war in 1973 armed for the 1950s, with semi-automatic FN rifles, short-range Uzi submachine guns, bazookas and recoilless rifles. More important, however, the potential of the infantry brigades was not used. Brigadier General Shaked, Chief Paratroop and Infantry officer, was frustrated when Chief of Staff Eleazar ignored repeated pleas for infantry or paratroop raids and attacks, and few such strikes, once the hallmark of Israeli operations, were launched. There were, as Dayan for one conceded, errors and mistakes; some senior officers faltered while others excelled, but the outcome, by all standards, was a victory limited only by an international political situation over which, as in 1949, 1956, and again in 1967, the IDF had no control. To be sure, Dayan was defending his own record. Neutral observers, however, agreed.

'When the war was over', Colonel Barker, a British officer, wrote, 'the Israelis could ponder on their victory – which militarily no one can question,' while an American expert concluded that despite the enormous advantage of surprise, the Israelis recovered within three days. Their performance, he suggested, showed that the 'qualitative gap had not narrowed between 1967 and 1973; if anything it had widened.'[18]

There also was no doubt that on the key question of morale, the IDF came out superior. As another British observer, Brigadier Barclay concluded, here 'the Israelis were comfortable winners.' He expressed, however, concern about civilian morale, all important for an army representing a large part of the electorate of a lively democracy. And morale on the home front, Barclay found 'vulnerable in a quite unexpected way'. Despite 30 years of intermittent wars, Israelis have a low tolerance of military casualties and the prime minister still is informed of every casualty and photographs with brief biographies of every dead soldier are carried on the front pages. This humane attitude may be admirable, but it has become something of a military handicap. As two Israeli analysts grumbled, while Israel often has been pictured as a modern Sparta, the complaints about the casualties suffered, heavy though by no means excessive, and the deep expressions of horror at the inevitable violence of war, had inhibited some operations and done little to strengthen Israel's bargaining posture in the aftermath.[19] It should be noted, however, that there was no decline in civilian morale as long as fighting continued. In fact, after it was revealed that the Arabs had scored unexpected advances, public confidence in the government's conduct of military affairs reached a high point; recriminations became a force only after the unsatisfactory end of the war.

During the fighting the Jewish state had found itself almost completely deserted, and while the United States had furnished vital supplies, it was not prepared to underwrite a clear-cut Israeli victory. It was prepared to counter Russian intervention but, as Kissinger informed the Israelis, it was not prepared to fight World War III so that Israel could destroy the 3rd Army. In fact, American efforts were designed to reduce the impact of Israel's success and produce a settlement based on a nearly total Israeli withdrawal to the pre-1967 lines. Although Israelis failed to see it, American policy had oriented itself towards establishing a 'quasi-alliance' with Cairo.

After considerable negotiations, including veiled and not so veiled pressures, Israel agreed to allow supplies to reach the encircled 3rd Army and made certain other concessions. An agreement to this effect was signed on 11 November by Israeli and Egyptian generals at Kilometre 101 on the Suez–Cairo highway. A general peace conference, co-sponsored by the Soviet Union and the Americans briefly met on 21 December in Geneva. At the same time the Israeli government, aware that its position in the salient across the Canal, constituted an irritant and required a high measure of military preparedness, initiated proposals for a disengagement of forces, which, after Kissinger had spent a great amount of time shuttling between the two sides, was signed on 18 January 1974 by the Israeli and Egyptian chiefs of staff in another meeting at Kilometre 101. Providing for a total Israeli withdrawal from the western side of the Suez Canal and a limited withdrawal east, though still west of the passes, the disengagement agreement limited forces to be deployed by both sides and placed UN troops as a buffer between them. Egypt and Israel agreed to 'scrupulously observe the cease-fire on land, sea, and air' and to refrain 'from all military and para-military action against each other'. Finally, both sides agreed to regard disengagement as a preliminary step to peace negotiations.

Syria, for the time being, remained adamant and during the winter there even was brief fighting along the cease-fire line. In the end, however, Syria signed an agreement following the general pattern of the Egyptian–Israeli disengagement on 31 May 1974, signalling a considerable success for Kissinger's efforts and apparently a substantial success in re-establishing the American position in the Middle East. Many regarded the two agreements as constituting the first steps on the road to peace, though the PLO had done its best to spoil negotiations by raids inflicting heavy civilian casualties on two Israeli towns in the Galilee. In the event, the agreements were signed and were followed by further disengagement steps. Israel now demobilized its reserves and began to consider steps to strengthen its armed forces while at the same time trying to cope, basically without much success, with its growing diplomatic isolation in an oil-hungry world.[20]

9

Between War and Peace: 1974-78

'But we made our prayer to our God and set watch against them day and night.'

Nehemiah 4: 3

For Israel an era opened in October 1973. Although 18 days of bitter fighting once again demonstrated the IDF's superiority in land, air, and naval warfare, the course and outcome of the conflict sorely bruised public confidence and morale – vital components of strengths for the citizen army of a democratic state. During the war, Israel had discovered that the Western European powers would not lift a finger to prevent her destruction. Only the United States, albeit tardily, had provided weapons and ammunition. Still, by 1974 it had become clear that there was a considerable gap between what most Israelis conceived as vital to national survival and what the United States regarded as its own, interest.

Rehabilitation of the armed forces, materially, psychologically, and organizationally proceeded, despite occasional difficulties and the Army that celebrated its 30th anniversary in May 1978 was in many respects as 'different from that of 1973 as the Army of 1967 was different from that of 1948'.[1]

Israel and the United States

The Arab–Israeli conflict always had been asymmetrical in character with Israeli resources being inferior to those of her adversaries. This asymmetry in the past had at least been partially compensated for by superior training, morale, endurance, and higher direction, supplemented since 1967 by a qualitative edge in certain weapons systems furnished by the United States and by the ingenuity of local industry. But, as the Yom Kippur War had demonstrated, the point was rapidly being reached at which courage and determination no longer would suffice against the sheer weight of numbers and when Arab access to Soviet,

European, and even American technology eroded qualitative advantages. Moreover, the dependence on American support, perhaps unavoidable, carried a price tag and soon after the air lift the bill arrived.[2]

The major item on this bill was American insistence on a speedy and 'comprehensive' settlement of the conflict and, while American and Israeli interests coincided on certain issues, the global interests of the United States made her conception of a settlement quite different from that of Israel. Summarized very briefly and simplistically, American policy was a revival of the stratagems of the 1950s when Egypt, not Israel, was sought after as the main partner in a regional policy. The energy crisis of the West required an accommodation with the Arabs and moreover, so American policy-makers argued, 'moderate' Arab states, a rather flexible term that included Egypt, Jordan, Saudi Arabia, even Syria, and sometimes even was stretched to cover certain PLO elements, were prepared to recognize Israel's existence provided that the territories occupied since 1967 were surrendered with, at best, minor modifications and that a solution be found to the Palestinian problem. To induce Egypt away from her dependency on the Soviet Union, the United States undertook to provide economic and ultimately military aid, while at the same time downgrading her relationship with Israel and pressuring her to make concessions.

To compel Israel to make concessions, the United States employed a carrot-and-stick approach, centring around the delivery or the withholding of military assistance. The approach had worked to produce the first round of disengagement agreements, and after an interval in which Israel's government, now headed by Rabin, was subjected to intensive pressure, including a complete embargo on arms transfers from March 1975 on, another withdrawal was arranged, the so-called Sinai II agreement of September 1975. Israel retreated east of the strategic passes and returned the Abu Rudeis oil fields to Egypt. Both sides agreed to limit their forces in the forward areas, while in the critical zone of the passes an American civilian-manned electronic warning station was to be installed. To reassure Israel for giving up valuable strategic and economic positions without reciprocal Egyptian concessions, the United States formally pledged to 'continue to maintain Israel's defensive strength through the supply of advanced types of equipment, such as the F-16 aircraft'. In addition, there were promises that other high-technology items, including Pershing ground-to-ground missiles and concussion bombs, would receive favourable consideration and the United States undertook to support Israel both diplomatically and economically. These pledges were substantial and hailed by some observers as an 'unwritten alliance' underwriting Israel's future security.[3] It was an over-optimistic appraisal. Far from constituting an 'unwritten alliance', they were at best a delicate balancing act concealing a major shift in the

American position.

This became manifest when Washington pressed Israel to make further withdrawals preliminary to any Arab–Israeli negotiations and when the Rabin government refused, the embargo was extended until January 1976 and for certain items into June. By that time, the Pershings already had been totally struck from the list, while other arms were delayed in the procurement process. Although Israel received massive aid after the October War, 4·2 billion dollars by mid-1976, Jordan also received significant aid and roughly twice as many dollars worth of American military equipment and assistance were provided to Saudi Arabia during the 1960–76 period as to Israel, almost all of this in the last few years. American military aid and sales to Arab countries in the period 1973–77 amounted to over 11 billion dollars. If transfers from the Soviet Union, Britain,and France were added, Arab arms acquisitions came to about 20 billion dollar outlay for weaponry since 1974. Translated into actual weapons, by mid-1976, Israel was at a 3:1 disadvantage in planes and tanks, 9:1 in artillery, 12:1 in missiles, and 5:1 in active duty manpower. In addition, in 1975–76, the American and Egyptian governments were conducting negotiations regarding a large-scale upgrading of the Egyptian armed forces. As revealed by the *Foreign Report* of the London *Economist* on 26 March 1976, the plan was to proceed in five stages, beginning with the delivery of C-130 transport aircraft, to communications equipment, ECW gear, armoured vehicles and missiles, and finally fighter aircraft. In addition, Egypt's Mig-21 force was to be improved by being retrofitted with more powerful American jet engines. To make this action acceptable to Congress and public opinion, there were articles and pronouncements by highly placed officials asserting that Israel never had been a strategic asset to the United States and in fact was fast becoming a liability. Israel in any case had more arms than she needed for defence and her arms-purchase plan, 'Matmon C', was designed for aggressive purposes. In the interest of peace, it was argued, the United States should adopt a hard-line policy, denying Israel arms and force her to come to terms with the 'moderate' Arab leadership.[4]

The media campaign and the arms embargo were relaxed during the presidential campaign in the autumn of 1976, during which candidate Carter accused the Ford administration of reneging on its promises and pledged that if elected there would be no more Kissinger-style 'reassessments'. Once elected, however, President Carter took a totally different approach. Delivery of concussion bombs and certain new types of night-fighting equipment were cancelled; there were delays in negotiations for new planes promised in 1975, while the new administration pushed for reconvening the Geneva Conference before the end of 1977. In fact, President Carter went far beyond any previous American position to appease the Arabs. He endorsed the concept of a

'Palestinian homeland', found 'moderation' in the radical Syrian regime, and on 1 October joined the Soviet Union in a declaration calling for Israeli withdrawal and recognition of the 'legitimate rights of the Palestinians', a euphemism that in Soviet and Arab parlance meant the establishment of a PLO state.

By this time Israel no longer was governed by the Labour Coalition. After 29 years of rule, only briefly interrupted by short periods of a national unity government, the Labour Party had become old and tired. It had managed to narrowly win the elections of 1973 held only three weeks after the war, though within four months the wave of protest against its handling of the war led to the resignation of the Meir cabinet. Another Labour Coalition government, with Rabin as prime minister and Peres holding the defence portfolio, managed to hold on until May 1977. It was, however, beset by mounting troubles – internal rivalry, runaway inflation, labour unrest, scandals and corruption at the highest level. American pressure for concessions did not help and in the eyes of many voters Rabin appeared weak and indecisive. When elections came in May 1977, Begin's opposition Likud block won an upset victory.

The new government continued to face the same American pressures, intensified when in November 1977, President Sadat made his dramatic journey to Jerusalem. During a visit to Israel that lasted only 44 hours, Sadat broke down many walls of distrust and enmity and established, albeit fragile, relations with the Jewish state. At the same time, however, Sadat had come to present demands. Addressing the Knesset, he asserted that peace required the return of 'every inch' of territory held since 1967 and recognition of Palestinian rights. Both demands, presented in this form, would have been unacceptable to any Israeli government and the key plank in the Likud platform was the principle that the 'Land of Israel', between the sea and the Jordan River would never be partitioned again. But in his response to Sadat, Begin declared that all issues, except Israel's security were negotiable, though he ruled out total withdrawal and a PLO state. He spelled out his negotiating position in December, reflecting a surprising shift in his known positions. In fact, they were more far-reaching than those offered by previous governments. Begin recognized Egyptian sovereignty over the entire Sinai Peninsula and announced that he had no intention of extending Israeli sovereignty over the West Bank. Instead he offered self-rule to the Arab inhabitants of the area, retaining, however, certain military safeguards. It was on this basis that talks opened in late December and proceeded until 18 January when Sadat suddenly broke off the negotiations and recalled his delegation. Contacts, especially between Sadat and Weizman, the new minister of defence, continued, but in the first half of 1978 peace prospects appeared to have dimmed.

American reaction, and perhaps this had been the objective all along, was to blame Begin for 'excessive rigidity' on the territorial issue. President Carter now announced his intent to sell the most sophisticated planes in the American arsenal to the Saudis and less sophisticated fighters to Egypt. To counter opposition, the administration linked this proposal with the sale of a sharply reduced number of planes to Israel. Linkage in an 'all or nothing' package was a breach of undertakings made during the Sinai II agreement and chilled relations between Washington and Jerusalem, and there also were reports that the administration planned to furnish Egypt with 3,000 APCs. And when in March, Israel replied to a series of PLO attacks from Lebanon, culminating in a particularly bloody raid into the Tel Aviv area, by sending troops to occupy a security belt along its northern frontier, the State Department was quick to demand a complete pull-back and censured the IDF for using cluster bombs against PLO positions.

American policy, however, seemed ambivalent and confusing. After several visits by Dayan and Begin had produced few results, Carter once again appeared to change his stand. In a press interview, he implied that Israel did not have to withdraw from all occupied territories and that a permanent settlement should not include an independent Palestinian state. And on 1 May 1978, during a White House reception for Prime Minister Begin, he pledged that the United States would never waver from its 'total absolute commitment to Israel's security'. Two weeks later, however, after considerable presidential pressure, Congress agreed to the administration's proposal to sell warplanes to Egypt and Saudi Arabia, a development hailed by some close to the administration as a major defeat for the 'Israeli Lobby'.

Military Problems of Withdrawal

Even when divorced from emotion and seen in pure military terms, territorial withdrawals remained a most difficult issue. Before 1967, Israel had lacked defensible borders and had solved this dilemma by opting for a first strike whenever deterrence had failed. After 1973, however, and barring unforeseen and dramatic shifts, either for the worse or better, such action no longer appeared feasible. Instead, while basing their planning on the 'maximum threat' concept, Israeli strategists worried about how to absorb a first blow and still be able to mount a counter-attack. An important part of their considerations was that the Middle East no longer was the region it had been before the 1967 war. All confrontation states had invested enormous sums in their arsenals; Saudi Arabia and Libya had joined the arms race, and weapons had become more sophisticated and deadly. Secure and defensible borders, giving both strategic depth and topographic positions, seemed to be more rather than less important.[5]

Although a few experts argue that medium-range ground-to-ground missiles, such as the SCUDs deployed by Egypt and Syria, and modern strike aircraft have made terrain and distances irrelevant, the majority opinion is that as long as conventional munitions only are employed, these strategic systems would not materially affect the outcome of a future conflict. They do, however, indicate the need for advanced warning stations and for greater dispersal of air bases and storage areas. Tactically, combat experience in 1973 indicated that the new technologies had increased rather than diminished the importance of terrain. Holding the high ground provided cover and observation necessary for directing artillery and the new terminally guided missiles. Conversely, forces assembling or manoeuvring on the low ground had become more vulnerable. And while there was an ongoing debate about the exact details of the future defence posture, there was near unanimity among military planners that mobilization and deployment of Israel's Army would become difficult, even impossible, if hostile forces were to re-establish themselves on the commanding ridges of the West Bank or the Golan. There appeared to be more flexibility in the Sinai, though here too the situation was not as clear cut as many civilians imagined.

For Israel the most vital part of the Sinai strategically was the northern approach and here, east of the strategic passes, there are no solid topographical obstacles. An exception are the hills of the Rafah–El Arish–Um Katef triangle, the historic assembly area for attacks north into the coastal area of Israel. Retention of a military presence here, especially in the Rafah approaches which cut off the Gaza Strip from the south and where a very large air field had been constructed, was regarded as desirable. To stabilize the position in this region the Labour government had established a few settlements. Whether these in fact were a military asset or a burden could be debated, though Sharon called them a 'psychological barrier, as important as a military'. In addition, military planners also had to consider relocation of the vast amount of stores transferred into the Sinai after 1973 to be closer to the potential front and, with the IDF grown by several hundred per cent since 1967, the loss of the Sinai as a manoeuvre area had to be taken into account. In the end, however, planners agreed that provided the Sinai was demilitarized, almost total withdrawal here was compatible with security needs.

By contrast there was little room for pull-outs on the Golan Heights or the West Bank. Moreover, here the issue was complicated by the danger of ever closer military co-operation between Jordan and Syria and by the rapidly growing Saudi Arabian forces. There was talk of an eastern front, between 14 and 18 divisions strong, a combination of Syrian, Jordanian, and Iraqi divisions, bolstered by contingents from Kuwait, Yemen, and other Arab states, and supplied from the large depots being built near the Jordanian frontier in Saudi Arabia. An even more immediate fear was that an Arab summit held in October 1974 at Rabat had designated the PLO as the 'sole legitimate representative of the Palestinian people', removing Jordan, at least temporarily, from the stage on the West Bank. And the PLO openly declared that it would regard a West Bank state merely as another step in its struggle for the ultimate eradication of Israel. Considering all these factors, Israeli soldiers and civilians alike regarded the retention of some security elements on the West Bank as essential. There exists a wide consensus that Jerusalem should remain united, that frontier rectifications in the coastal sector are essential, and above all that there should be an Israeli military presence on the Jordan ridge, a mountain range providing good defensive positions.

Militarily these considerations are logical. They provide Israel with secure borders and do not threaten any vital Egyptian, Syrian, or Jordanian objectives. Politically and emotionally, however, they were unacceptable to Egypt and Jordan, not to mention Syria, the radical Arab states and the PLO. They represent an improvement over the 'territorial compromise position' advocated by the Labour Coalition and have been, albeit reluctantly, accepted by the present cabinet. Though played up by the media, differences between 'hawks' and 'doves' on this issue are not all that great. A substantial majority will support territorial concessions provided they do not jeopardize basic security, but an even larger number will repudiate arrangements depriving the state of defensive capabilities. If faced with the destruction of their state and the annihilation of their people, still the avowed object of the PLO and the so-called Arab rejection front, Israelis will fight with all means at their disposal.

The Agranat Commission Report

Since the October War, Israel has faced difficult and uncertain circumstances, but it has managed to rebuild, reorganize, and re-equip its forces. The process began rather inauspiciously when the end of the war was followed by public recriminations among some of the leading soldiers. The dispute had professional, personal, and political overtones, the last hardly surprising in a citizen army where even ranking field commanders often were reservists with strong political ties and, on occasion, ambitions.

Sharon, representing the Likud opposition and an exponent of mobile warfare, fired the first volley, charging that the Bar-Lev Line had been a blunder that had deprived the army of its greatest asset, mobility. During the conflict, he continued, communications between the high command and the field had been poor and too many high-ranking officers had been promoted due to political favouritism. Finally, so he claimed, the Labour government had deliberately down-played his role in the Canal crossing and there had been an

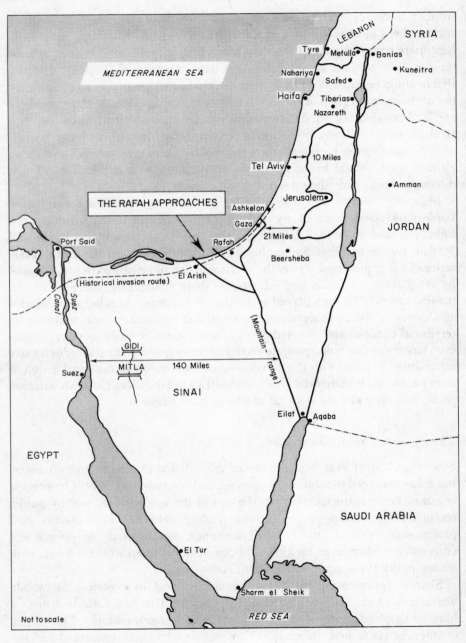

unwarranted and costly 36 hours' delay before reinforcements had been sent to his bridgehead. Appearing in the *New York Times* on 9 November 1973, these statements prompted Chief of Staff Eleazar to hint that he might take disciplinary action against Sharon for granting 'unauthorized' interviews. The same day, however, Bar-Lev, just returned to his civilian post as minister of industry, gave his side of the story in a signed article in Israel's top-circulation daily *Ma'ariv*. He claimed that those in charge of the Army since his retirement, namely Eleazar and his staff, and not the alleged fragility of his line, had been responsible for the setbacks during the initial phase of the war. In turn, Eleazar, once Bar-Lev's close friend, responded that such statements were irresponsible and that things would have gone differently if the reserves had been called out 8 to 24 hours earlier. And the decision not to call out the reserves had been made at the highest military and political levels – in other words Dayan and Mrs Meir.

Criticism did not remain confined to the generals. In Israel citizens take an active and highly vocal part in the political debate and with almost every man having served, or serving, in the armed forces, everyone is a 'general'. Serving soldiers, reservists, and civilians flooded the press, the Knesset, the state comptroller, and the Army's inspector general with complaints alleging incompetent leadership, equipment failures and shortages, and generalized complaints all demanding explanations for the *mehdal*, the blunder of October. Much of the criticism focused on Dayan, who vainly pointed out in speeches and in print that all armies experienced occasional setbacks, but that few had made such a spectacular comeback as the IDF.

On 21 November 1973 a public commission of inquiry, headed by Shimon Agranat, president of the supreme court, was appointed. The other four members were Moshe Landau, a supreme court justice, Yitzhak Nebenzahl, the state comptroller, and two former chiefs of staff, Yadin and Laskov. The commission was charged with investigating the 'intelligence information for the days preceding the Yom Kippur War' and the 'decisions taken by the responsible military and civil authorities in response thereto'.[6] It appears that the brief took for granted that greater vigilance and combat readiness would have decisively affected the outcome of the war. This is doubtful. To be sure, Arab penetrations might have been contained earlier and casualties might have been lighter, but ultimate results would have been the same. The two super powers, each for its own reasons, would have prevented the destruction of the Egyptian and Syrian armies and the oil-producing Arab states still would have imposed their embargo. The primary value of the inquiry was to settle internal disputes and assign responsibility.

The commission started its work on 23 November 1973, submitted a preliminary report on 1 April 1974, a secret paper on 7 July, and a final account on 30 January 1975. Most of the testimony and findings have remained secret; out of the 1,512 pages in the final report only 42 were released for publication.

The preliminary report of April 1974 placed the blame for Israeli unpreparedness squarely on the Intelligence Branch and recommended that its head, General Zeira, his deputy, and several senior officers be removed from their positions. Also, pending further investigation, it recommended the suspension of General Gonen, the former commander of the Southern Command. The report also criticized Chief of Staff Eleazar for claiming that Egypt would never attack until it had assembled enough air strength to destroy the IAF. As late as two days before the outbreak of the war, the commission stated, the Israeli general staff had believed that neither Egypt nor Syria, nor the two combined, had the capability. In the event, of course, the attacks were launched with only a few sorties against Israeli air fields. The initial report failed to address itself to the shortcomings of the government or the defence minister, though by holding Eleazar responsible, it left the strong impression that it absolved the government. Neither the public at large or even the Labour Party could accept these inconsistent findings. There was a storm of protest forcing the cabinet to resign.[7]

The final report, appearing some ten months later, did deal with the political leadership and concluded that if the intelligence at its disposal had been properly evaluated and if mobilization had been ordered earlier, the setbacks during the initial phase of the war could have been avoided. Dayan was faulted for believing that the covering forces of the active Army were adequate to protect an orderly mobilization. In the future, the committee advised, the country would have to mobilize as soon as a major threat was detected. Operations should be conducted by combined arms and the enemy's anti-air missile network would have to be suppressed before mobile action could begin.

Perhaps the most interesting finding, though hardly a surprise, was that there had been 'poor discipline, but high combat morale'. This, the commission argued, could no longer be tolerated. Other observers had come to similar conclusions. The egalitarianism and self-discipline, one British general commented, present in the IDF as late the 1960s, was 'all but gone' and external discipline would have to be imposed.[8] Of course, the IDF had been aware of this problem expressed in a high ratio of road and training accidents, low standards of dress, building, and vehicle maintenance. There had been repeated attempts to tighten up discipline, but with little effect. Even after 1973, the annual reports of the state comptroller continued to criticize the Army's handling of materiel, and soon after the Begin government assumed office, its new defence minister, Weizman, again issued orders that all regulations and prescribed standards, including proper uniforms, were to be rigidly enforced. But it is difficult to impose formal discipline on a citizen army, largely reservist, reflecting a society too much part of the Western intellectual world to escape the effects of the current widespread aversion to military forms. Combat spirit remains high, though dress and maintenance standards leave much to be desired. However, especially for weapons systems, they appear to be rather higher than those in first-line formations of other Western countries.

Command Changes and Force Structure

The war and the Agranat Commission's report forced major changes in command. Eleazar, Gonen, and Zeira resigned under protest, other major commanders such as Bar-Lev and Sharon returned to civilian life. Altogether, by May 1974 no fewer than 11 generals had left the Army. Rehabilitation of the IDF was supervised by General Mordechai Gur, the paratrooper hero of the 1967 battle for Jerusalem. Appointed chief of staff in April 1974, and with his term extended for an additional year, he served until 1978 when he handed over to General Raphael (Raful) Eytan, another paratroop officer.

Gur's appointment was regarded by some as signalling a turning away from the armour-dominated concepts that had prevailed under Tal and Eleazar, but this really was not the case. For one, Tal was appointed deputy chief of staff to back up Gur, and secondly, while lacking practical knowledge of tank warfare, Gur was far more than just a combat commander and had actually dealt with most aspects of the Army. After 1967 he had served as head of the military administration in the Gaza Strip, then he had been in charge of the important Northern Command, and had served as military attaché in Washington, a position giving him insight into Israel's complex military relationship with the United States. With a flair for public relations, a smooth talker and known to court the press, Gur was not an easy subordinate and on occasion clashed with his civilian masters in the ministry of defence.

His reputation for speaking his mind was legendary. As commander of the Gaza Strip he had a major row with Dayan, who wanted him to move his headquarters to a more secure area. Gur, arguing that this would be read as a sign of weakness, refused and in the end it was the minister and not the general who backed down. After he became chief of staff, Gur felt that in a country where security aspects were part of all policy decisions, the chief of staff should be consulted in the formulation of policy. This brought him into conflict with Weizman, who believed that the chief of staff should execute but not formulate policy and who, in contrast to practice under Dayan and Peres, rarely asked the chief of staff to attend cabinet meetings. Gur, however, was irrepressible. On the even of Sadat's visit, Gur declared in a press interview that Egypt's ultimate objective was war not peace. Weizman was incensed and ready to relieve Gur, but the prime minister refused, apparently feeling that the country could not afford to have two consecutive chiefs of staff resign under a cloud. However, both Begin and Weizman were determined to have as his successor a soldier and not a politician. The man they chose was General Eytan, an aggressive, hard-nosed disciplinarian, wounded five times, lacking a flair for dinner speeches and with a total disdain for the press, but regarded throughout the IDF as a soldier's soldier.

Eytan was born in 1929, the son of a farmer who had been one of the founders of the *ha-Shomer*. He joined the underground defence forces at age 16, fought in the battle for Jerusalem's Katamon quarter in 1948, and in the early 1950s joined the newly formed paratroop unit. As a battalion commander he fought at the Mitla Pass in 1956, commanded a brigade in 1967, and as chief infantry and paratroop officer led punitive strikes into Jordan, Lebanon, and Syria during the War of Attrition. Considered a fighting soldier, but not a planner, each of his promotions was regarded by some pundits as his last. Yet they were wrong. During the Yom Kippur War he received international attention when his outnumbered formations first repelled a Syrian assault and, reinforced, counter-attacked to a point just 20 miles from Damascus. At every command level, Eytan was known and admired by his men, infusing them with a desire to do their utmost for a man who had become a living legend to generations of young Israeli soldiers.

The Yom Kippur War propelled Eytan into contention for the highest position in the IDF. In April 1974 he was named to head the Northern Command, where he played an important role in aiding Christian forces in southern Lebanon to fight off Palestinian attacks, and in August 1977 replaced General Yekutiel Adam as chief of the operations branch, a job considered the stepping stone to the post of chief of staff. On 16 April 1978 he took over his new post, typically limiting himself to a laconic 20-second acceptance speech to the assembled ministers and other guests. His first major announcement came in the traditional Independence Day interview, given on Israel's 30th anniversary, when he stated that the IDF could not guarantee the security of the state without retaining control of the Golan Heights, the West Bank, and the Gaza Strip.

Eytan's promotion may be the harbinger of a return to the old-fashioned military ethos. The new chief of staff is deeply committed to the older values of Israeli society, unhappy about materialism and believes that the country is going soft, a development he considers as potentially destructive. At the same time, he realizes that the clock could not be turned back to the age of infantry. General Adan, the former chief of operations and a veteran tank officer, replaced in 1977 by Eytan, was brought back as deputy chief of staff and the IDF continued to place its faith in mobile armoured and mechanized forces.

As chief of staff, Eytan inherited an Army considerably larger, better armed, and differently organized from that of 1973, but also the problem of dealing with proposals for radically changing the command structure, a project under discussion since the summer of 1977. As it stood, the IDF command structure, a single chief of staff directing what in effect had become three different services – army, air force, and navy – basically was unchanged since its inception during and immediately after the War of Independence. Since then, both the air force and the navy had achieved operational independence, while the ground forces had become so large that it appeared questionable whether a single chief of staff could exercise effective control. In 1977, mobilization strength was estimated at over 500,000, with 150,000 on active duty. Since 1973, armour had increased by 35 per cent, artillery by 30, and air strength by 15, while the navy registered an increase of almost 45 per cent in combat effectiveness. The mobilized ground forces comprised a total of 47 brigades: 17 armoured, 9 mechanized, 9 infantry, 9 artillery, and 3 paratroop-air mobile, grouped into divisional task forces, *ugdot*, and with corps formations, *gayessot*, introduced late in 1975 and tested during the manoeuvres of 1975–76. To retain maximum flexibility, the composition of each corps differed according to its individual mission.[9]

The much-enlarged size and number of field formations required a more complex command and control system and in August 1977, General Tal was appointed to study the organization of the Army to determine whether an independent ground forces command, paralleling the autonomous IAF and IN, should be established. Apparently Tal recommended the creation of such a command which not only would provide better control in the field, but also abrogate much of the independence enjoyed by the ground branches. In effect, the IDF was to move from a theoretically unified command structure to a three services arrangement, with each service chief responsible for day-to-day operations, and the IDF chief of staff functioning in a fashion similar to the chairman of the Joint Chiefs of Staff in the United States. Gur made no attempt to hide his opposition to a separate ground force command. As he saw it, not only would it mean a decentralization of control and a duplication of effort, placing more senior officers in desk jobs, but also remove the chief of staff from supervising training and combat readiness, though he still would retain responsibility for leading the forces in an eventual war. The matter remained unresolved when Eytan assumed office.

There was less controversy over another major scheme, a new infrastructure for the land forces. After the Yom Kippur War it was felt that the delay in transporting troops and materiel to the front had given the enemy a considerable tactical advantage and it was decided to move mobilization depots and stores closer to the potential combat areas. Relocation had begun late in 1974 and was supposed to be completed by 1980. As it was, this move constituted yet another headache for planners in the event of withdrawals following Sadat's initiative. A corollary part of this scheme was an effort to increase reserves, especially combat formations, and speed up the process of getting these units into action. Additional manpower was found by reclassifying and reassigning men and relaxing physical qualifications and age limits for combat service. The reserve call-up system was streamlined and computerized. Trials made in 1975 and 1976 showed the system to be 90 per cent effective and the majority of units combat ready within 48 hours.

Manpower, however, remained, and is likely to remain, a problem for the IDF. With a nearly static population of three million Jewish citizens, and with immigration just barely matching emigration, the Army has tried to fill a wider range of jobs with women. This became more difficult when the Begin cabinet, in order to enlist the support of the National Religious Party, agreed to liberalize rules governing exemptions for women from military service. Even before this, only between 51 to 54 per cent of potential female recruits had been inducted, with about 20 per cent exempted on religious grounds. Orthodox religious groups always had opposed all military service for women and liberalizing exemptions, by no longer requiring rabbinic certification but only a personal declaration, may lead to a significant drop in the number of women soldiers.

Increased combat readiness required larger career cadres, nearly doubling the number serving in 1973. To attract and retain qualified specialists, pay and benefits were raised and new senior non-commissioned grades created. Even so, as in other Western countries, it was difficult to retain qualified technicians in uniform.

New Weapons and Tactics

Although in the wake of the October war many commentators hastened to assert that the *Blitzkrieg* was dead, these announcements, to say the least, were premature.[10] In the first days of the 1973 war, Israeli armoured units, advancing without close air, infantry, or artillery support, attacked in the face of large numbers of ATGMs and suffered heavily. But this did not mean that the tank was finished. In 1974, the deputy chief of staff chaired deliberations to assess mistakes and find ways to improve organization and tactics in the light of recent experience. There was agreement that tanks on their own indeed had become vulnerable, especially when strong air-defence systems prevented close air support. On the other hand it rejected the concept that infantry had once again become the 'queen of battle'. Israel, in any case, did not have the manpower to flood the battlefield with infantry masses and, being forced because of its quantitative inferiority to wage a mobile offensive war, could look only to armoured forces to achieve victory by rapid penetration into enemy territory.

Only the tank with its heavy armament, armour protection and cross–country mobility could achieve this. 'The tank', Tal wrote, 'is the core and the backbone of the armoured formations, all of whose arms are mobile and some of them armoured. The tank bears the brunt of the assault and is the decisive weapon of land warfare. All other arms are integrated into the formation in order to support the tank and serve it by dismounted fighting, providing protection, breaching obstacles, and giving fire cover and logistic support.'[11]

In organizational terms this meant that the traditional branches, infantry and artillery, were being absorbed in an army comprised almost entirely of armoured and mechanized formations, differing only in the proportion of tanks to other armoured vehicles. This, of course, did not mean that there was no infantry. In fact the new armoured formations included a higher proportion of infantry than those before 1973, with more infantrymen riding and fighting from APCs and with the pre–war ratio of one APC for every two tanks changing to an even number. But in the IDF, mechanized infantry always had been part of the Armoured Corps, wearing the black beret and training in corps schools. Artillery, one brigade in each armoured division, became an organic component and no longer an assigned formation, though it remained a separate branch.

Israeli planners recognized that the integration of SAMs and short-range air-defence weapons had seriously compromised close air support. However, the IAF had sustained a relatively low overall sortie loss rate and it was concluded that tactical air operations – control of the airspace over the battlefield, suppression of air defences, and even direct ground support – still were possible, albeit requiring greater use of both passive and offensive devices. In addition, with Arab air strength growing, ground troops were provided with more air-defence weapons, including twin 20mm half-track mounted guns, single-barrel 40mm Bofors guns, commonly towed behind trucks, and the American-supplied Chaparral system. The latter consists of a modified M-113 carrier, carrying converted Sidewinder-type missiles. Normally the system is deployed in conjunction with radar directed XM-163 20mm cannon anti-aircraft vehicles. Reported under development is a personal shoulder-fired missile based on captured Strela prototypes.

The new 'combined arms' doctrines, some might call them old, were tested in several large-scale manoeuvres in the Sinai. In 1975 the manoeuvre plan called for the attacker to break through a strongly defended zone. Paratroops were dropped behind the enemy defences, while combat engineers, infantry, and armour, covered by a heavy artillery barrage launched frontal and flank attacks. An even larger exercise was conducted the following year. This time it began with a night attack, a traditional Israeli speciality neglected between 1967 and 1973. Preceded by a heavy artillery barrage, infantry worked its way into the enemy defences and aircraft came into action at dawn, attacking selected targets, dropping paratroops and landing helicopter-borne commando forces to attack missile batteries and command posts. When the enemy was thrown into confusion and breaches had been made, armour passed through to open a mobile exploitation phase. In many ways this combination of night operations, frontal pressure and manoeuvre on the rear, with armour assuming its pursuit role only when the battlefield became fluid, was reminiscent of Sharon's attack against Um Katef in 1967.

The conversion of the ground forces into an all-armoured or mechanized army required a substantial increase in armoured vehicles. Israel could not afford the expense of introducing an entirely new family of armour and most of the IDF armour continued to consist of obsolescent, even obsolete, types, with rehabilitation still the prime source. Overblown estimates by foreign sources credit Israel with over 3,200 tanks, but this would include the World War II Shermans, last seen in action in 1973, and withdrawn in 1975. More realistically, the IDF probably can deploy some 2,700 medium tanks, including about 600 M-48s, 650 M-60-A1s, 900 Centurions, and about 600 captured Soviet tanks, mainly T-54/55s, but also some 140 T-62s. All vehicles have been extensively modified. Commanders' cupolas have been fitted to the American tanks and additional bottom armour has been provided for the M-48s. The Centurions all have been converted to diesel engines, new guns, rangefinders and other improvements, and are said to have nearly 60 per cent new parts. Captured T-54/55s have been refitted with the standard 105mm gun and spare parts are being produced. It is unclear whether any major work has been done on the T-62s.

In addition, Israel also has a limited number of heavy tanks, the 60-ton Merkava or Chariot. Since the late 1960s there were reports that the IDF was developing its own tank and in May 1977, Defence Minister Peres announced that such a vehicle was indeed in production and service. The Merkava was a rather unique hybrid, combining the features of a tank with that of an APC. Having suffered almost two-thirds of all casualties in 1973, the Armoured Corps looked for the greatest possible crew protection. The result was a heavy vehicle, with a four-man crew protected by British-developed Chobham armour and a frontal engine. This design traded tank kills for crew casualties, but also provided a large rear compartment carrying, depending on ammunition load, up to ten infantrymen. The Merkava carries the 105mm gun and an array of gadgets for protection against atomic, biological, and chemical warfare. Other novelties included a laser-beam rangefinder, infrared night sights, and an Israeli-made artillery computer. With its 900 horsepower engine, the tank was underpowered by American standards and the same was true of the Merkava II, appearing late in 1977, featuring a modified German 120mm gun and a 1,200 horsepower engine. The design reflected Tal's view that battlefield mobility and not theoretical speed mattered and that survival on the battlefield depended on heavy armour and armament.

In October 1977, Major-General Moshe Peled, Armoured Corps commander since April 1974, expressed his satisfaction with the Merkava, a tank of the 1980s generation. Production figures for the vehicle are unknown, though probably do not exceed a maximum of 50 a year. The IDF, therefore, will have to rely on its older tanks for some time to come and it has been rather successful in upgrading obsolete models.

The same, of course, was true of APCs. The IDF, despite its new emphasis on mechanized infantry, is short of tracked vehicles and the Merkava's dual functions pointed up the lack of real infantry fighting vehicles. Both the old M-3 half-tracks, rehabilitated again and again, and now diesel-engined, certainly the oldest armoured vehicles in service anywhere, as well as the new M-113s, of which over 800 had been received after 1973, lacked adequate protection and firepower. Acquisition of additional APCs remains a high priority.

The new role assigned to artillery required it to match the off-road mobility of armour. By the end of 1977, the IDF had an estimated 750 heavy and medium guns, with 90 per cent self-propelled compared to 75 per cent in 1973. Artillery ammunition, in short supply during the 1973 war, has been increased and stocks now are thought to be adequate for 30 days of intensive fighting. In addition, IDF artillery employs captured Russian materiel, including various models of 122, 130, and 203mm towed gun-howitzers, supplemented by truck-mounted Katyusha barrage rockets.

Probably the most potent weapon in the artillery inventory is the Lance, a supersonic ballistic missile, inertially guided, with a range of over 60 miles. Equipped with a cluster-bomb warhead, spreading some 800 smaller explosive missiles either anti-personnel or armour-piercing over a controlled area, the Lance seems especially useful against SAM batteries, though less useful as an ATGM suppressant because of its 4- to 5-mile minimum range. For suppressive fire at shorter ranges, the IDF has developed a new ground-to-ground missile, the Zeev. There exist two configurations. The first, with a 70kg warhead, has a range of up to 4 miles, while the second, carrying a 180kg warhead, has a range of 1 mile only. No details regarding the type of warhead or the guidance system, if any, are available.

There also are questions about the existence and configuration of another ground-to-ground missile, the so-called Jericho rocket. At the time of the Sinai II agreement the United States had indicated willingness to consider supplying Israel with Pershing missiles, an inertially guided ballistic missile with a range of over 500 miles. These missiles were supposed to counter-balance the SCUDs furnished by the Soviet Union to Egypt and Syria. Pershings, however, existed only in a nuclear warhead configuration and it was deemed too expensive to produce them in limited numbers with a conventional warhead. This may have been a pretext, but, in any case, the item had been shelved. Israel then is said to have gone ahead with the development of the Jericho missiles, a product of the IAI, based on the French–Israeli Topaz-Shavit II rocket and the Dassault M-620 missile. The status of this solid-fuelled 300-mile-range missile has never been clarified, though Western analysts assume that it exists.[12]

The Jericho missile was a sensitive issue because in a conventional configuration its effectiveness would be small. Certain defence analysts claimed that the missiles were nuclear-tipped with a warhead in the 20-kiloton range. They pointed out that Israel's reactor at Dimona in the Negev, originally built in 1958 with French help, is capable of producing weapon's grade material and there were stories that during the darkest days of October, Dayan called for the activation of such 'last resort' weapons. Finally, some experts believe that Israel should develop and publicly announce possession of such weapons as a deterrent.[13]

There are weighty arguments against this course of action. Apart from the problems that such a policy would raise with the United States, it would compel the Arabs to seek the protection of a nuclear umbrella. Already during the Yom Kippur War, so it is reported, nuclear warheads for the SCUDs were deployed, though not released from Soviet custody. The Middle-East countries, and Israel in particular, are extremely vulnerable to nuclear weapons. Industry, population, and critical oil installations all are concentrated in a small number of areas. Israel's government, therefore, has consistently denied rumours about possession of nuclear weapons and declared that it never would be the first to introduce them into the region. Both statements are very likely correct. Yet, when the level of conventional forces on the side of its adversaries would seem to threaten the elimination of the state, Israel would have a strong temptation to develop a secondary deterrent, based perhaps on the concept of a nuclear weapon 'one step away'.

On a less dramatic level, the IDF has greatly enlarged its inventory of anti-tank missiles and guns. American TOW missiles, launched from a tube, optically tracked and wire-guided, and capable of being ground-, vehicle-, and helicopter-mounted have been provided and are in use with armoured and mechanized units. Shoulder-fired Dragon missiles also have been furnished by the United States, and the IDF also utilizes the large quantities of captured Soviet-made anti-tank weapons, ranging from 100mm guns to squad-level RPGs.

Air and Naval Developments

The IAF and the IN also responded to the lessons of the 1973 war. Faced by new

Arab capabilities, both in anti-air defences and in the air, the IAF was forced to reconsider its priorities, while the navy continued expansion of its combat-proven missile-boat concepts. Both services expanded personnel, though given the weapons systems, the increase was small compared to the ground forces.

Before 1973, the IAF had two major missions – command of the air and ground support. Its air superiority had not been seriously challenged, though Arab acquisition of large numbers of first-line combat aircraft both from the Soviet and Western suppliers meant that in a future conflict Israel once again would have to be concerned about her major population centres and no longer could expect her lines of communications to remain immune to air or helicopter-borne attacks. The second main mission, ground support, has been difficult. New tactics and weaponry had to be devised for integrating ground and air forces, and the problem loomed larger as defensive systems became more numerous and sophisticated, yet simple to operate and lethal. Neutralizing these defences obviously is a very high priority. ECM capabilities are a must, but aggressive operations also must be mounted against enemy weapons and control systems. This requires both close-in as well as stand-off capabilities with ranges out to 30 miles. The IAF acquired a variety of American ECM and stand-off systems from 1970 on and in 1977 the IAI unveiled the Luz 1, a television-guided air-to-ground missile with a 200-kg conventional warhead and a range of 40 plus miles.

Nonetheless, short-range air-defence weapons deployed in the battle area are the least vulnerable to suppression and as already had been decided, the IAF no longer would function as 'flying artillery'. Remotely piloted vehicles, drones, especially in expendable strike versions, may be partial answer for battlefield use and the IAF has some American as well as locally produced vehicles. In another development, helicopters, limited until recently to troop lift and evacuation, have received new emphasis. Armed attack helicopters, especially the TOW-armed Huey Cobra, are now in service and the IAI is reported to be working on its own design for a rotary wing aircraft. In July 1977, General Benyamin Peled, IAF commander, told reporters that armed helicopters would play a major role in any future operations and that their pilots now received the same intensive training given to fighter pilots.

Indications are that in the future the IAF will concentrate on retaining air superiority, coupled with interdiction strikes against enemy lines of communications and his infrastructure well behind the battle area. This will require more intelligence acquisition capabilities. Grumman E-2C Hawkeye reconnaissance planes have been received and some large jets have been equipped for airborne command roles. These, however, remain improvisations. When Major-General George J. Keegan, retired chief of US Air Force intelligence, visited the IAF in the summer of 1977, he recommended that Israel acquire a modified version of the AWACS (Airborne Warning and Control Systems) aircraft. The reason, he pointed out, was that Israel had but few ground radars and these were vulnerable. It was, and remains, however, highly unlikely that the United States would authorize transfer of these expensive and extremely sophisticated systems, even in modified form.

In fact, even replacement of the ageing force of Phantoms, Skyhawks, and Mirages with new planes became an issue between Israel and the United States. By late 1976 losses of the Yom Kippur War had been replaced and the IAF inventory included about 600 planes – 250 Skyhawks, 200 Phantoms, 50 Mirages, and an undisclosed number of Israeli-built Kfir aircraft. The Magisters, sometimes figured in the inventory, can no longer be counted as combat aircraft. To update this force, Israel submitted purchase requests based on the American commitments made in 1975. These requests ran into opposition both from the State Department and the Pentagon, which argued that the IAF did not need the total requested – 50 F-15s and 150 F-16s – and that requests for co-production rights, that is Israeli manufacture of certain components, was undesirable. Israel felt that it needed the planes to counter the rapidly growing Arab air potential, the air forces of the confrontation states as well as those of Saudi Arabia, Iraq, Morocco, Kuwait, and Libya, which in the event of another conflict were likely to come into action against her. As for the co-production rights, these were important not only for economic reasons, but with the United States also supplying the same types of planes to the Arabs, it was hoped that co-production might permit the incorporation of special modifications.

Twenty-five F-15s were contracted for as a first instalment and the first three planes, Eagles or *Nesherim* as they were called, arrived on 10 October 1976 and were welcomed by Prime Minister Rabin, Generals Gur, Peled, and other dignitaries. Rabin proclaimed their arrival 'a holiday for Israel', while Gur noted that they gave the IDF new strategic capabilities. The F-15s indeed were uniquely potent planes, air-superiority fighters as well as long-range ground-attack aircraft. A US Air Force publicity release asserts: 'Over 15,000 pounds of air-to-surface ordnance can be carried . . . in addition to four Sparrow and four Sidewinder air-to-air missiles, two ECM pods and the internally mounted 20mm cannon. . . . The F-15 also has the potential to utilize the latest in the family of air-to-surface weapons without losing any air-to-air capability.' The plane had a range of over 2,800 miles and a speed of Mach 2·5.

When the F-15s arrived in Israel, the United States had already promised the same aircraft to Saudi Arabia. Although announcements of the plane sale were delayed by production schedules, the need to build a Saudi infrastructure, and by political considerations on 28 April 1978 the administration submitted letters to Congress for the sale of 60 F-15s to Saudi Arabia, 50 F-5E fighters to Egypt, and 15 F-15s and 75 F-16s fighter-bombers to Israel. The package approach was selected to minimize the chance of rejection of the most objectionable sale, that to the Saudis, though from Israel's point of view, the F-5Es also raised grave concern. The F-5E is definitely not a 'tenth-rate plane', as President Sadat called it. It carries air-to-air missiles, cannons, and nearly 7,000 lb of ordnance and in US Air Force tests was able to fight superior F-14s and F-15s to a deadly draw. The combination of massive Soviet equipment with high-quality American weapons has truly threatening implications for Israel.

Although the planes in the package would not be delivered until 1982, they caused a stiffening of Israel's negotiating position and forced the government to take a second look at domestic production capabilities. The IAI, an efficient enterprise with several subdivisions, already was producing the Kfir CII, a refinement of the original plane with a more powerful GE J-79 engine. Manufactured in two versions, a pure interceptor and a fighter-bomber version, the plane had impressed foreign observers, though sales abroad had been disappointing, in part because of American intervention and in part because of Arab pressures. The IAF had about 150 Kfirs in service or on order, but to keep its research and production lines going at full capacity, the IAI required additional business. By 1977 it was ready to proceed with the development of a third generation Kfir, the so-called Aryeh, with capabilities roughly equal to the F-16 and expected to become operational in the mid-1980s.

The Knesset Foreign Affairs and Defence Committee endorsed this scheme, though some defence officials and politicians were opposed. Developing such a plane would be more expensive than purchasing F-16s from the United States. Moreover, though airframes, avionics, and armament could be manufactured locally, the engine still would have to be American and to produce an Israeli plane without producing an Israeli engine afforded little more than an illusion of independence. And to develop an Israeli jet engine, though possible, would raise the price considerably. No final decision has as yet been made. General David Ivri, who in October 1977 succeeded Peled as IAF commander, has not committed himself, while Defence Minister Weizman has stated that he prefers getting the most for the least. However, with the package approved by the Senate on 15 May 1978, amid rhetoric that US commitment to Israel's security was as firm as ever, it appears that the Israeli government will have to reconsider this option.

By contrast the IN encountered fewer problems in procuring additional units, including additional *Reshef*-class missile boats as well as several larger Q-class vessels, all built by the Israel shipyards in Haifa. The Q-class, becoming operational in late 1976, had a displacement of 850 tons, a range of 5,000 miles, a top speed of 42 knots, and a powerful armament – Gabriel II and American

Harpoon ship-to-ship missiles, anti-submarine gear, and dual-purpose automatic guns. Altogether, in size, range, and armament these vessels far outclassed the *Reshef* boats and appear to posses strategic capabilities.

The same also appeared true of the two 600-ton submarines, the *Gal* and the *Rahav*, acquired from England in 1977. A third boat of this type is being completed at Vickers. The question whether Israel needed a submarine force had been the subject of debate ever since the IN purchased its first boat in the mid-1950s. At one time the possession of a sizeable submarine force by Israel's enemies – Egypt alone had 12 – was a major consideration. The new boats, however, appear to be built largely for durability and protracted periods at sea. They are believed capable of reaching any point in the Mediterranean or Red Sea. Armed with torpedoes and, according to reports, Blowpipe missiles, and operating jointly with the Q-class vessels, they should be able to carry out missions far from Israeli shores.

Israel's 'high seas' navy is backed up by a number of smaller craft – motor-torpedo and patrol boats. The most interesting development here is the *Dvora*-class patrol boat, designed and manufactured by Ramat Systems and Structures, an IAI branch. Although small, 71-foot long, the boat has considerable firepower carrying both Gabriel missiles and two 20mm cannons. Although powerful for its size, the *Dvora* class, with an operational range of 700 nautical miles and a top speed of 36 knots, seems designed primarily for coastal protection.

Overall, naval personnel has reached 10,000 – 3,500 career sailors, 1,000 conscripts, 5,000 reservists, and a small number of frogmen commandos, about 500 at the most. Morale and proficiency appear high and its commander, *Aluf* Michael Barkai, well respected. On the other hand, the image of the navy was blemished when on several occasions since 1973, seaborne Palestinian terrorists groups managed to evade its coastal cordon and twice inflicted heavy civilian casualties in the Tel Aviv region.

Anti-Terrorist Operations

These incidents highlighted one of Israel's ongoing security problems, the fight against terrorism. Since September 1970, when the PLO had been bloodily suppressed by the Jordanian Army, it had concentrated in Lebanon, establishing its bases and operational centres in Beirut, in the crowded refugee camps along the coast, and in the southern hill country. Liberally financed by the oil-rich Arab countries, and openly supported by Libya and Iraq, the PLO and its splinter groups, especially the Popular Front for the Liberation of Palestine, established intimate connections with radical terrorist groups in Western Europe and Japan, and backed by the Arab countries, the Communist bloc and the so-called Third World, managed to gain respectability in the UN. Its highpoint came when in December 1974, its leader, Yasir Arafat was invited to address the United Nations General Assembly. For all that, the various Arab states continued to regard the PLO and its terrorist groups with ill-concealed suspicion. Egypt, though vociferously supporting it, did not permit operations from its territory and in February 1978, Egyptian commandos and PLO fighters fought a bloody battle in Cyprus following the assassination of an Egyptian editor. Jordan remained hostile, and even Syria and Iraq, each maintaining its own Palestinian forces, kept them under close control.

Lebanon therefore remained the main base for the Palestinian operations against Israel, which continued in their pattern of indiscriminate attacks, purposely directed against civilians and showing a clear desire to avoid encounters with military forces. To be sure, this was part of a clear design to create fear and confusion and not because of any reluctance to fight. Although many Palestinians long had found jobs and homes in other countries, a hard core were prepared to sacrifice their lives during missions. But indiscriminate terrorism, while on occasion spectacular and always attracting attention of the media, was not enough to constitute a major resistance movement endangering the existence of the Jewish state and the IDF devoted only a very small part of its resources to this fight.

For operational purposes there exists a division of responsibility between the Army and the police. Together with the paramilitary Border Police, the IDF is responsible for the security of the frontiers and for a 10-mile stretch into the country itself. In practice this applies only to the Lebanese frontier where barbed-wire fences, mines, and infiltration-detection devices are assisted by roving patrols and observation posts. In addition, together with the civilian General Security Service, the IDF maintains, on occasion heavy-handedly, order in the occupied territories. Along the sea frontiers, the navy was supposed to maintain a tight cordon, though its responsibility ended on the shore line. Within Israel proper, a Civil Guard, over-age men and women, only partially armed with hand-me-down small arms, is supposed to assist in patrolling their neighbourhoods. The military or the Border Police are called in only if a major group of terrorists penetrates into Israeli territory. Liaison between the various bodies and agencies has, on occasion, been far from perfect, though on balance the IDF has done rather better than the overworked, undermanned and poorly armed police.

In 1974–75, terrorist groups carried out a number of bloody actions inside Israel. In April 1974 they massacred several families in Kiryat Shemona and the following month seized a school in nearby Maalot, an affair ending in the death of scores of children. In December, local sympathizers or infiltrators, exploded bombs in a Tel Aviv movie theatre and on Zion Square in Jerusalem. In January

1975, Lebanese-based groups fired Katyusha rockets into Israel and the same month made a rocket attack against an El Al plane at Orly Airport in Paris. While vigilance along the Lebanese frontier increased, the terrorists took to the sea and in March executed an attack into Tel Aviv, seizing the Savoy Hotel and killing several civilians, before being wiped out by an IDF unit. Throughout the year, the IDF retaliated with air and commando attacks against Palestinian bases, though these could not halt terrorist activities. And operations against civilian targets outside of Israel, attacks against airliners, air terminals, and other such objectives encountered little effective resistance and, when caught, the terrorists normally were freed within a few days.

In April 1975, however, the PLO and its various splinter groups, became enmeshed in a 19-months' civil war against the Lebanese Maronite Catholic community that absorbed most of its energies and killed over 60,000 people, more than had died in all Arab–Israeli wars. Fighting started when the Christian community, seeing the Palestinian armed presence as a threat to Lebanese sovereignty, attempted to drive the guerrillas out. In turn, many, though by no means all, Lebanese Moslems joined the Palestinians and in the end, after Beirut had been left in ruins, Lebanon was in effect partitioned along religious lines, with Moslems and Palestinians in control of perhaps two-thirds of the country. The Christians were left with the eastern part of Beirut and a stretch of territory extending into the mountains to the north, as well as seven enclaves in southern Lebanon. Receiving little support from the Christian world, midway in the civil war, the Christians had entered into a military alliance with Israel, receiving sanctuary, some arms, and occasional artillery and armour support for the enclaves in the south.

The situation was complicated by Syrian intervention. Initially the Syrians supported the Moslems, but, soon after their first appearance in strength in June 1976, changed sides and turned armour and artillery on Palestinian camp strongholds. Even so, the presence of some 30,000 Syrian troops in Lebanon opened the prospect of yet another front in a future conflict. Israel repeatedly warned that if the Syrians crossed the 'red line', undefined but commonly believed to be the Litani River, the IDF would enter the country. But when Syrian-trained and equipped Palestinian forces, with medium tanks and artillery, did appear in southern Lebanon during March and April 1977, the IDF did not act. Apparently regarding the Syrians as a 'stabilizing influence', Washington had exerted its leverage on the Rabin government. Only when these Palestinian units began to threaten the last Christian enclaves did the IDF intervene. In September 1977, artillery began to support the embattled Christians and small mechanized units began operations across the frontier. American mediation arranged a truce. A reconstituted Lebanese Army was to police the area and secure it against the PLO, but no such units appeared and the

Palestinians remained entrenched on hills overlooking Israel repeatedly firing at the northern Galilee settlements. In February 1978, they became more active and overran yet another Christian village.

For the first time the Palestinians were perceived as a military threat. Syria's military presence and deployment in northern Lebanon was regarded as highly undesirable, though the nature of the terrain precluded its employment in an armoured thrust south against Israel. But from the Palestinian strongholds along the border, long-range artillery could fire as far as Haifa, its port and other vital installations. Removal of this potential artillery base appeared a military necessity. This was the situation when on 11 March 1978, a seaborne terrorist attack into the Tel Aviv area caused 37 civilian casualties. Three days later, the IDF mounted a major operation, a preventive measure and not a retaliatory strike as Begin stressed. Although not a particularly dangerous foray, the operation revealed that Israel had learned one of the lessons of the 1973 war: planes and tanks alone are insufficient and must be supported by artillery.

The immediate objective of the Israeli forces – two mechanized infantry brigades and one tank brigade – striking across a 75-mile frontier in three main thrusts, were the forts on a string of rough hills running north and north east from the Israeli–Lebanese border. Neutralization of two PLO camps in the Tyre area was a secondary objective. The initial attack was preceded by heavy artillery barrages and by repeated fighter-bomber attacks. In addition, Israeli missile boats off the coast launched short-range missiles and fighters also struck the large PLO base camp at Sabra outside Beirut. Although the Israeli government first announced that it would limit operations to a belt 6 miles deep along the frontier, troops eventually reached the Litani River, except in the area of Tyre where they approached but did not enter the town. American military analysts described the operation as 'well prepared and executed', and claimed that it showed that the 'Israelis are as strong as ever and as competent as ever.'[14]

On the other hand, the PLO was not destroyed. Though several veteran PLO units were chewed up during the attack, most had withdrawn in anticipation of the action and Israeli military sources acknowledged that limiting the initial attack to a 6-mile depth had been a mistake. It has been reported that this restraint came in response to American pressure and out of a desire to keep casualties to a minimum. Some analysts argue that Israel should have seized the Litani bridges in an air landing to cut off the retreating Palestinian forces. But that would have entailed much higher troop losses. General Gur claimed that there had been significant gains. The PLO infrastructure in southern Lebanon was destroyed, some 300 PLO fighters killed or captured, substantial quantities of arms and equipment seized. At the same time, Syria, for all her belligerent rhetoric had not intervened. The permanence of the achievements claimed, however, will depend on the effectiveness of a hastily dispatched United Nations Interim Force in Lebanon.

Past experience indicates that these troops will not be very effective. Numerically weak, armed only with light weapons, and with orders only to fire in self-defence, it seems more likely that their presence in the area will not inhibit the return of the guerrillas, while making future Israeli action, either retaliatory or in support of the Christian enclaves, more problematic. In fact, when PLO elements clashed with French troops of the UN force, the response of the UN command was to withdraw its forces from a number of key positions. By this time, Israel, acting under American and UN pressure, actually had withdrawn its soldiers to the original 6-mile zone. Further pull-out, so Jerusalem declared, would depend on effective UN or Lebanese Army presence in the area. Neither developments seem likely, but, bowing to American pressure, the IDF scheduled a total withdrawal for 13 June 1978.

On balance, the operation showed that the IDF was well prepared and capable, but that its power was subject to political pressures which could make its employment counter-productive. There also were reports that in the wake of the affair, Moscow had decided to initiate a direct Soviet arms-supply relationship with the PLO, providing anti-aircraft guns, medium artillery and communications equipment. And this in turn would make the PLO a more dangerous adversary in the future, though this development will hardly be welcome to the various Arab states.

No such ambiguities surrounded Israel's second major anti-terrorist operation, the first ever IDF operation mounted outside the Middle East. When following the hijacking of an Air France plane by PFLP elements, European as well as Arabs, on 27 June 1976, 105 Jewish and Israeli hostages were held at Entebbe Airport in Uganda, the government, fearing for their lives and reluctant to bow to escalating terrorist demands, decided on military action. On 3 July 1976, 'Operation Thunderbolt', later renamed 'Operation Jonathan' to commemorate Lieutenant-Colonel Jonathan Netaniahu who commanded the assault force and was killed in the fighting, sent a mixed force of paratroopers and Golani infantrymen over 2,000 miles to rescue the hostages held by the terrorists, reinforced by Ugandan troops.

The operation, undertaken after considerable soul searching, and only after Gur had declared it feasible, sent three C-130 Hercules transports and several Boeing passenger jets down the Red Sea into Africa. It was supervised from the air by the chief of operations, General Adan, while command on the ground was held by Brigadier Dan Shomron, chief paratroop and infantry officer. After swooping down on the runway, the troops rapidly stormed the old terminal building where the hostages were being held, while other elements neutralized interference from Ugandan troops. Within an hour, the entire operation was completed with minimal casualties and the elimination of the hijackers. Perhaps the most daring long-range rescue mission in history, its success was applauded throughout the Western World, although the Austrian UN Secretary General, Mr Kurt Waldheim, complained that the sovereign territory of a UN member had veen violated. But Israel long had given up expecting much from the UN.

The other sour note came from France. Although a French plane and crew were involved, and though France had elite troops available in nearby Djibouti, it did not employ them and the French government did not even bother to congratulate Israel. It did not matter. The Entebbe rescue, 'salvation from the sky', lifted Israeli morale and dispersed some of the gloom that had settled over the country after 1973. Isolated, scorned, and attacked from many quarters, Israelis felt that their Army still was capable of unprecedented achievements.

Israel's Strategic Situation into the 1980s

Forecasting is an undertaking full of pitfalls and all that can be said with confidence about the future is that the IDF will remain the cornerstone of Israel's security and that the unexpected will happen frequently. Beyond this, it is possible to make some assumptions as to the near future, say five to seven years ahead, based on developments and trends already apparent.

There are a number of permanent principles governing IDF strategic planning. They include the realization that in any future war the IDF is likely to be out-numbered in weapons systems, firepower, and men; and secondly, that given the asymmetry in resources, outside support and the intervention of the super powers, Israel must fight short wars that will always stop short of complete victory. Israel cannot assume that only Egypt and Syria will join forces in a future conflict against her. Past experience indicates that Israel must plan for a multifront war contingency, including a far greater threat from Jordan. Jordan has established close military ties with Syria, including a joint military commission, and has stepped up arms purchases. Saudi Arabia, Kuweit, Libya, the United Emirates, and other Arab states, all have pledged to transfer weapons and manpower to the confrontation states on Israel's borders.

Israel has traditionally attempted to maintain a 1:3 balance of military power in favour of the confrontation states and for the moment, provided American supplies promised are delivered, it actually enjoys a somewhat more favourable ratios vis-à-vis Egypt, Jordan, and Syria at the present time.

	Military establishment manpower		Tanks		Combat planes	
	1973	1977	1973	1977	1973	1977
Egypt	298,000	342,000	2,000	2,200	620	500
Syria	182,000	227,000	2,000	2,220	325	440
Jordan	72,000	67,000	420	490	52	72
Total	552,000	637,000	4,420	4,890	997	1,012
Israel	300,000	450,000	1,700	2,700	448	550+

If, however, the total Arab potential is considered, the ratios become much more unfavourable and will soon grow even larger. In certain weapons categories it will become truly staggering (see table below).

Military balance of power ratios against Israel

	1976–7		1980–1 (Assuming full funding of $1 billion requested in February 1977)	
	Confrontation states*	Confrontation states plus anticipated contribution by states outside confrontation area**	Confrontation states*	Confrontation states plus anticipated contribution by states outside confrontation area**
Combat aircraft	2·8:1	3:1	3·2:1	3·8:1
Tanks	2·7:1	3:1	3:1	3·6:1
Artillery	6:1	9:1	8:1	9:1
Armed forces *** (divisions)	4:1	5:1	5:1	6:1
SAM batteries	10:1	12:1	18:1	20:1

* *Egypt, Syria and Jordan.*
** *Egypt, Syria, Jordan, Iraq, Saudi Arabia, Kuwait, Libya, Algeria, Morocco, Sudan and Tunisia.*
*** *This ratio includes all of Israel's reserves – not its much smaller standing army.*

What the Arab states are expected to contribute
in a future war with Israel (1980)

Eastern front (Syria, Jordan, Iraq, Saudi Arabia, Kuwait)		Western front (Egypt, Libya, Algeria, Morocco, Sudan, Tunisia)	
20	divisions	15	divisions
1,000	combat aircraft	1,150	combat aircraft
5,400	tanks	3,500	tanks
5,000	armoured personnel carriers	3,850	armoured personnel carriers
3,000	artillery pieces	2,800	artillery pieces
150	SAM batteries	250	SAM batteries

Note: These projections include realistic assessments of the percentages of forces the non-confrontation Arab states will be able to supply. They do *not* include all available resources and are based on past contributions and logistical improvements now going on.

Many analysts believe that current political and military circumstances prevent Israel from exercising a first-strike option. On the other hand, soldiers have stressed that this option remains a vital requirement. A defensive war, Tal wrote in 1977, was a luxury which only the quantitatively superior side could enjoy. The 'few', he asserted, 'must adopt the principle of delivering the "first blow" and conduct an offensive rather than a defensive blow.'[15] This, course, is the rationale behind Israel's concentration on mobile armoured formations, designed to achieve a decision before the much more extensive resources of the Arab states are fully brought into action. In such a conflict, victory conditions for Israel would not correspond to Clausewitz's classical definition of 'making the enemy do our will', that is the imposition of a political solution, but by creating a threat to the enemy's vital strategic targets and the survival of his field army compel him to end the war. Survival and not supremacy is the ultimate national strategic goal.

The entire question of strategic means and national goals will undoubtedly be examined and re-examined at Israel's National Defence College which, ten years after its predecessor had been dissolved, started up again in September 1977. Whatever becomes eventual doctrine, and there are those who favour the strategic defence coupled with a tactical offence, choices will be required. Even if the first-strike doctrine remains, a multifront war will require making priorities. The IDF will not have the time or the means to win decisively on all four possible fronts. One will have to be given priority and geopolitical considerations, above all the proximity to major population centres, even if present lines are maintained, point to the Syrian front with a massive attack delivered across the relatively open terrain of northern Jordan into Syria proper. Another possible line of approach would be through the Bekaa Valley of southern Lebanon, which would bypass Damascus and threaten the key communications centre of Homs. Any of the two approaches would tend to disrupt the development of an 'eastern front' threat and place the Syrian Army, massed in its defences before Damascus, in a precarious situation.

If, on the other hand, Egypt should become the primary objective, an Israeli advance would have to be along the lines of 1956 and 1967, though indications are that airborne operations, both in the Sinai and perhaps in upper Egypt, combined with a naval amphibious sortie across the Gulf of Suez, would be diversionary manoeuvres.

Both against Egypt or Syria, control of the airspace over Israel and in the theatre of operations, including protection of the lines of communications, would assume new importance. Most of the air power on both sides would still be deployed in tactical operations, though all sides now possess much greater strategic capabilities than ever. It does not seem likely, however, that Israel would dilute its effort to attack population centres. Instead it most likely would concentrate on enemy installations and infrastructures and here the new missile craft may also come into their own.

In the near time frame, the next five to seven years, most experts agree that the IDF is still more than a match for the combined Arab armies. On the other hand, the Arabs can afford to launch a war they are sure to lose, secure in the knowledge that it may bring them political advantages. Whether Israel can maintain this posture over the long run is debatable. To a large degree this does not depend on Israel alone but it becomes a test whether the free world has the political will and cohesion to translate into reality its repeated commitments to the survival of the state. This casts doubts on the wisdom of supplying ever-larger arsenals to the Arabs and on the tendency of the United States and its European allies to try to solve their immediate economic problems by hacking away another support of their defence structure. The latter, of course, does not just apply to their relationship with Israel, but to the whole spectrum of confrontation facing the West.

In the last analysis, however, the state of Israel has always relied on its own efforts and the achievements of independent Israel have been impressive. A nation of less than 700,000 has absorbed so many immigrants that its population has quintupled. They came from more than a hundred countries and all were different. And in its 30-year history, the state has also fought and won four wars against nations that outnumbered her 40 to 1. Israel at thirty has many troubles – economic, political, cultural – but she has remained a democracy defended by a citizen army. If for the first time in three decades there is talk and the hope of peace, it may well have come about because the Arab leaders have recognized that they cannot destroy the state by military means. And this may well be the proudest achievement of the Israeli Army.

Notes

Notes

Chapter 1

1 Probably the best and most balanced history of modern Zionism is W. Laqueur, *A History of Zionism*, Holt, Rinehart & Winston Inc., New York, 1972.

2 For a fair survey of the earliest defence efforts see Y. Allon, *Shield of David*, Random House, New York, 1970, pp. 11–73.

3 Cited in J. Kimche, *There Could Have Been Peace*, Dial Press, New York, 1973, p. 91.

4 Allon, op. cit., pp. 75–108. It should be noted, however, that Allon, second commander of the Palmach, and later a general officer and member of various Labour cabinets, was not always fair to the right-wing defence groups. For a corrective view see J. Bowyer Bell, *Terror out of Zion*, St Martin's Press, New York, 1977, and M. Begin, *The Revolt*, Nash Publishing House, Los Angeles, 1948

5 On Wingate see C. Sykes, *Orde Wingate*, Collins, London, 1959.

6 The intricate story of British–Jewish relations as well as the development of the Haganah and Palmach is told in the superb study by Y. Bauer, *From Diplomacy to Resistance*, trans. A.M. Winters, Atheneum, New York, 1973.

7 Printed in Y. Allon, *The Making of Israel's Army*, Bantam Books, New York, 1971, pp. 147–8.

8 J. Weller, 'Sir Basil Liddell Hart's Disciples in Israel', *Military Review*, January 1974, pp. 13–20. B. Bond, *Liddell Hart: A Study of his Military Thought*, Rutgers University Press, New Brunswick, NJ, 1977, pp. 240–6.

9 Israel, General Staff, Historical Section, *Toldot Milchemmet ha-Kommeiyut*, Maarachot, Tel Aviv, p. 78, and D. Gutmann, 'The Palestinian Myth', *Commentary*, 19 October 1975, p. 44.

10 Among the many accounts of these activities see L. Slater, *The Pledge*, Simon & Schuster, New York, 1970.

11 Begin, op. cit., pp. 42–3.

12 Bauer, op. cit., pp. 325–9, and also his remarks in the Preface to the paperback edition cited, p. viii.

13 The British view in J. Paget, *The Story of the Guards*, Osprey, London, 1976, p. 241

237

and G. Blaxland, *The Regiments Depart*, William Kimber & Co., London, 1971, pp. 30–47.

Blaxland, *The Regiments Depart*, William Kimber & Co., 1971, pp. 30–47.

14 Thus the revealing account by Sir A.S. Kirkbride, *A Crackle of Thorns*, John Murray, 1956, passim.

15 Bowyer Bell, op. cit., p. x.

16 Slater, op. cit., pp. 121–3.

17 On this and other information see the excellent volume by E. Luttwak and D. Horowitz, *The Israeli Army*, Allen Lane, 1975, pp. 23–9. Also cf. J. and D. Kimche, *A Clash of Destinies*, Praeger, New York, 1960, pp. 160–1.

Chapter 2

1 N. Lorch, *Israel's War of Independence 1947–1949*, Hartmore House, Hartford, Conn., 1968, p. 46.

2 Kimche, *Clash of Destinies*, p. 79.

3 C. Sykes, *Crossroads to Israel*, Indiana University Press, Bloomington, In., 1973, p. 343.

4 Blaxland, op. cit., p. 51.

5 B. Dunkelman, *Dual Allegiance*, Crown Publishers, New York, 1976, p. 185.

6 R.D. Wilson, *Cordon and Search*, Gale & Polden, Aldershot, 1949, p. 106.

7 D. Joseph, *The Faithful City: The Siege of Jerusalem 1948*, Simon & Schuster, New York, 1960, p. 25.

8 A. Krammer, *The Forgotten Friendship: Israel and the Soviet Bloc 1947–53*, University of Illinois Press, Urbana, 1974, pp. 83–8; B. Kagan, *The Secret Battle for Israel*, World Publishing Co., Cleveland, 1966, pp. 56–7; Lorch, op. cit., pp. 93–4.

9 A fair summary of the evidence in Bowyer Bell, op. cit., pp. 294–6.

10 See the photostat reports in M. Pearlman, *The Army of Israel*, Philosophical Library, New York, 1950, pp. 116–7.

11 Bowyer Bell, op. cit., pp. 299–302.

12 Blaxland, op. cit., p. 59.

13 Luttwak and Horowitz, op. cit., pp. 29–30; P.J. Vatikiotis, *Politics and the Military in Jordan: A Study of the Arab Legion 1921–1957*, Praeger, New York, 1967, pp. 77–8.

14 Luttwak and Horowitz, op. cit., p. 34.

15 Kirkbride, op. cit., p. 160.

16 Allon, Appendix II, in B.H. Liddell Hart, *Strategy*, Praeger, New York, 1962, p. 396, n. 1.

17 *Toldot*, p. 290; the higher estimate in J.A. Heckelman, *American Volunteers and Israel's War of Independence*, Ktav, New York, 1974, passim.

18 Lorch, op. cit., p. 388.

19 James S. Metcalfe, 'Foot Soldiers War', *Infantry Journal*, March 1949, pp. 23, 29.

20 Dunkelman, op. cit., pp. 201–2.

21 Bowyer Bell, op. cit., pp. 324–7.

22 E.B. Glick, *Between Israel and Death*, Stackpole, Harrisburg, Pa., 1974, p. 137; A. Avi-Hai, *Ben Gurion State Builder*, John Wiley & Sons and Israel Universities Press, New York–Jerusalem, 1974, pp. 117–18.

23 Krammer, op. cit., pp. 105–6.

24 E. Weizman, *On Eagles' Wings*, Weidenfeld & Nicolson, 1976, pp. 75–6.

25 S.K. Crosbie, *A Tacit Alliance: France and Israel from Suez to the Six Day War*, Princeton University Press, Princeton NJ, 1974, pp. 29–33.

26 *Toldoth*, op. cit., pp. 337–40.

27 Metcalf, op. cit., p. 29.

28 I. Tal, 'Israel's Doctrine of National Security', *The Jerusalem Quarterly*, Summer 1977, pp. 47–8.

29 Luttwak and Horowitz, op. cit., p. 66.

Chapter 3

1 Avi-Hai, op. cit., p. 119.

2 Ibid., pp. 142–5.

3 S. Teveth, *Moshe Dayan: The Soldier, the Man, the Legend*, Houghton Mifflin, Boston, 1973, p. 284.

4 Avi-Hai, op. cit., pp. 123–5; A. Perlmutter, *The Military and Politics in Modern Times*, Yale University Press, New Haven and London, 1977, pp. 262, 268–9.

5 Dayan, op. cit., pp. 149–50.

6 M. Ben Shaul (ed.), *The Generals of Israel*, trans. I. Hanoch, Hadar, Tel Aviv, 1968, p. 205.

7 Dayan, op. cit., pp. 149–50.

8 Luttwak and Horowitz, op. cit., pp. 94–8.

9 Weizman, op. cit., p. 196.

10 Yadin, 'Learning from Experience', pp. 247–9 in Allon, *Making of Israel's Army*.

11 Weizman, op. cit., pp. 88–9.

12 R. Porath, 'The Israeli Navy', *US Naval Institute Proceedings*, September 1971, pp. 34–5.

13 Weizman, op. cit., pp. 88–9.

14 Z. Schiff, *A History of the Israeli Army 1870–1974*, trans. R. Rothstein, Straight Arrow Books, San Francisco, 1974, pp. 97–8; Teveth, op. cit., pp. 287–8.

15 Schiff, op. cit., p. 59.

16 Teveth, op. cit., pp. 195–8.

17 Anon., 'Israel's Defence Plans', *Zionist Review*, 12 January 1951, p. 10.

18 Avi Hai, op. cit., p. 199.

19 S. Peres, *David's Sling*, Random House, New York, 1970, p. 40.

20 Dayan, op. cit., p. 159.

21 Ben Shaul, op. cit., p. 207; Luttwak and Horowitz, op. cit., p. 106.

22 Dayan, op. cit., p. 173.

23 Teveth, op. cit., p. 214.

Chapter 4

1 Dayan, op. cit., p. 178.

2 Ibid., p. 172.

3 Luttwak and Horowitz, op. cit., pp. 110–12. On the paratroop and commando actions in general see also D. Margalit, *Yehidat komando* 101, Moked, Tel Aviv, 1968, and U. Milstain, *Milhamot ha-tsanhanim*, Ramdor, Tel Aviv, 1968.

4 M. Dayan, *Diary of the Sinai Campaign*, Weidenfied & Nicolson, 1966, p. 27.

5 Luttwak and Horowitz, op. cit., pp. 116–17.

6 Dayan, *Diary*, pp. 4–10, 130–1; N. Safran, *From War to War*, Pegasus, New York, 1969, p. 45.

7 Dayan, *Diary*, p. 57.

8 Figures adapted from Safran, op. cit., pp. 216, 228, 234. There is, however, a discrepancy regarding Jordan between Safran and Vatikiotis, op. cit., p. 81. Also

note that J.D. Glassman, *Arms for the Arabs: The Soviet Union and War in the Middle East*, John Hopkins University Press, Baltimore, MD., 1975, pp. 12–13 provides somewhat lower figures for Soviet deliveries to Egypt prior to October 1956.

9 S.K. Crosbie, *A Tacit Alliance*, Princeton University Press, Princeton, NJ, 1974, pp. 43, 60.

10 Teveth, op. cit., p. 189; Luttwak and Horowitz, op. cit., pp. 130–1.

11 Ben Shaul, op. cit., p. 236; Dayan, *Diary*, p. 20, and Teveth, op. cit., pp. 236, 262–3.

12 Dayan, *Diary*, pp. 29–30, 68.

13 Weizman, op. cit., p. 142; Crosbie, op. cit., pp. 38–46; Schiff, op. cit., pp. 63–5.

14 Weizman, op. cit., p. 133.

15 The best account from the Israeli military side in Dayan, *Life*, pp. 223–9.

16 Dayan, *Diary*, pp. 39–40.

17 S.L.A. Marshall, *Sinai Victory*, Morrow, New York, 1967, pp. 26, 142–4.

18 Order of battle in Dayan, *Diary*, pp. 220–1.

19 There is some doubt regarding the actual strength of the IAF. Dayan, ibid., indicates 53 jets and 63 piston planes, while Weizman, op. cit., pp. 148–9 gives 100 jets. Crosbie, op. cit., p. 79 suggests that one French jet squadron actually operated in Sinai.

20 Dayan, *Diary*, p. 103, and *Life*, pp. 241–4.

21 Dayan, *Diary*, pp. 164, 227–9, and passim.

22 R. Henriques, *A Hundred Hours to Suez*, Viking, New York, 1957, p. 12.

23 Marshall, op. cit., p. 127.

24 Weizman, op. cit., p. 165.

Chapter 5

1 W. Byford-Jones, *The Lightning War*, Bobbs-Merrill Co., Indianapolis–New York, 1968, p. 97.

2 W. Schneider, *Das Buch vom Soldaten*, Econ Verlag, Düsseldorf–Vienna, 1964, pp. 309–10, presents an interesting German view.

3 Allon, *Making of Israel's Army*, p. 291.

4 Dayan, *Diary*, p. 165; A. Shapira, ed., *The Seventh Day*, Scribner's Sons, New York, 1970, pp. 130–5.

5 S. Rolbant, *The Israeli Soldier*, Yoseloff, New York–London, 1970, pp. 261–3, 265–7.

6 Brigadier Peter Young, talk at the Royal United Service Institute, London, 6 June 1967; cf. Luttwak and Horowitz, op. cit., pp. 181–4.

7 The fluid number of regular, conscript, and reserve formations has continued to baffle observers. Published sources vary greatly. For a discussion see 'Will Israel's Real Order of Battle Please Stand Up?', *Armed Forces Journal*, October 1973, p. 40; cf. Luttwak and Horowitz, op. cit., pp. 216–17.

8 A. Perlmutter, *Military and Politics in Israel*, Praeger, New York–Washington, 1969, pp. 105–9.

9 Luttwak and Horowitz, op. cit., pp. 186–91.

10 S. Teveth, *The Tanks of Tammuz*, Weidenfeld & Nicolson, 1969, pp. 55–7, 63–7, 71–3.

11 J. Lartéguy, *The Walls of Israel*, O. de Kay trans., Evans and Co., New York 1968, pp. 161–6.

12 Weizman, op. cit., pp. 176–7.

13 Crosbie, op. cit., p. 197.
14 Weizman, op. cit., pp. 263–4.
15 Ibid., pp. 192–9, passim.
16 Safran, op. cit., pp. 205–44, passim; Glassman, op. cit., pp. 28–35.
17 Interview, *Jerusalem Post*, international edition, 7 June 1977.
18 On the command crisis of May–June 1967, see Perlmutter, op. cit., pp. 110–12; for an insider's view see Weizman, op. cit., pp. 217–21.
19 Dayan, *Life*, pp. 321–9.

Chapter 6

1 Weizman, op. cit., pp. 221–7.
2 A.J. Barker, *Six Day War*, Random House, New York, 1974, p. 73; cf. Luttwak and Horowitz, op. cit., pp. 226–9. There exists a large literature on the war, most of a sensational and often sloppy nature. The magnificent work by Luttwak and Horowitz stands out as one of the best accounts. Both Dayan and Weizman have provided illuminating insights on various major command decisions.
3 ibid., pp. 237–9. One battalion of Eytan's brigade was detached for the Sharm el Sheik operation.
4 Dayan, *Diary,* p. 35.
5 Dayan, *Life*, p. 362.
6 The controversy ably discussed in Luttwak and Horowitz, op. cit., pp. 258, 285–6.
7 Dayan, *Life*, p. 356.
8 The best account of the battle for and around Jerusalem is A. Rabinovich, *The Battle for Jerusalem*, Jewish Publication Society of America, Philadelphia, 1972.
9 Dayan, *Life*, p. 373.
10 Luttwak and Horowitz, op. cit., pp. 274–7.
11 Weizman, op. cit., pp. 258–9.
12 P. Young, *The Israel Campaign 1967*, William Kimber, 1967, p. 240.

Chapter 7

1 Teveth, *Dayan*, p. 357.
2 For an overall view see N. Safran, *Israel – The Embattled Ally*, Harvard University Press, Cambridge–London, 1978, pp. 222–3, 257–8.
3 F.B. Horton et al., eds., *Comparative Defense Policy*, John Hopkins University Press, Baltimore–London, 1974, p. 393.
4 Weizman, op. cit., p. 288.
5 Major General (ret.) M. Peled in W. Laqueur, *Confrontation: The Middle East War and World Politics*, Abacus, 1974, pp. 86–7, cf. the bitter charges in Y. Porat et al., *Yom Kippur*, Special Editions, Tel Aviv, 1973, pp. 132–48 and passim.
6 Perlmutter, *Military and Politics*, pp. 270–1.
7 Y. Peri, 'Ideological Portrait of the Israeli Military Elite', *Jerusalem Quarterly*, Spring 1977, pp. 34–5.
8 cf. C. Herzog, *The War of Atonement*, Little, Brown & Co., Boston–Toronto, 1975, p. 272, and Laqueur, *Confrontation*, p. 100, with Luttwak and Horowitz, op. cit., p. 336.
9 Tal, op. cit., p. 48.
10 Dayan, *Life*, p. 438; Safran, *Israel*, p. 274.
11 ibid., pp. 280–2.

12 Luttwak and Horowitz, op. cit., p. 298.

13 J. Kimche, *There Could Have Been Peace*, p. 338.

14 A summary of the overall development of the IDF 1967–73 in Luttwak and Horowitz, op. cit., pp. 327–36.

15 Dayan, *Life*, pp. 413–15; Weizman, op. cit., pp. 268–9.

16 Dayan, *Life*, p. 425.

17 For the debate see Peled in Laqueur, *Confrontation*, pp. 83–6; Dayan, *Life*, pp. 438–9; Luttwak and Horowitz, op. cit., pp. 317–20; and Rabin in *Jerusalem Post*, international edition, 7 June 1977.

18 I. Szanto, 'Die militärische Lage im Nahosten', *Österreichische Militärische Zeitschrift*, September 1972, pp. 350–1.

19 Weizman, op. cit., pp. 273–6.

20 ibid., pp. 274–5; Peled in Laqueur, *Confrontation*, p. 85. The most detailed, if on occasion controversial, analysis of the War of Attrition along the Canal, is L.L. Whetten, *The Canal War: Four Power Conflict in the Middle East*, MIT Press, 1974, passim.

21 A. Eban, *An Autobiography*, Random House, New York, 1977, p. 498.

Chapter 8

1 For this phenomenon see J. Weller, 'Armor and Infantry in Israel', *Military Review*, April 1977, pp. 4–5.

2 Peres, op. cit., pp. 18, 135–6.

3 Dayan, *Life*, pp. 468–9; Herzog, op. cit., pp. 60–1.

4 Safran, *Israel*, pp. 286–8.

5 Dayan, *Life*, pp. 472–3; Herzog, op. cit., p. 41.

6 Dayan, *Life*, p. 461; Herzog, op. cit., pp. 53–5, and Luttwak and Horowitz, op. cit., pp. 341–4.

7 Herzog, op. cit., pp. 279–80.

8 Dayan, *Life*, p. 510.

9 US Army, TC 71-4-2.

10 Safran, *Israel*, p. 489.

11 Dayan, *Life*, pp. 494–5; discussion in Luttwak and Horowitz, op. cit., p. 377.

12 Herzog, op. cit., p. 191.

13 Dayan, *Life*, p. 502.

14 ibid., pp. 511–13.

15 Herzog, op. cit., p. 145.

16 Figures follow Safran, *Israel*, p. 311. Other sources differ but slightly. By types the IAF lost 57 Skyhawks, 37 Phantoms, 8–10 Mirages.

17 Herzog, op. cit., pp. 251–9 for air and naval operations.

18 Dayan, *Life*, pp. 619–20; A.J. Barker, *The Yom Kippur War*, Random House, New York, 1974, p. 149; T.N. Dupuy, *Elusive Victory: The Arab–Israeli Wars, 1947–1974*, Harper & Row, New York–London, 1978, pp. 598–99.

19 C.N. Barclay, 'Lessons from the October War', *Army*, January 1974, p. 27; Luttwak and Horowitz, op. cit., pp. xiii, 397; Weizman, op. cit., p. 293.

20 Safran, *Israel*, pp. 495–534 passim. Safran appears, however, to be overly optimistic regarding the direction of US policy.

Chapter 9

1 Luttwak and Horowitz, op. cit., p. 397.

2 Weizman, op. cit., p. 116.

3 Thus Safran, *Israel*, pp. 554–60.

4 See for instance the peculiarly vitriolic attack by A.H. Cordesman, 'The Arab–Israeli Balance. How Much is too Much?', *Armed Forces Journal*, October 1977, pp. 32–41. In the same issue there also appears a report on massive Egyptian arms modernization launched with Saudi funds, reporting the transfer of 76 French-built combat planes from Saudi Arabia, purchase of 200 Alpha Jets from Britain, contracts for 400 helicopters and 21,000 Swingfire anti-tank missiles. Additionally, the report adds that 200 Mig-21 fighters would be overhauled, T-55 tanks modernized, and improved shells provided for Egypt's Soviet-supplied 122mm and 130mm artillery weapons.

5 M. Van Creveld, 'Military Lessons of the Yom Kippur War', *Jerusalem Quarterly*, Autumn 1977, p. 115.

6 Dayan, *Life*, pp. 591–2.

7 Eban, op. cit., pp. 568–9.

8 Brigadier General Farrar-Hockley in E. Monroe and A.H. Farrar-Hockley, *The Arab–Israeli War, October 1973*, Adelphi Papers No. 111, Institute for Strategic Studies, 1975, p. 84.

9 Order of battle taken from M. Meisel, 'Der Nahost Konflikt 1973–77', *Österreichische Militärische Zeitschrift*, December 1977, pp. 299–303. The London Institute for Strategic Studies gives a somewhat different order of battle. It credits the IDF with 20 armoured, 9 mechanized, 9 infantry, and 5 paratroop brigades, with 5 armoured, 4 infantry, and 2 paratroop normally near full strength. See *The Military Balance 1977–1978*, The Institute, 1977, p. 37.

10 For instance J. Record, 'The October War: Burying the Blitzkrieg', *Military Review*, April 1976, pp. 19–21.

11 Tal, op. cit., pp. 55–7; J. Weller, 'Armor and Infantry in Israel', *Military Review*, April 1977, pp. 4–10.

12 Thus T.N. Dupuy, *The Almanac of World Military Power*, 2nd ed, Barker Co., 1976, p. 171, asserts that Israel has started serial production of the Jericho, producing 60 to 80 yearly; cf. RUSI and Brassey's *Defence Yearbook 1974*, Brassey's Ltd., 1974, p. 157.

13 Safran, *Israel*, pp. 488–9, 596–7; cf. S. Aronson, 'Nuclearization of the Middle East: A Dovish View', *Jerusalem Quarterly*, Winter 1977, pp. 27–44.

14 Quoted by D. Middleton, *New York Times*, 16 March 1978.

15 Tal, op. cit., p. 55.

Selected List of Books in English

The literature on the Israel Defence Forces and the Middle East conflict is extensive and includes not only books but also a plethora of articles in many journals. Some have been listed in the notes. The following select book list is designed to provide a guide for further reading. It is by no means inclusive and stresses works which bear on the development of the Army as an institution, though, invariably, works on war and operational history also have been listed.

Allon, Y., *The Making of Israel's Army*, Bantam Books, New York, 1971.

Allon, Y., *Shield of David: The Story of Israel's Defence Forces*, Random House, New York, 1970.

Avi-Hai, A., *Ben Gurion State Builder: Principles and Pragmatism 1948–1963*, John Wiley & Sons and Israel Universities Press, New York–Toronto–Jerusalem, 1974.

Baer, S., *The Weekend War*, Yoseloff, New York, 1960.

Bashan, R., *The Victory: The Six Day War of 1967*, Quadrangle Books, Chicago, 1967.

Barker, A.J., *Six Day War*, Random House, New York, 1974.

Barker, A.J., *The Yom Kippur War*, Random House, New York, 1974.

Bauer, Y., *From Diplomacy to Resistance: A History of Jewish Palestine 1939–1945*, Atheneum, New York, 1973.

Begin, M., *The Revolt: The Story of the Irgun*, Nash, Los Angeles, 1972.

Ben-Porat, Y., Carmel, H., *et al.*, *Kippur*, Special Edition Publishers, Tel Aviv, 1974.

Ben Shaul, M., ed., *The Generals of Israel*, Hadar Publishing Co., Tel Aviv, 1968.

Bond, B., *Liddell Hart: A Study of his Military Thought*, Rutgers University Press, New Brunswick, NJ., 1977.

Bowden, T., *Army in the Service of the State*, University Publishing Projects, Tel Aviv, 1976.

Bowyer Bell, J., *Terror out of Zion: Irgun Zvai Leumi, LEHI, and the Palestine Underground, 1929–1949*, St Martin's Press, New York, 1977.

Byford-Jones, W., *The Lightning War*, Bobbs-Merrill Co., Indianapolis, IN., 1968.

Churchill, R.S.., *The Six Day War*, Houghton Mifflin, Boston, 1967.

Crosbie, S.K., *A Tacit Alliance: France and Israel from Suez to the Six Day War*, Princeton University Press, Princeton NJ., 1974.

Dayan, M., *Diary of the Sinai Campaign*, Schocken, New York, 1967.

Dayan, M., *Story of my Life*, W. Morrow & Co., New York, 1976.

Dayan, Y., *A Soldier's Diary, Sinai 1967*, Weidenfeld & Nicolson, 1968.

Dekel, E., *Shai: The Exploits of Hagana Intelligence*, Yoseloff, New York, 1959.

Deacan, R., *The Israeli Secret Service*, Hamish Hamilton, 1977.

Dunkelman, B., *Dual Allegiance*, Crown Publishers, New York, 1976.

Dupuy, T.N., *Elusive Victory: The Arab–Israeli Wars, 1947–1974*, Harper & Row, New York–London, 1978.

Gilbert, M., *Atlas of the Arab–Israeli Conflict*, Macmillan, New York, 1974.

Glassman, J.D., *Arms for the Arabs: The Soviet Union and War in the Middle East*, John Hopkins University Press, Baltimore, MD., 1975.

Glick, E.B., *Between Israel and Death*, Stackpole Press, Harrisburg, PA., 1974.

Gur, M., *The Battle for Jerusalem*, Popular Library, New York, 1978.

Heckelman, A.J., *American Volunteers and Israel's War of Independence*, Ktav, New York, 1974.

Henriques, R., *A Hundred Hours to Suez*, Viking Press, New York, 1957.

Herzog, C., *The War of Atonement*, Little, Brown & Co., Boston–Toronto, 1974.

Hutchinson, E.H., *Violent Truce: A Military Observer Looks at the Arab–Israeli Conflict, 1950–1955*, David Adair, New York, 1956.

Irving, C., *The Battle of Jerusalem: The Six Day War of June 1967*, Macmillan, New York, 1970.

Israel, Ministry of Defence, Publications Division, *The Six Day War*, Tel Aviv. n. d.

Jackson, R., *The Israeli Air Force*, Tom Stacey, 1970.

Joseph, B., *The Faithful City: The Siege of Jerusalem, 1948*, Simon & Schuster, New York, 1960.

Kagan, B., *The Secret Battle for Israel*, World Publishing Co., Cleveland–New York, 1966.

Katz, S., *Battleground: Fact and Fantasy in Palestine*, Bantam, New York, 1973.

Kimche, J. and Kimche, D., *A Clash of Destinies*, Praeger, New York, 1960.

Kimche, D. and Bawly, D., *The Six Day War: Prologue and Aftermath*, Stein & Day, New York, 1968.

Krammer, A., *The Forgotten Friendship: Israel and the Soviet Bloc 1947–53*, University of Illinois Press, Urbana, IL., 1974.

Laqueur, W., *The Road to Jerusalem*, Macmillan, New York, 1968.

Laqueur, W., *Confrontation: The Middle East War and World Politics*, Abacus, London, 1974.

Lartguy, J., *The Walls of Israel*, M. Evans & Co., New York, 1968.

Lev, A., *With Plowshare and Sword: Life in the Army of Israel*, Herzl Press, New York–London, 1961.

London *Sunday Times*, Insight Team, *The Yom Kippur War*, Doubleday & Co., Garden City, NY, 1974.

Lorch, N., *Israel's War of Independence 1947–1949*, 2nd ed., Hartmore House, Hartford, CT., 1969.

Lorch, N., *One Long War: Arab versus Jew since 1920*, Keter, Jerusalem, 1976.

Luttwak, E., and Horowitz, D., *The Israeli Army*, A. Lane, 1975.

Mardor, M., *Haganah*, New American Library, New York, 1966.

Marshall, S.L.A., *Sinai Victory*, W. Morrow & Co., New York, 1967.

O'Ballance, E., *The Sinai Campaign of 1956*, Faber & Faber, London, 1959.

O'Ballance, E., *The Third Arab–Israeli War*, Archon Books, Hamden, CT, 1972.

Ofry, D., *The Yom Kippur War*, Zohar Publishing Co., Tel Aviv, 1974.

Pearlman, M., *The Army of Israel*, Philosophical Library, New York, 1950.

Peres, S., *David's Sling: The Arming of Israel*, Random House, New York, 1971.

Perlmutter, A., *Military and Politics in Israel*, Praeger, New York, 1969.

Rabinovich, A., *The Battle for Jerusalem, June 5–7, 1967*, Jewish Publication Society of America, Philadelphia, PA., 1972.

Rolbant, S., *The Israeli Soldier: Profile of an Army*, Yoseloff, New York, 1970.

Safran, N., *From War to War: The Arab Israeli Confrontation, 1948–1967*, Pegasus, New York, 1969.

Safran, N., *Israel – The Embattled Ally*, Harvard University Press, Cambridge–London, 1978.

Schiff, Z., *A History of the Israeli Army (1870–1974)*, Straight Arrow Books, San Francisco, CA., 1974.

Schiff, Z., and Rothstein, R., *Fedayeen*, McKay, New York, 1972.

Shapira, A., *et al.* eds., *The Seventh Day: Soldiers' Talk about the Six-Day War*, C. Scribner's Sons, New York, 1970.

Slater, L., *The Pledge*, Simon & Schuster, New York, 1970.

Stevenson, W., *Zanek: A Chronicle of the Israeli Air Force*, Viking, New York, 1971.

Sykes, C., *Crossroads to Israel*, Indiana University Press, Bloomington–London, 1973.

Tadmor, J. and Rothstein, R., *The Silent Warriors*, Macmillan, New York, 1969.

Teveth, S., *The Tanks of Tammuz*, Viking, New York, 1969.

Teveth, S., *Moshe Dayan: The Soldier, the Man, and the Legend*, Houghton Mifflin Co., Boston–New York, 1973.

Weizman, E., *On Eagles' Wings*, Weidenfeld & Nicolson, London, 1976.

Whetten, L.L., *The Canal War: Four Power Conflict in the Middle East*, Massachusetts Institute of Technology Press, Boston, 1974.

Young, P., *The Israeli Campaign 1967*, W. Kimber, London, 1967.

Index

Index